MW00658001

SEEING *the* TEXT

EXEGESIS FOR STUDENTS OF GREEK AND HEBREW

Mary H. Schertz
&
Perry B. Yoder

ABINGDON PRESS / Nashville

SEEING THE TEXT
EXEGESIS FOR STUDENTS OF GREEK AND HEBREW

This book is printed on recycled, acid-free, elemental-chlorine–free paper.

Library of Congress Cataloging-in-Publication Data

Schertz, Mary H.
Seeing the text : exegesis for students of Greek and Hebrew / Mary H. Schertz & Perry B. Yoder.
p. cm.
Includes bibliographical references.
ISBN 0-687-09114-4 (alk. paper)
1. Bible—Hermeneutics. I. Yoder, Perry B. II. Title.

BS476 .S325 2001
220.6'01—dc21

2001035289

01 02 03 04 05 06 07 08 09 10—10 9 8 7 6 5 4 3 2 1

MANUFACTURED IN THE UNITED STATES OF AMERICA

To

the Associated Mennonite Biblical Seminary faculty

who taught us,

our colleagues who supported us,

and our students from whom we learned

PREFACE

In biblical studies, we often ask how the text is related to its context. The context for *Seeing the Text* is the art and practice of teaching. If we were not teachers, if we did not spend the hours of our lives in classrooms with students studying the biblical text, we could not have written this book. Our students are its heroes. Their enthusiasm for our suggestions, their willingness to try these approaches and their ability to teach us what works and what does not work is the foundation of our satisfaction with what we have done in this volume. The insights into the biblical text that they acquired using these skills were the impetus to our beginning and continuing the road to publication. Along the way, our students kept us focused on the "payoff." Which study disciplines yield the most understanding? What is really worth doing? Because the approaches we suggest here emerged and were tested in the classroom, practicality has been our guiding principal and "operational" the word that we used most in our many discussions about the manuscript. What we wanted to achieve above all else was to help students actually use, in their theological studies and in their work as pastors, teachers, or related vocations, the skills that they work so hard to acquire in the biblical language classroom. We wrote and taught, taught and wrote to that end.

If it takes a village to raise a child, it takes a community to write a book. In addition to our students, there have been many other people over the years that have contributed in significant ways to this effort. A Teaching and Learning Grant from the Association of Theological Schools funded by the Lilly Foundation helped us do some experimentation with computer technology for the project. Associated Mennonite Biblical Seminary has been generous with sabbaticals and grants from the

Faculty Scholarship Development Fund that supported our research in various ways. We were enriched and stimulated by colleagues who gathered and discussed our project in formal and informal settings. A series of breakfast meetings in which we demonstrated our approach to colleagues from other disciplines was especially influential in the shaping of the last half of the book. In addition, we are especially grateful to the fellow members of the Bible department, Jacob W. Elias and Ben C. Ollenburger, who read and commented on parts of the manuscript at critical junctures. Students who served as departmental assistants were also vital members of the team. Patrick Preheim, Julia Zacharias, and Brad Schantz patiently assembled bibliography, read copy and attended to many details with unfailing good humor and cheer. All of these people and many others contributed to the strengths of the book and corrected many of its weaknesses. Any glitches that remain are certainly due to our own limitations or stubbornness.

Our families and friends were other important participants in this project. They kept us sane, provided perspective, and made us laugh. Community and human relationship are the grounding of all significant labor and we were well grounded. Last but not least we are grateful to each other. Two opinionated authors working on a single project is neither the easiest nor the quickest way to write a book. Many days were fueled by simple, dogged perseverance. But then there were those moments when, after yet another of our endless discussions, we would grin with relief and agree, "Now, that's operational." It is certainly a different book and a better book for having emerged from two minds and two hearts.

CONTENTS

INTRODUCTION

In the twentieth century there was a significant shift in how interpretation was understood. When the century began, authors were central to the understanding of their work. Texts were understood to represent the intentions of their authors. Knowledge of the writer and the writer's context was pivotal for critical study. History became the dancing partner of biblical studies as scholars sought to reconstruct the historical context of a work, the circumstances of its writing, and the situation or audience to which it was addressed. From this historical foundation inferences were made as to the intentions and meaning of the work.

Historical reconstruction and development were at the heart of higher criticism—the *who, what, where, when,* and *why* questions addressed to biblical texts—and these historical questions were discussed at length in commentaries and introductions to the Old and New Testaments.[1] Interpretations were sponsored and supported by the historical context assumed for a writer and the writing. "A text out of context is a pretext" might serve as a slogan for this approach. This historical-critical approach to interpretation dominated biblical studies for at least the first seventy years of the twentieth century.[2]

However, in time, such an approach came to be discouraged as naive. Who can know the mind of another, let alone the mind of a person writing long ago in another culture? The term *intentional fallacy* became used in literary studies to describe what was considered wrongheaded about the historical approach. Instead of the author's mind, which we don't have, the interpreter should look at what we do have—the text. Besides, who is to say that the text actually represents authorial intention or that authors are cognizant of their real intentions in writing?

For this literary approach, labeled *new criticism,* the close reading of the text was the appropriate technique for interpretation, and the text itself was the court of last appeal for conflicting interpretations.[3] Historical circumstances, it was agreed, could be neglected in appraising a literary work of art. Although historical research continued in biblical studies, literary questions began to emerge as a major focus after the middle of the twentieth century.[4] A comparison of the introductory matter in Burton's commentary on Galatians in the *International Critical Commentary* series with Betz's in the *Hermeneia* series is a remarkable illustration of this shift.[5] The slogan for this development might be "A text is a text is a text!"

More recently, questions have been raised about the status of the written text itself. The slogan "There are as many texts as there are readers" names a problem that comes with making the text central in interpretation. Meaning, after all, is a construct of the human mind and does not spring unmediated from the text itself. In this sense, a text does not have meaning: meaning is recreated each time a text is read.[6]

The reader, in this view, becomes central as the creator of a text's meaning. With this emphasis on readers, interpretations became readings. Furthermore, since a reader's understanding of a document is colored by his or her context, ideology, or social identification, a variety of readings are possible. As a result, a plethora of different kinds of readings came to the fore—Marxist readings, feminist readings, and liberationist readings, among others. These readings were often attempts to address the concerns of contemporary audiences. They were also, at least tacitly, critiques of readings in which the concerns or issues of different constituencies were not adequately represented, or ignored altogether, by "mainline" interpretation.

The expanding variety of readers and readings has enriched the heremeneutical circle and widened the horizons of possible interpretations. The expanding universe of readings also makes the subjective dimensions of interpretation more obvious. Interpreters constrained by social location and ideology will reflect social, political, or theological commitments in their interpretations. In short, how a text is read depends on where the reader is sitting when reading!

As we look back on these developments in the twentieth century, we see a journey from authors to texts to readers as the determining element in the interpretive process. A way to understand this shift from author to reader is that, although context is still determinative for interpretation, the focus has shifted from the context of the author to the context of the reader. In keeping with this shift there is a movement from arguing about the merits of differing interpretations based on historical or literary considerations to explaining why different interpreters produce the differing results that they do.[7]

At least part of the energy for this pilgrimage has been the lack of agreement among serious, well-intentioned, critical-historical exegetes. Take, for example, the translation of Genesis 1:1-3 in the *Good News Bible.* One translation appears in the text, but a number of other possibilities are mentioned in a footnote. Or compare several scholarly commentaries on these verses. Good arguments have been given for alternative ways of understanding and translating these verses.[8] Neither historical research nor close attention to grammar and syntax brought about a single agreed upon interpretation of these verses. This is not a unique case. Historical-critical scholars were often unable to come to unanimity when there were well-founded, but competing, interpretations and interpretative assumptions.[9] If historical-critical biblical scholarship was an objective "scientific" enterprise, how could this be?

After a history of more than two thousand years of biblical interpretation, it seems unlikely that there will ever be a time when readers of the Bible will accept a single interpretation for many texts or that a given interpretation will not be disputed in the course of history. This reality forces us to consider the nature and process of interpretation itself. The movement of biblical studies during the last century from author of the text to the reader of the text has made the subjective nature of interpretation more apparent, since inevitably interpretations are shaped by the subjective experiences, values, and beliefs of their sponsors. However, it is also the case that interpretations are *not* spun out of thin air by a reader. In the end they are based on something—a text—and formed by someone—a reader.

The Path Ahead

The plurality of interpretations accepted as a given in the late twentieth century indicates that *the* meaning of a text is a chimera. There will continue to be a plurality of interpretations as long as there are different readers and different communities that sustain different parameters for understanding texts. Pragmatically, rather than trying to repress this fact by continuing to talk about "the one true meaning" of a text, we should be more modest and content ourselves with talking about *a* meaning of a text or a reading. Interpretations have been plural and will continue to be plural.

Nevertheless, while accepting the inevitability of the plurality of interpretations *we need not accept every interpretation as an equally valid understanding of a text.* Variety does not negate the need for critical thinking and validation in interpretation. Some interpretations will seem more probable than others, since some interpretations will be more cogently supported and coherently argued. Consequently, we are more likely to accept those understandings of a text that have greater evidential support as more appropriate than those not so supported or argued.

The beginning question of interpretation now becomes: How do we find a place to stand in sorting through the probabilities of differing interpretations? First, although we obviously do not have immediately available the thoughts of an author or speaker, *past or present,* we can and do make judgments about what information, presuppositions, or expectations could have guided his or her speaking or writing.[10] We might judge, for example, that anachronistic interpretations are quite unlikely. Thus, an interpretive consideration is what an author likely could or could not have known, what he or she might or might not have expected the audience to know in context. In this regard, we can learn much from the work of historical criticism, which researched the background of the biblical authors and their writings.[11]

Second, language is a shared public phenomenon, and shared public conventions govern its operation in the areas of lexical meaning, grammar, syntax, and rhetoric. These governing conventions are the stuff of grammars and dictionaries, and help us distinguish between the appropriate and inappropriate uses of a word or between the proper and improper formulation of a sentence. When different readers construe a text differently, appeals to these governing conventions can discriminate between more likely and less likely readings. Determining what senses the wording of a text will allow and what senses are unlikely is a necessary interpretive judgment.

Third, the rule-governed phenomenon of language is used to communicate. Our basic experience of language is that we use it to *convey* meaning to another. Speakers and writers formulate texts, using the words they do in the way they do, in order to communicate something to someone. In this sense it is helpful to think of the words in a text as *conveying* meaning rather than as *having* meaning. As language users, we know that authors have expectations about what the listener or reader is "to get." Authors do contest some understandings of their words as *misunderstandings.*[12] To what degree a reader understands or misunderstands begins, in large measure, with whether the reader construes a text according to the communicative expectations that governed how its words were used.[13]

The words *likely* and *unlikely* have been used above rather than *correct* and *incorrect.* It is important, as interpreters, that we take our limitations seriously. Our knowledge is relative. We can only understand in part. In the end, we choose more probable interpretations over less probable ones. Our limitations, however, may be regarded as a challenge: as responsible interpreters we need to rigorously pursue every available avenue of study in order to make the most informed interpretive decisions of which we are capable.

As we shall see in the course of this book, many factors must be considered in arriving at the most likely interpretation. However, the most important ones, and our starting point, come from the wording or language of the text itself. From the use of language in a text we begin to grasp the communicative expectations that shaped the text. Because of the primacy of a text's language for understanding, *the primary goal of this book is to enable students to progress from their ability to read a biblical language to making considered judgments about the meaning of texts and their significance then and now.*

Unfortunately, in seminary studies there is often a chasm between instruction in the biblical languages and the study of the Bible in other courses—courses devoted to book, text, and theme studies. At best this chasm is crossed by references to Hebrew and Greek words or to the grammatical and rhetorical features that are found in the Greek or Hebrew text. However, we believe the reason for learning the languages is to interpret Scripture and the payoff should be the joy and prize of personal discovery. Consequently, the process presented below makes knowledge of Hebrew and Greek a necessary and integral part of the interpretive process. To this end, we have attempted to create *a seamless web from reading the languages to interpreting texts.*[14] Students who have had at least a semester of Hebrew or Greek can use this book to establish their interpretive practice on their knowledge of the language of the text.

To be sure, in the seminary environment there are courses in which the languages are taken seriously in the study of Scripture. These are usually called "exegesis courses."[15] In these classes, typically, the biblical text is read and translated verse by verse. The major project is often a substantial exegetical paper. Although writing exegetical papers is a very important and valuable learning experience, seminary students usually do not have time to write exegetical papers after they graduate—unless they move on to graduate school. As a result of associating the languages with doing exegesis, in the press of ministry, students' knowledge of the biblical languages frequently languishes.[16]

This need not be! *The process we present below is doable in the midst of active pastoral ministry.* Although learning new skills and ways of working takes time, once the requisite procedures are understood and assimilated much less time is actually needed in study than was previously thought necessary. From experience, we can say that *what is taught here can be practiced after seminary and will sustain the practitioner.*

A Textcentric Approach

Because our emphasis is on the text, we offer a textcentric approach rather than one governed by methodology.[17] This is a practical consideration. Students and ministers normally begin with a text—a lectionary reading, for example. They sit at their desks and ask, Now that I have a text, what do I do? By beginning with the text and working up and out from it in a disciplined and systematic way, time can be saved by using it more productively. Consequently, in the first four chapters, the aim is to guide you toward the production of a **textual topography.** You will begin by reading through the text. Being able to read the text, you can go on to produce a *visual reading,* the depicting of textual contours and regions. By marking these features on the text, you will make it three-dimensional and begin to see how and what it is saying. This first phase of study is crucial in order to discover the communicative dynamics of the text, and you will begin to see things in texts that you most certainly would have missed with a simple, flat, linear reading. At the end of this process of visual reading, you will have produced a textual topography through which you can see into the text and grasp its gist—what it is saying.

In chapters 5 and 6, the **contextual function** of the text is explored. Language is used not only to communicate content, but also to bring something about, to accomplish an objective. For example, at a meal, the question Is the salt down there? is not a request for information, but for action! The speaker wants the salt passed. To uncover this functional aspect of meaning, you will need to move beyond a visual reading to discovering its location within a literary, historical, intellectual, and social horizon. After placing a text within a context, you will be asked to make an assessment of the text's communicative intent—What was your text to accomplish? What was it to achieve?—in its context. That is, within the horizon of the text, how would its communicative force have been understood?

Finally, in chapters 7 and 8, you will move toward **appropriating and applying** your text. First, the matter of a text's function within the canon needs discernment. When we apply a text we do so in light of what else the Bible has to say on the topic. Here you will need to consider the weight of a passage in dialogue with other passages. Sometimes it is not the meaning of a passage that is disputed but the use made of a passage. It is here that your work in the first six chapters is vital for your confidence. We will again provide a perspective and tools for drawing on your new understandings within the context of a canonical conversation with other texts.

Having considered canon, you will be prompted to move with integrity from text and canon to your context. Without leaving the text behind, you will be shown how to find and use what we will call *points of attachment*—anchors for linking the text to the present.

Although this book may be viewed as a "method" book, two important caveats must be made. First, *method does not mean a linear process.* Consequently, we will stress the interconnections and overlap between the different phases of the study process. Initially, learning may take place in a more linear fashion, but practice should be interlinear! When the process of interpretation is understood, certain phases may be lumped together, others may be expanded or contracted. Experience leads to an interactive process in study and to flexibility in practice.

Second, *interpretation is a personal and creative enterprise.* It depends on the "aha!"—the moment of insight. By presenting a series of techniques for understanding texts, we do not mean to suggest that understanding is the result of a mechanical process. Rather, we have found the processes presented below to be a powerful means for promoting critical and creative understanding. By covering the basics, a method can free the student for creative, imaginative, and empathetic interaction with the text. What follows represents a starting point. We expect the student to adapt the practice of exegesis to his or her skills, needs, and situation, as well as to the passages studied.

Finally, *pragmatism* and *common sense* are invaluable aids to productive study. Keep in mind the question of payoff—how much interpretive "bang" will you get for a given line of inquiry. Everybody has a limited amount of time. Don't be afraid to spend it wisely! Common sense will often protect you from wild-goose chases and getting carried away by a personal, although rather speculative, insight. Bible study is exciting. It is easy to get carried away. Use common sense and the techniques presented here to get carried in the right direction.

A Note to Students

One of the most important aspects of this study process is its cumulative nature. Much of what you learn from one text will be applicable to other texts. For that reason it is important to establish a study notebook and get into the practice of placing entries in it. In the course of this work we will suggest the material you should collect in your notebook for each passage you study. At the end of each chapter we have placed a "checkpoint." These checkpoints will summarize the important work you have done in the chapter and indicate what you should place in your notebook.

A Note to Teachers

As suggested above, the techniques and stages of study taught here are not in direct or necessary conflict with the "normal" scholarly approaches, for which there are many helps already existing.[18] Rather the aim here is to provide the student with a simple and coherent way of proceeding from the reading of a text to understanding and appropriating it. Once the student has grasped this path, he or she can profitably be shown the forest of academic scholarship since they will have in place an interpretive framework that can be elaborated and enlarged by further study. Also, being anchored in the text, the student can view scholarly approaches critically with an eye for their efficacy in solving the real problems that they meet in the texts they study.[19]

The present book can function as a supplemental or standalone text for classes in the biblical languages and in exegesis. We have striven to make it both clear and simple. Many examples are provided. However, classroom demonstrations of the techniques described in the first four chapters will pay big dividends for the student. Since this material is linked to language learning, such demonstrations need not be intrusive or detract from the learning of the languages.

Finally, and uniquely, this book can be used in either Hebrew or Greek classes. A great advantage of this approach is that the student can see how the same interpretive process works in both Testaments and, second, the student can follow the same method in both Greek classes and Hebrew classes. Such double usage reinforces and enhances the students' interpretive skills and facilitates additional learning. Consequently, we believe that consistency in interpretive method between Hebrew and Greek texts is a major pedagogical gain.

CHAPTER 1

READING THROUGH THE TEXT

For most of us, reading is so natural that we rarely, if ever, reflect upon how we go from squiggles on paper to understanding a text. As easy at it seems, however, reading is a rather remarkable feat! It involves several interrelated and simultaneous activities. You must assign provisional meanings to words. You then confirm or change these meanings on the basis of further reading. You need to decide grammatical relationships—for example, what serves as the subject and object of the verb. Normally, you make these connections automatically. In the sentence "John kissed Sue," you know who kissed whom even if you do not know how to explain the connections between the words in grammatical terms. On the basis of these posited relationships, you group words into sense units—phrases, clauses, and sentences, and assign a meaning to them. Finally, you group the clauses and sentences together into paragraphs and larger units of communication that in turn influence your understanding of how the clauses and sentences hang together and what they mean.

There is no particular order in which these activities take place. Since you are unconscious of them, they all seem to happen at the same time. If you were to think about what you do when you read, you might assume that understanding words comes first since this step logically precedes a comprehension of phrases and sentences. In fact, reading is an interactive process that does not proceed in a linear, logical fashion. In the sentence cited above, "John kissed Sue," did you decide on the meaning of the words first and then decide who kissed whom? Both processes seem to occur at the same time.

Because we simultaneously decide on the meanings of individual words and how they go together, the larger linguistic units influence and sometimes even determine our understanding of the smaller ones. Therefore, as we read a sentence we assign meanings to its words, but these meanings are only provisional. Sometimes we change the meanings we have assigned in light of the larger whole. For example, in a sentence beginning "the boy's favorite bat was . . . ," the meaning of "bat" depends on how the sentence is finished. If the ending is "a vampire" one meaning is assigned to the word "bat." If the ending is "a Louisville Slugger" a different meaning is assigned. This process of grasping wholes and understanding the parts from the whole happens so quickly and naturally that we would not consider "bat" to be an ambiguous word in either of these alternate sentences.

Our knowledge of a world outside the text also affects our judgments about the meaning of words and how they go together. We understand some words and phrases as metaphors. Others we understand as symbolic. If someone says, "He grew a foot overnight," we construe this statement as an exaggeration or hyperbole based on our knowledge of the world—where children may grow fast, but not that fast!

The larger context of understanding that frames our reading also includes our knowledge of how language itself functions. For example, in some cases we realize that the importance of words lies in what they do, as in, "I now pronounce you husband and wife." For such a sentence, the external frame consists both of the wedding ceremony and the role the sentence plays in that ceremony. Likewise, the greeting How are you? is not really a request for information but a conventional way of establishing contact with another person.

Reading is a complex interactive activity involving different types of information. It depends on knowledge of parts and of wholes, of how words and phrases are used, and even of the external world. Consequently, and most important for our purposes, understanding a text requires more than assigning a meaning to each word.

So much to keep in mind! It is a wonder that we can ever understand letters on a page. But thanks to what is called *working memory* we have the capacity to understand as we read. Our working memory, like a skilled juggler, keeps the requisite blocks in the air and facilitates their interaction. The result is our comprehension of the squiggles on a page.

Because it is fairly easy, most of the time, to keep all the necessary information in mind when reading English, we take our knowledge of language and the world, as well as our working memory, for granted. However, it is a different matter when we turn to biblical texts. Our knowledge of the biblical world may be thin, our grasp of the language halting, our working memory inadequate. Consequently, we are forced to read in a more linear fashion. We pause to look up the meaning of unfamiliar words. Once we think we understand the words, we try to understand their relationship, unscrambling the linear flow of words on a page so they make sense to us. Finally, we try to understand the connection between clauses and sentences.

With our attention focused so closely on the basic elements, rarely does our understanding involve larger textual units such as clusters of clauses or whole units of text. There may be little interaction between our understanding of a word and the relationship of its clause to other clauses. Unfortunately, as a result, we often read biblical Hebrew and Greek as codes to be deciphered rather than as texts to be understood.

Our aim in what follows is to help you become a reader of the biblical texts. The skills covered in this chapter are beginning skills. Later chapters will introduce further skills that can increase your ability to read interactively. In the end, our hope is that reading the Bible can become more than a process of deciphering code. Instead, you will be reading texts.

A Visual Reading

With the exception of poetry, most texts are printed in a linear, wrapped fashion. Although this convention saves millions of trees, it also means that, in itself, a line of printed prose has no particular meaning or significance. It may contain the end of one sentence and the beginning of another, or it may contain a fragment of a clause or sentence. If you compare a line of prose text and a line of poetry, the difference the "layout" makes for analysis and understanding is clear. It makes sense to ask what a particular line of poetry means. It makes little sense to ask what a line of prose means.

What we are proposing in the first two chapters is to line out biblical texts so that each line has meaning. Arranging the text this way does not make prose into poetry. But it does break it into meaningful lines and makes the text much easier to read. A layout also makes it much easier to see how the author designed the text and what significance the design has for understanding it, hence a visual reading—one in which it is easy to see how the text is designed and "works."

In your native language you could easily line out a text as you read through it, perhaps placing each clause on its own line. But neither biblical Hebrew nor Greek is your first language. Consequently, before you can line out the clauses or other units of meaning, you must first read through the text for basic word meanings, grammatical forms, and syntactic structures. "Pencil in" where the clauses begin and end once you have a basic understanding of these features.

But before we begin working with clauses we face a catch-22 situation: Where do we begin and end our reading of the text? How many verses constitute a literary unit of some type?

Where Does a Text Start and Stop?

In classes, texts are often assigned, but on the job you will usually need to make your own decisions about where a text starts and stops. Lectionaries, for example, are notorious for chopping passages awkwardly and sometimes even bundling disparate verses into a "text." Nor are the traditional markers, such as verses or chapters, very helpful. Verses are short and manageable, but not a very satisfactory point of departure for interpretation. Verses may not even represent a single sentence, as in Ephesians 1:5-6, which together form a single sentence in the NRSV.[1]

> He destined us for adoption as his children through Jesus Christ, according to the good pleasure of his will, to the praise of his glorious grace that he freely bestowed on us in the Beloved.

Chapter divisions may be no more satisfactory since chapters normally contain several literary units. Further, chapter divisions do not always agree between the biblical text and its English translation. Deuteronomy 12:32 in English is verse 1 of chapter 13 in Hebrew. As a preface to a warning about false prophecy (Hebrew text), this verse about not adding to or subtracting from the law takes on a different dimension than when it is attached to the treatise on idolatry with which chapter 12 (English text) concludes. In short, the divisions of the Bible—verses and chapters—while serviceable as reference marks, do not make a good starting point for interpretation. The first is too brief—not enough context—while the second is frequently too broad. Both may be at odds with the flow and coherence of the material.

In most modern translations, as well as in printed editions of the Hebrew and Greek texts, there is an intermediate-sized textual unit between verse and chapter that is found either in the manuscripts or given by their modern editors. These variously sized units may be marked by indentation or by spaces in the text, designating a break in the flow of the text.[2] Pragmatically, these divisions are a good starting point for identifying a suitable text for study. Keep in mind, however, that the textual divisions identified by your text may not agree with your final assessment as to where the boundaries of the literary unit lie. But these divisions do form a convenient base from which to begin your investigations. Here, as usual, our approach is pragmatic. If the marked divisions seem to make sense, use them. If they do not, make your own.

Whether you use divisions already marked in the text or make your own, you still need to understand why a chunk of text makes an appropriate unit for study. What justifies a text as a unit for exegesis? First, it should have unity. If it is a narrative text, it should not contain radical shifts in character, setting, or plot. If it is an expository text, it should not contain a major shift to a different argument. When the characters, locale, plot, or argument are the same throughout, the text hangs together. Second, it needs to have adequate size for the interpretation of its parts. It should have adequate scope and horizon for the explanation of what lies within it. Third, the material needs a sense of completeness. Does it have a beginning and an ending that marks a conclusion? Fourth, is it set off in some way from the material around it?

There should be some discontinuity between what goes before it and what follows it. Depending on your level of proficiency, you may need to have in hand an English translation as well as your Hebrew or Greek text. Scan the English version for the larger context and the structural markers. Inevitably, however, your decisions as to the limits of your unit will need to be based on the Hebrew or Greek text.

Let's look at Genesis 12:10-20 to illustrate how a textual unit might be identified. In the NRSV the text reads:

> 10 Now there was a famine in the land. So Abram went down to Egypt to reside there as an alien, for the famine was severe in the land. 11 When he was about to enter Egypt, he said to his wife Sarai, "I know well that you are a woman beautiful in appearance; 12 and when the Egyptians see you, they will say, 'This is his wife'; then they will kill me, but they will let you live. 13 Say you are my sister, so that it may go well with me because of you, and that my life may be spared on your account." 14 When Abram entered Egypt the Egyptians saw that the woman was very beautiful. 15 When the officials of Pharaoh saw her, they praised her to Pharaoh. And the woman was taken into Pharaoh's house. 16 And for her sake he dealt well with Abram; and he had sheep, oxen, male donkeys, male and female slaves, female donkeys, and camels.
>
> 17 But the LORD afflicted Pharaoh and his house with great plagues because of Sarai, Abram's wife. 18 So Pharaoh called Abram, and said, "What is this you have done to me? Why did you not tell me that she was your wife? 19 Why did you say, 'She is my sister,' so that I took her for my wife? Now then, here is your wife, take her, and be gone." 20 And Pharaoh gave his men orders concerning him; and they set him on the way, with his wife and all that he had.

The unit begins with an expression that often begins a new narrative in Hebrew—וַיְהִי (compare the beginning of Ruth and Esther, for example). It is translated "Now there was" in the NRSV. This beginning clause sets off verse 10 from the verses that have gone before, and introduces a new theme, a famine. At the end, in verse 20, the episode is over—Sarai is saved and Abram is safe and sound, in fact wealthy. In narratives, the resolution of a tension or problem marks the end—or the beginning of the end. Furthermore, if we look at the following material, the stage is once more Canaan. At that point, Lot also enters the story once again. As suggested, a change in setting and actors is a strong indication that one unit has ended and another has begun. It would seem that Genesis 12:10-20 is a basic unit suitable for study.[3]

READING YOUR TEXT

When you feel that you have defined a unit that has integrity, the next step is to make a *working copy* of it, one that you can mark up. The best way to prepare a working copy is to copy your text from a Bible computer program into your word processor. You may want to enlarge the type and indicate the reference for your text. Generally it is easier to work with a text at this point if you can get it all onto one page. If the verse numbers distract you, delete them. The important thing is to have a text that you can read and work with easily. If you do not have access to a computer, photocopy the text, cut away everything outside of the selected text, center the text on a piece of white paper, and recopy it. You may also wish to use the machine's enlarging function to make the text easier to read.[4]

Glosses

In reading Hebrew and Greek texts, of course you must figure out the meaning of unfamiliar words. Glosses are the initial meanings you assign to words so you can read the text. They are simple semantic equivalencies. In practice, you will be equating Hebrew or Greek words with English ones as you work through a text. It is efficient to maintain a glossary of these equivalencies by entering unknown words and their glosses together with their lexical form, root, and parsing on your working copy of the text as needed.

The need to look up words can be the most laborious part of reading. There are, however, several tools that can make this task lighter. Probably the quickest and easiest way to work through a passage is to use a computer program such as Bible Windows, BibleWorks, or Logos that have an online dictionary and parsing guide. At the click of a mouse button you can find the gloss of a word, its lexical form, and its morphology. Since it is easy to copy text from these programs into a word processor document, you can easily enter your glosses on your working copy.[5]

Similar tools in printed form are Armstrong, Busby, and Carr, *A Reader's Hebrew-English Lexicon;* Zerwick, *An Analysis of the Greek New Testament;* Rienecker and Rogers, *Linguistic Key to the Greek New Testament;* and Han's *Parsing Guide.* These are "speed" tools. They "run" with the biblical verses—they are organized in a convenient verse-by-verse format. However, as you gain greater reading competency, you will want to use tools of greater precision. In dictionaries like *BDB, NKBE, DCH, Lidell-Scott,* or *BAGD,* the uses of words and the constructions in which they occur are illustrated. In these tools you can ask which usage and construction seems most relevant to your passage, or which sense seems most appropriate in your context. Commentaries also contain discussions of key words in a passage. Choose a volume that comments on the Greek or Hebrew text, such as those in the *ICC* or *Hermeneia* series. However, keep focused on reading the text and do not get sidetracked, at this point, into investigations of interesting words.

Parsing

One half of an initial reading of a biblical text is glossing the words. The other half is knowing how they fit together within their clauses. This business of "fitting together" is known as grammar and syntax.

In order to determine the grammatical role of words in a clause it is necessary to parse the words of which you are unsure. For verbs, indicate their tense, aspect, and mood. Here again the "running" tools can aid you. Computer programs are the quickest, but for Greek you can also use the analytical lexicons (Zerwick, Rienecker and Rogers, and Perschbacher are all good) to find the parsing for words that stump you. For Hebrew, Einspahr's *Index to the Brown, Driver, and Brigg's Hebrew Lexicon* is a helpful tool. Note any pronouns attached to verbs and their function. In the case of nouns, be clear about case, number, and gender and their relationship to other nominals (e.g., genitives or constructs) as well as to verbs. For example, subjects and verbs are marked by agreement in person and number, and in Hebrew, gender as well. Nouns and their adjectives are marked by agreement in number, gender, definiteness, and in Greek, case. This morphological and grammatical analysis of words is the foundation for the next step—understanding the role of words in a clause and how they function together as a unit of communication.

In reading through a passage, when you come upon constructions and word combinations that puzzle you, your initial source of help is a short guide to syntax, such as Ronald Williams, *Hebrew Syntax in Outline;* or Merwe, Naude, and Kroeze, *A Biblical Hebrew Reference Grammar*[6] for Hebrew; or Brooks and Winbery, *Syntax of New Testament Greek* for Greek. Also, there is nothing wrong with continuing to use whatever grammar you used in your introductory course. You will know it best and be able to find information quickly. Just remember that the information in it is basic and may not be adequate to meet your growing needs for understanding.

If you cannot get an answer to your question in these materials, check a reference grammar. For Hebrew, use resources such as Gesenius-Kautzsch, *Gesenius' Hebrew Grammar,* the old standard, translated from German by A. E. Cowley, or use Jouon and Muraoka, *A Grammar of Biblical Hebrew,* which is the best reference grammar available in English. A recent work on syntax is Waltke and O'Connor, *An Introduction to Biblical Hebrew Syntax.* For Greek, look at Blass and de Brunner, *A Greek Grammar of the New Testament and Other Early Christian Literature,* or Robertson's *A Grammar of the Greek New Testament.* One of the best from the wider perspective of classical Greek is Smyth's *Greek Grammar.* Two newer and more user-friendly intermediate grammars are Wallace's *Greek Grammar Beyond the Basics* and Young's *Intermediate New Testament Greek.* The most efficient ways to use any of these reference works is to consult their indices. You will find not only subject indices, but indices listing scriptural citations and discussions of grammatical and syntactic forms as well.

A strange or puzzling combination of words may be an idiom. In this case a dictionary like *BDB, NKBE,* or *DCH* will list the usages of a word in idioms and provide you with their translation. A good source of Greek idioms is Zerwick's *Analysis of the Greek New Testament* or C. D. F. Moule, *An Idiom-Book of New Testament Greek.*

When reading through a text for the first time it can be a problem to know how much to look up and how much to write down. Perhaps a few simple guidelines can help. Do not look up words or parsing you think you know, even if you are not 100 percent sure. You want to maintain, use, and increase your language facility and working knowledge. Exercise your memory whenever possible. It is like taking the stairs instead of the elevator—every little bit helps. But if you look up a new word or the parsing of a difficult form, by all means write it down. Remember your goal is to read the passage and be able to reread it easily.

Where Does a Clause Start and Stop?

Now that you have read through your text, you are ready to go through your copy and mark with a light pencil slash where the clauses begin and end. This is the first step toward lining out your text. You may have already begun to get a feel for which words cluster together into basic units of meaning and clauses. If, at this point, you need additional help with understanding what a clause is, what kinds of clauses there are, and how clauses relate to one another we encourage you to read or review Excursus 1 on clause structure and type.

In designating clauses, here are several basic markers for which to look. First, the most important clue for finding the end of a clause is *the appearance of a second finite verb,* since most clauses in Greek and Hebrew will contain a single finite verb and its complements. Second, look back at the words between the two verbs you have identified. Can you determine which words go with the first verb and which seem like they belong to the second verb? If so, go ahead and put a tentative slash between the two clauses.

Then proceed to find the third verb and work in the same way to identify and mark the second clause. In a way you will be leapfrogging through the text, using the following verb to assess the words in between it and the preceding verb in order to divide the text into its clauses.

Third, look for *syntactic markers*. In Hebrew, for example, the *waw conversive* almost always marks the beginning of a new clause, as do the subordinating conjuctions כִּי and אֲשֶׁר. In Greek, many clauses begin with καί unless it is clearly being used to link a compound complement. Also, in the printed Greek text, commas, colons, and periods are usually reliable as clause markers. A comma is a particularly good clue, especially if it is followed by a conjunction such as καί or δέ.[7]

In Hebrew, accents play a role in the quick identification of clauses. These accents are divided into two classes, conjunctive and disjunctive. The latter divides word groups, phrases, and clauses from one another. Learning the strongest or heaviest of these disjunctive accents can point you to where clauses begin and end.[8]

The major disjunctive accent within a verse is the *atnach*, which normally divides a verse into its two major parts. These parts, however, may not be the same in length. Also, this accent does not necessarily divide a verse into clauses, since a verse may only have a single clause, as is the case in Genesis 1:1. However, it is good to look first for the *atnach* to see how it divides the verse. Three other accents to look for are the *segolta*, the *zaqef*, and the *rivia*, which divide the major verse parts into yet finer parts.

Let's look at an example from Ruth 1:11. In this verse you can see that the *atnach* lies under the word "with me," which divides the verse into its two major parts.

וַתֹּ֤אמֶר נָעֳמִי֙ שֹׁ֣בְנָה בְנֹתַ֔י לָ֥מָּה תֵלַ֖כְנָה עִמִּ֑י
הַֽעֽוֹד־לִ֤י בָנִים֙ בְּמֵעַ֔י וְהָי֥וּ לָכֶ֖ם לַאֲנָשִֽׁים׃

> And Naomi said, "Return now my daughters. Why would you come with me? // Do I yet have sons in my womb that they might become your husbands?"

However each of these two major divisions of the verse is divided yet again by the *zaqef*. In this way the verse is divided into four clauses:

> And Naomi said, "Return now my daughters. / Why would you come with me? // Do I yet have sons in my womb? / that they might become your husbands?"

Participial and infinitival clauses sometimes cause problems. A good guideline is that if a participle or infinitive has its own complements, consider it a clause in its own right. If a participle has no complements, it is usually best to consider it a part of the clause in which it is found. If an infinitive completes the verbal idea of the finite verb, it is best to treat the verb and the infinitive together.

For the sake of manageable units, you may want to divide a clause into more than one line. For this reason we speak of semantic units, normally a clause, but sometimes less than a clause, for example, a phrase.

Examples

By this point, you will have a pretty good idea of where the clauses start and stop. Except for nominal clauses, each clause should have a finite verb, a participle, or infinitive. Let's turn now to working with a real text. We will work through Genesis 12:10, discussing as we go how we might divide the material into appropriate semantic units.

In the Hebrew Bible, Genesis 12:10 (NRSV) appears like this:

וַיְהִי רָעָב בָּאָרֶץ וַיֵּרֶד אַבְרָם מִצְרַיְמָה לָגוּר שָׁם כִּי־כָבֵד הָרָעָב בָּאָרֶץ׃

> Now there was a famine in the land. So Abram went down to Egypt to reside there as an alien, for the famine was severe in the land.

In reading through this verse in Hebrew, we look first for the verb and its complements, stopping when we reach the second verb since it has a *waw conversive*. This means placing a divider before "went down." וַיְהִי רָעָב בָּאָרֶץ would represent the first clause.

Now we look for the end of the second clause. This time we stop before the כִּי, which we know normally begins a dependent clause. So we would place our second mark after וַיֵּרֶד אַבְרָם מִצְרַיְמָה לָגוּר שָׁם ("So Abram went down to Egypt to reside there.") This clause is a bit more complicated than the first since it contains a second verbal form, an infinitive לָגוּר. In this case we have kept the infinitival phrase with its main clause since it is short—a pragmatic decision.

The last line would then contain the last clause of the verse, which is linked to the main clause by the conjunction כִּי כִּי־כָבֵד הָרָעָב בָּאָרֶץ׃ ("for the famine was severe in the land").

This dependent clause seems to deserve a line of its own both because of its length—to put it with the preceding main clause would make it too long—and because it forms a near inclusio with the first clause. Note the repetition of "famine" and "land." Our final product would look like this:

וַיְהִי רָעָב בָּאָרֶץ / וַיֵּרֶד אַבְרָם מִצְרַיְמָה לָגוּר שָׁם / כִּי־כָבֵד הָרָעָב בָּאָרֶץ׃

Here is a longer text in Greek with the clauses marked. Your text should look something like this example from Luke's Beatitudes in 6:20-24 (clauses are divided by virgules):

> Μακάριοι οἱ πτωχοί / ὅτι ὑμετέρα ἐστὶν ἡ βασιλεία τοῦ θεοῦ. / μακάριοι οἱ πεινῶντες νῦν, / ὅτι χορτασθήσεσθε. / μακάριοι οἱ κλαίοντες νῦν, / ὅτι γελάσετε. / μακάριοί ἐστε / ὅταν μισήσωσιν ὑμᾶς οἱ ἄνθρωποι, / καὶ ὅταν ἀφορίσωσιν ὑμᾶς / καὶ ὀνειδίσωσιν / καὶ ἐκβάλωσιν τὸ ὄνομα ὑμῶν ὡς πονηρὸν ἕνεκα τοῦ υἱοῦ τοῦ ἀνθρώπου· / χάρητε ἐν ἐκείνῃ τῇ ἡμέρᾳ / καὶ σκιρτήσατε, / ἰδοὺ γὰρ ὁ μισθὸς ὑμῶν πολὺς ἐν τῷ οὐρανῷ· / κατὰ τὰ αὐτὰ γὰρ ἐποίουν τοῖς προφήταις οἱ πατέρες αὐτῶν.

This passage is an example in which there are both nominal and verbal clauses. It is also an example of how useful the punctuation as well as the καί are in identifying clauses. Also remember that these marks (light pencil, after all) are tentative. You will have plenty of opportunities to reconsider what you have done and make appropriate changes.

Checkpoint

At the end of this chapter you should have in hand:

- A text to study with a beginning and ending you can justify.
- A working copy of this text—either in a word processor or on a photocopied sheet.
- Notes on glosses and parses—any information that you need to read the text efficiently.
- Penciled slashes on the text that tentatively identify where the clauses begin and end.

CHAPTER 2

TABLING THE TEXT

In chapter 1 you did the spade work for reading a text visually. This is necessary work because you are not a native reader of Hebrew or Greek. In this chapter you will be doing the actual lining out of the text. The way you will do this is to transfer each clause, or a major semantic part of one, from your linear copy to a table. Each row in the table will represent one line. Using a table, as you will find, keeps your formatting of the text uniform and allows you to add other information to your layout in an unobtrusive manner.

Transforming your slashed text into a clause layout is largely a mechanical exercise but, on the other hand, we do not use the term *transforming* lightly. There is often something quite illuminating about simply moving the text from its linear, wrapped format, in which a line has no particular significance, to a layout wherein each line represents a unit of meaning. This is the beginning of a visual reading because suddenly the text begins to stand out in a new way.

If you are working through a text on a computer screen, simply push "enter" at each penciled slash mark on your working copy. If you are working on paper, cut your text at the slash marks and paste each clause onto its own line. Once your text is lined out, transfer it to a table that has three columns.[1] In one column place your text. In the next one place your reading notes. In either the first or last column place the verse numbers. This can be a very narrow column.

Although a clause will normally occupy a single line, if it is long or complicated break it into several parts. Subordinate clauses may be kept with their main clause, but often it is best to give them a line of their own. To indicate a subordinate relationship, you might want to indent these lines. As you grow more skilled in laying out texts, decisions as to how to line them out will become increasingly automatic. But, beware! This practice can be habit forming. You may find that having begun lining out texts, you will feel that you have not really grappled with the passage until you have tabled it.

Although layouts can be done securely only from the Greek or Hebrew text, for purposes of demonstration we present the following example from Amos in English.[2] In the NRSV it is printed:

> Thus says the LORD:
> For three transgressions of
>   Damascus,
>   and for four, I will not revoke
>   the punishment;
> because they have threshed
>   Gilead
>   with threshing sledges of iron.
> So I will send a fire on the house
>   of Hazael,
>   and it shall devour the
>   strongholds of Ben-hadad.
> I will break the gate bars of
>   Damascus,
>   and cut off the inhabitants
>   from the Valley of Aven,
> and the one who holds the
>   scepter from Beth-eden;
>   and the people of Aram shall
>   go into exile to Kir,
>   says the LORD.
>   (Amos 1:3-5)

In a layout, we might arrange the text as follows in order to show the relationship of the clauses. (For this example, we have retained the NRSV text and have dispensed with the table.)

> Thus says the LORD:
>
> For three transgressions of Damascus,
>   and for four, I will not revoke the punishment;
>   because they have threshed Gilead with threshing sledges of iron.
>
> So I will send a fire on the house of Hazael,
>   and it shall devour the strongholds of Ben-hadad.
>   [and] I will break the gate bars of Damascus,

and cut off the inhabitants from the Valley of Aven,
  and the one who holds the scepter from Beth-eden;
    and the people of Aram shall go into exile to Kir,
says the LORD.

(Amos 1:3-5)

Because this passage is poetry, each line may not represent a complete clause, but depends on its fellow to complete its sense. This is the case in the second and third line in which the line with "three" is completed by its parallel line with "four." After the introductory formula, we have divided the passage into three sections, each with three lines. The passage concludes with another formula.

The line groupings are based on the similarities of their content. The first three lines focus on the wrongs done. The second set of three mentions physical items as objects of destruction—although "house" may be used metaphorically since it can either refer to a "house" or a "dynasty." The final triad has people as the objects of punishment.

ANNOTATING THE TABLED TEXT

In the last chapter we used Genesis 12:10 (NRSV) as an illustration of how to mark off the clauses of a text. In this chapter we take the slashed text and convert it into a table and add two additional columns. The *before* looks like this:

וַיְהִ֥י רָעָ֖ב בָּאָ֑רֶץ / וַיֵּ֨רֶד אַבְרָ֤ם מִצְרַ֙יְמָה֙ לָג֣וּר שָׁ֔ם / כִּֽי־כָבֵ֥ד הָרָעָ֖ב בָּאָֽרֶץ׃

Now there was a famine in the land. So Abram went down to Egypt to reside there as an alien, for the famine was severe in the land.

The *after* looks like this:

וַיְהִ֥י רָעָ֖ב בָּאָ֑רֶץ
וַיֵּ֨רֶד אַבְרָ֤ם מִצְרַ֙יְמָה֙ לָג֣וּר שָׁ֔ם
כִּֽי־כָבֵ֥ד הָרָעָ֖ב בָּאָֽרֶץ׃

Reading Notes

As you line out the text, place the notes you still need in the center column. This would include the gloss for a word you keep forgetting or the parse of a second aorist that gives you fits. If you are not sure about a particular gloss, you may record several senses for later consideration. It is also helpful to make a brief notation of any idioms or unusual wordings. Sometimes in glossing a text, you will come across a discussion of some conundrum hinging on word usage. Any observations or information that would unbalance your chart can be entered in notes following your table. In the table cell itself just indicate the number of the note where your discussion can be found. For example, for the word לָגוּר you might want to indicate that it may have the meaning of "taking up temporary residence" and list other places in which it occurs with this meaning.

Grammatical Notes

Record items of interest. Ask yourself, is there a shift from third person to second person? Is there a pattern in the distribution of tense or aspect in the passage? Is there a move from plural to singular? If you record this type of information now, you will be able to draw upon it later when you examine more closely the language used in your text. As you gain experience, you will gain confidence in knowing what are significant features to record and what are not.

Syntactical Notes

In your syntactical notes, you might note the distribution of clause types in your passage. Is a clause independent or dependent? If it is independent, note whether it is syndetic or asyndetic. Also note the types of dependent clauses you find. Identify verbal and nominal clauses. Again, if you have any uncertainty about what a clause is, what kinds of clauses there are, and how they function in relation to other clauses, refer to Excursus 1. In addition, most intermediate grammars contain information about clauses, especially the dependent clauses.

There may be other information that you want to save as well. You may want to note where the discussion of a feature is found in a grammar. What you should have by the end of this process is a table that has philological notes and other notes that seem to mark interesting features about the language of the text. A table for Genesis 12:10 might look like this:

וַיְהִי רָעָב בָּאָרֶץ	Predicate first, topic second.
וַיֵּרֶד אַבְרָם מִצְרַיְמָה לָגוּר שָׁם	Main clause + infinitive.
כִּי־כָבֵד הָרָעָב בָּאָרֶץ׃	Subordinate nominal clause.
	Note inclusio with the first line of the verse.

The following is a Greek example from Matthew 12:31-32.

For this reason I say to you,
every sin and blasphemy will be forgiven humanity.
But blasphemy against the spirit will not be forgiven.
Indeed whoever speaks a word against the Son of Man,
it will be forgiven him,
but whoever speaks against the Holy Spirit—
it will not be forgiven him neither in this age nor in the coming age.

	CLAUSES	PHILOLOGICAL NOTES
31	Διὰ τοῦτο λέγω ὑμῖν,	Independent, asyndetic. Present.
	πᾶσα ἁμαρτία καὶ βλασφημία ἀφεθήσεται τοῖς ἀνθρώποις,	Independent, syndetic. Future, passive. Object complement in dative. Blasphemy = Language irreverent or hostile to God.
	ἡ δὲ τοῦ πνεύματος βλασφημία οὐκ ἀφεθήσεται.	Independent, syndetic. Future, passive. Objective genitive.
32	καὶ ὃς ἐὰν εἴπῃ λόγον κατὰ τοῦ υἱοῦ τοῦ ἀνθρώπου,	Dependent, syndetic. Aorist, subjunctive.
	ἀφεθήσεται αὐτῷ·	Independent, asyndetic. Future, passive.
	ὃς δ' ἂν εἴπῃ κατὰ τοῦ πνεύματος τοῦ ἁγίου,	Dependent, syndetic. Aorist, subjunctive.
	οὐκ ἀφεθήσεται αὐτῷ οὔτε ἐν τούτῳ τῷ αἰῶνι οὔτε ἐν τῷ μελλοντι.	Independent, asyndetic. Future, passive. Common rabbinic designation for an indefinite, long period.

To place your semantic notes as well as your information about the syntactical and grammatical relationships on the same sheet as your layout, as we have done, is a handy and helpful trick. In this way, all of your work is accessible at a single glance—the clauses of the text as well as the supporting material needed to read them. Now you are free to attend to other aspects of reading and the text will become more familiar and intimate.

Having lined out your text and placed it in a table, there are three tasks that need attention now. They are examining the word order of the lined out clauses, further exploration of the meaning of some words in your passage, and finally, a consideration of the text. We insert these inquiries here because they entail looking at each clause rather than the passage as a unit. Methods for recording your work on these issues will vary widely. Your observations can either be added directly to your table or appended as notes after it.

Word Order

English is a word-order language. There is relatively little flexibility in the order of words in a clause because changing the order of words is likely to change the meaning. Compare:

John kissed Jane.

Jane kissed John.

For English, the order of words is a key indicator of their grammatical function. Subjects come before the verb; objects follow it. Change this order and you change the subject and object of the sentence, as in the above example.[3]

Greek, especially, but also Hebrew, are inflected languages and consequently there is more flexibility in word order since the words retain their grammatical and syntactic function regardless of word order. Note the following example from Deuteronomy 5:22:

אֶת־הַדְּבָרִים הָאֵלֶּה דִּבֶּר יְהוָה אֶל־כָּל־קְהַלְכֶם

These are the words the LORD spoke to your entire assembly at the mountain.

In this sentence the direct object comes first, then the verb, and then the subject.

Since authors had a choice among a variety of word orders in biblical Greek and Hebrew, the order of words became part of an author's expressive repertoire. Nevertheless, certain patterns were more frequent or the standard patterns while others were less frequent and more unusual. In language analysis the patterns that are frequent, that call no attention to themselves, are termed *unmarked.* They are not distinctive. The patterns that are unusual and distinctive and thereby can call attention to themselves are the *marked* patterns.

In reading texts it is important to note the marked patterns, clauses with less frequent word orders. In order to see what is unusual, however, you need to know the standard from which it is deviating. Since basic grammars and courses in Greek and Hebrew vary widely in how much attention is paid to word order, we have included an excursus, excursus 2, on marked and unmarked word order for both Greek and Hebrew. We will assume this knowledge in our analysis below. If this is new material, please review it.

As you look over the lined out clauses in your table, note instances of unusual word order. If you find marked word orders, especially if they seem to be significant or form a pattern in their distribution, you should note them on your table. There are several ways to do this. You may wish to note standard and unusual word order for each clause. Alternatively, you may wish simply to mark in some way those clauses that depart from standard word order. Or, particularly if the passage is highly structured or poetic, you may wish to label with numbers or letters the various components of the clause that appear in different word orders. In the following illustration, from Genesis 1:27, we have used several of these techniques for the purposes of demonstration.

וַיִּבְרָא אֱלֹהִים אֶת־הָאָדָם בְּצַלְמוֹ	Unmarked order: w=V+S+O+Satellite	ברא only used of God צלם used of material objects that resemble or signify the object they model. 1 Sam. 6:5, 11; of idols, 2 Kings 11:18
בְּצֶלֶם אֱלֹהִים בָּרָא אֹתוֹ	The satellite shifted to first position Satellite+S+V+O	
זָכָר וּנְקֵבָה בָּרָא אֹתָם׃	The satellite remains in first position Satellite+V+O	Biological terms used for gender rather than social ones—man and woman

A visual representation of these word orders would look like this:

Created	God	*the human*	in His image	**A**	*B*	C	D
In the image of God	**he created**	*him*		D′	**A′**	C′	
Male and female	**he created**	*them*		D′′	**A′′**	C′′	

Although it is not always possible to translate the word order of the text into English, it is helpful to do so when the sense of the clause can be maintained.

Lexical Analysis

Frankly, our tendency is to be quite cautionary about extensive word study, especially at this stage. It is easy to become fascinated and overly invested in this part of the process, producing beautiful and extensive word studies of a passage—leaving little time and energy for much else! Having said this, however, the study of words is important and intriguing. Indeed, some words are pivotal for understanding a passage. Following your reading and lining out of a passage it might be evident to you that investigating the meaning of particular words is an important task. In such cases you should now proceed to a more careful analysis of the sense of these words.[4]

First, consult a dictionary to gain an overview of the word's meaning. Some dictionaries, like *DCH* will list all of the constructions within which a word occurs. This may help you narrow down your investigations. For example, you may decide you need only study a verb when used with a certain preposition since that is how the verb is used in your passage.

Next, use a concordance.[5] A concordance lists all occurrences of a word in the Bible. In consulting a concordance you are searching for ways in which the distribution—the use of the word—is skewed. Begin by noting the environments in which the word occurs. Does a word tend to cluster with certain other words or in a certain predicate frame? For example, scholars have noted that the word *create* in Hebrew, ברא, has only God for its subject and only the product of the action for its object. A material or substance from which creation might have proceeded is never mentioned. We can represent this predicate frame schematically as:

ברא + Divine subject + product as object. [material never mentioned]

In looking at the frames within which a word occurs, it is important to observe how different prepositions are used with a verb to connect it with its oblique complements. For example, the Hebrew verb ישב can have two different meanings. When accompanied by the preposition על it means "sit"; when accompanied by ב it means "reside, live." We can readily recognize this phenomenon in English from a word like *put*. It has a wide variety of meanings depending on the preposition used with it—put up, put up with, put on, put off, and so forth. The meaning of *put* depends, in part, on how it is linked to its complements. Compare "he put on his clothes" with "he put off his meeting."

Besides noting what words cluster with another, also note other dimensions in which such skewing takes place. Looking again at the word *create* in Hebrew, we note that it clusters in Isaiah chapter 40 and following—often considered to date from the exilic period—as well as in Ezekiel, again from the same period. On the other hand, the word almost never occurs in the earliest strata of biblical literature (in the Torah outside of the "P" material). Although you may not know what to do with this information at this stage, such a skewing in the diachronic distribution of a term may be significant to your later work.[6] A handy tool for finding this type of information is Jenni and Westermann, *Theological Lexicon of the Old Testament.* Also articles in the standard Hebrew and Greek lexicons may cite all occurrences of a word. From these articles you may find a peculiar distribution of a word.

Another question to ask is, What other choices were available? Usually in a language there is more than one way to say something. In Genesis 1–3 we not only find ברא (create) used of God's activity, but also the words עשׂה (make) and יצר (form). The latter is used in Genesis 2:7 for the "creation" of humankind. The question is, on what basis did the author select these various terms to describe the creative activity of God? In the case of יצר (form), the answer seems quite straightforward: according to *BDB* the dominant use of this word in the human sphere is to describe the activity of a potter shaping or forming clay. From this distribution, we can understand why it was an appropriate term for the divine activity in making humankind—they were formed from the earth.[7]

As for preserving this work, the easiest and best way is to attach a sheet of notes to your analysis. Such notes should include comments from lexicons and concordances as well as commentaries and other resources that you consult. Be sure to include decisions you make about the senses of words in your passage.

Textual Criticism

In the course of reading through your passage, looking up word meanings, and analyzing grammar and noting syntax, you will occasionally encounter texts that just don't seem to make good sense as written. For example as you begin reading Amos 6:12, הֲיְרֻצוּן בַּסֶּלַע סוּסִים אִם־יַחֲרוֹשׁ בַּבְּקָרִים you would probably translate it: "Do horses run on rocks, or does one plow with oxen?" If you thought about this construction a bit, you would see that the first question demands a "no" answer—it is a rhetorical question—but the second needs a "yes" answer! Then if you checked the NRSV you would find: "Do horses run on rocks? Does one plow the sea with oxen?" which makes sense, but is not what is in the text. Where do they find "the sea"? We have here a textual issue—not because we cannot read the text as it stands, but because what it says does not make sense. Briefly put, the word for "oxen" can be divided into two words, בַּבָּקָר יָם by detaching the plural ending. The noun is now singular, "ox," and the plural ending, now detached, can form the word for "sea." Alternatively, one could reason, the word for "sea" was left out because it is identical to the plural ending and the scribe's eye skipped over it.

In cases in which the biblical text is so difficult or unclear that you cannot read it sensibly, you might begin by comparing several translations to see how others have coped with the problem. Commentaries also provide discussions of various options for construing a text. Be sure you understand what the problem is—state to yourself the exact reasons the wording is a problem. What problem is text criticism to solve?

Textual criticism is a very specialized and technical discipline. You are not, nor are you expected to be, an expert textual critic. However, textual criticism does play a fairly dominant role in the secondary literature, especially for the New Testament. You should become adept at using Metzger's handbook, *A Textual Commentary on the Greek New Testament.*[8]

As suggested above, you might place text critical matters after your table, or with more difficult or controversial texts, you may find it useful to summarize the fruit of your textual work on a table like the one below. In this case you will devote a separate section, following the tabled text, to your text critical chart. Following such a worksheet as you make text critical decisions will help you understand the issues and not get lost in the forest.

One of the more dramatic variants in the New Testament occurs in Luke 24. Some ancient manuscripts omit verse 12, which reads, "But Peter got up and ran to the tomb; stooping and looking in, he saw the linen cloths by themselves; then he went home, amazed at what had happened" (NRSV). Manuscripts that omit this verse move straight from the disciples' dismissal of the women's news to the narrative of the two disciples going to Emmaus. This variant is still being debated. If you look at the RSV you will see that it omits verse 12. The NRSV, however, includes it. Below is a chart that summarizes and evaluates the information:

Variants	External Evidence	Internal Evidence	Commentaries	Decision
Luke 24:12 is omitted completely by some ancient manuscripts. Other manuscripts retain this verse.	This verse is omitted in the Western text (D) but appears in papyrus 75. Normally, one is cautious about the realiability of D when it differs from other major texts such as papyrus 75.	The fact that Peter responds to the empty tomb with wonderment or puzzlement (not a positive emotion or state of being in Luke-Acts) is a possible reason for its omission in D, which tends to omit references that make the disciples look bad.	Both the UBS committee (Metzger) and Brown *(A Risen Christ in Easter Time)* argue for the retention. The committee "regarded the passage as a natural antecedent to verse 24 and was inclined to explain the similarity with the verses in John [20:23, 5, 6, 10] as due to the likelihood that both evangelists had drawn upon a common tradition" (184).	Based on both the external manuscript evidence and the internal evidence, the decision is for retention of the verse.

Begin by noting the *possibilities* offered by the most important variants, the ones that make a difference in how the text is translated and understood. Second, proceed to fill in the information in the columns in a systematic way. At the end of the process come to a decision as to the most *probable* reading.

For the Hebrew Bible, textual criticism plays a less important role, because the textual variants are usually found in ancient translations, like the Septuagint, rather than in differing Hebrew texts. In fact, the printed Hebrew text normally follows a single manuscript, whereas the Greek text is an eclectic text—it chooses its wording from a wide variety of texts and the final product does not represent the text of any single manuscript. For the advanced Hebrew student, two works with which to be familiar are: Emanuel Tov, *Textual Criticism of the Hebrew Bible,* and J. Weingreen, *Introduction to the Critical Study of the Text of the Hebrew Bible.* These works will provide a wider point of reference for your understanding of how we got the present form of the Hebrew Bible and what it represents.

What the Hebrew does have, however, are Masoretic notes. An indispensable aid for the student is Kelly, Mynatt, and Crawford, *The Masorah of Biblia Hebraica Stuttgartensia: Introduction and Annotated Glossary* (Grand Rapids: Eerdmans, 1998).

CHECKPOINT

At the end of this chapter you should begin your study notebook. It should contain the following items:

- A **table or chart** with each unit of meaning, normally the clause, having its own line.
- Notes about **grammatical or syntactical** features entered into your table or appended to it.

Depending on your text, you may also include the following material:

- Any necessary reading helps and important discoveries regarding words.
- Marks indicating unusual word orders.
- A table or notes indicating your conclusions about significant textual difficulties.

CHAPTER 3

CONTOURING THE TEXT

The work of this chapter and the next is to prepare a textual topography. Your tabled text may be compared to a flat road map, which shows the horizontal plane, the location of towns, rivers, highways, and distances but does not show the vertical dimension, the ruggedness of the terrain, the height of mountains, or the depths of valleys. Topographical maps represent this third dimension by contour lines, colors, and symbols. Similarly, a textual topographic map adds marks and colors to a layout in order to place its contours of expression in relief and to designate the various regions of the text.[1]

Discovering and bringing out the textual terrain of a biblical passage is one of the most exciting phases of study. The interpreter, seeing the shape of the text emerge, comes to know the text in a new and intimate way. It's like meeting someone in person after studying his or her photograph. And, like meeting a person, it requires interaction. The reader must participate; the reader must use all the empathy, creativity, reflection, and intuition that she or he has to give to the art of biblical interpretation.

Your goal in producing a textual topography is to make visible the expressive features of your text. Discovering these features will require looking carefully at the unit to see how what is said, is said. Since language normally affords several ways of saying something, speakers and writers make choices about how they word what they want to say. For example, the sentence "Bill bought Bob's boat" could be transposed into the passive "Bob's boat was bought by Bill." Or one could say, "It was Bill who bought the boat from Bob." These three expressions all convey with different nuances and communicative force the notion that Bill now owns Bob's boat.

In addition to choosing among the available ways of saying

something, writers may also repeat themselves, creating refrains and other patterns. These choices about the words used and the patterns of expression adopted are not value neutral. Meaning is communicated through these choices. How something is said is part of what is said!

However, before you begin searching for the contours of your text, just a reminder that while the following discussion and your learning will be linear, as you gain proficiency your analysis will become more holistic, constantly shifting from one aspect of analysis to another. Indeed, as you become proficient, you will do several sequential steps simultaneously. This is how it should be and demonstrates your mastery of the method. Consequently, you will find the processes outlined in the next two chapters to be interrelated and perhaps overlapping. Feel free to disregard the order of presentation given here. Above all, don't become mechanical—operate intuitively and creatively.

The basic technique for illuminating a text's topography is to *mark its features*. One of the great advantages of the computer is the ease with which a text can be readily manipulated and marked. Bold print, italics, underlining, different font faces and sizes are all useful for calling attention to the features of a text. But *coloring makes contours leap to the eye*. If you can, mark the text with colors on the computer screen and print them out. If not, print or photocopy your layout and then color it manually. Or you might use an overhead transparency on which you can mark the text with erasable transparency markers. These markers allow false trails to be erased and, therefore, promote experimentation. You can also use lines to indicate textual features. The possibilities are limited only by your insights and ability to make them visible.

Because contouring a text will mean marking up the Greek or Hebrew text, first copy your text from its column in your table to a new page. You can "untable" your text by copying the contexts of the text column to a new page. Or you can copy the whole table, delete the other columns, and then remove the table lines from around the text.[2] The end product should be a clean lined out text that you can now mark. At this point you should also make a spare copy of your clean layout. You will probably use one copy on which to mark the different features that you find as you work through this chapter. The second copy you will use at the end when you reach the checkpoint for this chapter. There you will prepare your final contoured text, which can then be placed in your notebook.

SEMANTIC REPETITIONS AND PATTERNS

What are you looking for when setting out to discover the expressive features of a text? The most obvious features are repeated words and phrases, although these repetitions are frequently accompanied by other forms of repetition as well.[3] Notice that in the following example the repeated words are also accompanied by repetitions in the grammatical and syntactical patterns.

Romans 8:30

οὓς δὲ προώρισεν,	**whom** he set apart
τούτους καὶ ἐκάλεσεν·	***these*** he also *called*
καὶ οὓς ἐκάλεσεν,	and **whom** he *called;*
τούτους καὶ ἐδικαίωσεν·	***these*** he also *justified*
οὓς δὲ ἐδικαίωσεν,	and **whom** he *justified*
τούτους καὶ ἐδόξασεν.	***these*** he also glorified.

Word repetitions stand out in this text and catch the eye first. But other kinds of repetitions and patterns are also visible. Notice, for instance, how the relative pronoun, "whom" alternates with the demonstrative pronouns, "these." Also, all of the verbs are aorist, a repetition of a grammatical feature. This grammatical pattern includes the two verbs, "set apart" and "glorified," that are not repeated. They are, however, integrated into the regularity of the passage through this grammatical pattern. Although this particular passage is more highly structured than most, it does demonstrate that frequently word repetitions will be accompanied by other kinds of repetitions as well.

Now go through your layout and mark repeated words that you believe could be significant.[4] Look for the repetition of key words and phrases. Sometimes it may be a single word or a cluster of words. Sometimes it may be entire phrases or clauses. As you mark these occurrences, take careful note not only of the repetition, but also of any variation in the repetition. Is the repetition exactly word for word, or are there changes in the wording of the second or third instance? If there are changes, what is changed, what is different, what is omitted, and where are the expansions? Bear in mind that even if a phrase or clause is repeated exactly, it may have a different nuance in a different context. There is an ancient proverb to the effect that one never steps into the same river twice! Even a word for word repetition is different the second time around because the verbal context has changed—there's different water flowing around it.

For example, in the Balaam story, Numbers 22, we find an artful and quite humorous use of repeated clauses. In his journey, we find first:

> The donkey saw the angel of the LORD standing in the road, with a drawn sword in his hand. (Numbers 22:23 NRSV)

The donkey saw, but Balaam did not.

The first part of this clause is repeated in verse 25, "the donkey saw the angel of the LORD," and in 27 "the donkey saw the angel of the LORD." Finally in verse 31, the entire clause is repeated, but this time with Balaam as the subject:

> He [Balaam] saw the angel of the LORD standing in the road, with his drawn sword in his hand.

Finally Balaam sees what the donkey has seen from the very beginning! This refrain tracks the perception, or lack of perception, of the main character.

Another interesting feature of some biblical narratives is the close repetition of large blocks of material. These larger repetitions function similarly to the repetitions that we have been examining. Repetitions of this scope stand out, especially if you are reading in Greek or Hebrew—suddenly you find yourself zipping through big chunks of text that are virtually repeated. For instance, the story of the sheep and the goats in Matthew 25:31-46 consists of two segments. Except for the negations, what the Son of Man says to the goats, in a somewhat abbreviated form, is a mirror image of what he has already said to the sheep. What is repeated as well as what is left out is an important expressive feature of this passage and should be marked.

In addition to these general occurrences of repetition, some types of repetition form *patterns* that belong to the stock-in-trade of biblical writers. The most important ones are: *parallelism, chiasm, anastrophe*, and *inclusio*.[5]

Parallelism

Parallelism is the basic building for these important patterns. A good understanding and recognition of parallelism will help you become a good interpreter of biblical texts. Parallelism is the correspondence between two or more words, phrases, or clauses in biblical prose or poetry.[6] It can and does function on many different levels, using correspondences in semantics, grammar, syntax, and even sound to achieve its effect.[7] These correspondences show a balance and symmetry in thought and form that may be characterized as synonymous, antithetic, or synthetic.

Synonymous parallelism is a pattern in which two or more lines say similar things. Of course, since different words are used, the semantic significance is not exactly the same. Still, the two meanings are roughly equivalent.

An example is Psalm 29:4:

קוֹל־יְהוָה בַּכֹּחַ
קוֹל יְהוָה בֶּהָדָר׃

The voice of the LORD in strength / the voice of the LORD in majesty.

We can scan these lines as follows: a b c / a b c´. Because the first two words are repeated in the second line, no prime was used. The third word is different and indicated by the pairing c / c´. This bicolon is unusual because ordinarily the repetition will not be as exact and so symmetrically ordered, as a reading of the whole of Psalm 29 will show.[8]

Matthew 7:2 is another example of parallelism, this time in a prose context.

ἐν ᾧ γὰρ κρίματι κρίνετε κριθήσεσθε,
καὶ ἐν ᾧ μέτρῳ μετρεῖτε μετρηθήσεται ὑμῖν.

For with the judgment you judge, you will be judged,
And with the measure you measure, you will be measured.

Notice in these examples that it is not only the words that stand in parallelism but also syntactic and grammatical components. For instance, both members of the couplet end with a future, passive verb. The scansion would be: a b c / a´ b´ c´.

Antithetical parallelism is a type of parallelism in which the two lines articulate a contrast. The second line opposes the first. Often one is negative; the other positive. Or the two lines may be connected by an adversative conjunction, such as "but." Wisdom literature abounds in this kind of parallelism. Proverbs 16:22 reads:

Wisdom is a fountain of life to one who has it,
but folly is the punishment of fools.

Or Matthew 6:19-20 (RSV):

Do not lay up for yourselves treasures on earth,
where moth and rust consume
and where thieves break in and steal,

but lay up for yourselves treasures in heaven,
where neither moth nor rust consumes
and where thieves do not break in and steal.

Climactic parallelism describes the semantic relationship between lines that form a progression or climax. The second clause may intensify or clarify the meaning of the first clause. Or the second builds on the first in some way, perhaps extending it in a stair-step fashion. Psalm 146:1 offers an example:

Praise the LORD!
Praise the LORD, O my soul!
a b
a b c

Notice that the shape of the scansion forms a stair step.

The well-used doxology at the end of Jude, verse 24, is an example of *synthetic parallelism.*[9] The parallelism is developed with two infinitives, but the motion developed with the semantic choices is much more climactic than parallel.[10]

Now to him who is able to keep you from falling
and to present you without blemish before his glory
with jubilation.

Chiasm

Chiasm builds on parallelism, taking it, in a sense, one step further. In chiasm, the word order of the first phrase or clause is repeated in reverse order in the second. Obviously an inflected language such as Hebrew or Greek has greater flexibility than English, making it easier to invert the order of semantic, grammatical, and syntactical components. An inverted order creates a mirror image between the two clauses. The simplest chiasm may be represented by an **a b c / c b a** pattern as in the examples below.[11]

Mark 2:27:

Τὸ σάββατον διὰ τὸν ἄνθρωπον ἐγένετο
καὶ οὐχ ὁ ἄνθρωπος διὰ τὸ σάββατον·

The Sabbath for humankind was made/
a b c
and not humankind for the Sabbath.
b a

Matthew 6:34:

μὴ οὖν μεριμνήσητε εἰς τὴν αὔριον,
ἡ γὰρ αὔριον μεριμνήσει ἑαυτῆς·

Therefore, do not be anxious for tomorrow,/
a b
for tomorrow will be anxious for itself.
b a

Chiastic constructions can be both forward moving and concentric. Reading a chiasm may mean reading from the extremities of the construction inward to the center as well as progressively from the beginning to the end.[12] Reading from the ends toward the middle is apparent in those cases in which there is a hinge or central unmatched member of the construction. A chiasm may also be formed by whole lines as part of a much larger chiastic structure. Below is a paragraph from a narrative in Jeremiah with a chiastic arrangement.

Jeremiah 28:2-4 (NRSV, arranged and contoured):[13]

Thus says the LORD of hosts, the God of Israel:

A **I have broken the yoke of the king of Babylon.**

B Within two years *I will bring back to this place*

C ***all the vessels of the LORD's house,***

X which King Nebuchadnezzar of Babylon took away
from this place and carried to Babylon.

C′ King Jeconiah son of Jehoiakim of Judah,
and ***all the exiles from Judah*** who went to Babylon

B′ *I will also bring back to this place,* says the LORD,

A′ **for I will break the yoke of the king of Babylon.**

The contouring indicates the elements that are repeated in a chiastic arrangement and marks their chiastic partner.[14] Notice the practically verbatim repetitions in the first two and last two lines. The phrase "from this place" is also picked up in the central, unpaired member of this chiasm.

A new feature of this chiasm is the center element marked with an X. It has no parallel member but marks the pivot or the hinge around which the chiasm is formed. As such it is the center of the chiasm and calls for particular attention in the exegesis of a passage. At this point in your work it is adequate to note the patterns of expression and mark the significant ones on your layout.

Chiasms can be used to organize texts at a variety of levels—from a simple four-word pattern to a discourse as long and complex as the Sermon on the Mount. One of the great joys of biblical study is spotting a chiasm for oneself.[15]

Anastrophe

Anastrophe is picking up a word that appears at or near the end of one clause and repeating it at the beginning of the next. Notice in 1 John 4:15 (RSV) that the first clause ends with "God" and the second clause begins with "God," as shown by the underlining in the Greek and the bold print in the English.

> ὃς ἐάν ὁμολογήσῃ ὅτι Ἰησοῦς ἐστιν ὁ υἱὸς τοῦ θεοῦ,
> ὁ θεὸς ἐν αὐτῷ μένει καὶ αὐτὸς ἐν τῷ θεῷ.

> Whoever confesses that Jesus is the Son of **God, God** abides in him, and he in God.

In Genesis 13 we find two paragraphs linked by anastrophe, providing a smooth transition from one to the other. *LORD* is the final word of one paragraph. It is also the first word of the next paragraph, which opens a new scene.

> Now the people of Sodom were wicked, great sinners against the LORD.
> The LORD said to Abram, after Lot had separated from him... (Genesis 13:13-14 NRSV)

Inclusio

Finally, words or other features from the beginning of a unit may be repeated at the end of a unit, forming a frame around the unit. This arrangement is rather like a chiasm at the outset and at the end, but does not necessarily follow the structure of a chiasm for the body of the text. Psalm 8 (NRSV) is a classic example. The first half of the first verse and last verses are the same.

> O LORD, our Sovereign, how majestic is your name in all the earth!
> You have set your glory above the heavens.
>
> O LORD, our Sovereign, how majestic is your name in all the earth!

Pay special attention to this arrangement, called *inclusio*. Inclusios can be found in a single passage, marking off sections of text within a book, or even framing an entire book. Here is an example from Matthew.

The list of beatitudes in Matthew 5:3-10 is framed by an inclusio. In this passage there is a list of eight beatitudes. They are sometimes called the "third-person beatitudes" because they are distinct from the beatitude in verse 11 that is addressed to "you," second person. The first and last of the third-person beatitudes end with the phrase "for theirs is the kingdom of the heavens."

Matthew 5:3

> Μακάριοι οἱ πτωχοὶ τῷ πνεύματι,
> <u>ὅτι αὐτῶν ἐστιν ἡ βασιλεία τῶν οὐρανῶν·</u>

Matthew 5:10

> μακάριοι οἱ δεδιωγμένοι ἕνεκεν δικαιοσύνης,
> <u>ὅτι αὐτῶν ἐστιν ἡ βασιλεία τῶν οὐρανῶν·</u>

These two beatitudes form a frame for the third-person beatitudes. Because these blessings are framed by this phrase, we understand verses 3-10 to be an integrated unit of expression.

Word Plays

Before we leave the subject of repetition we need to deal with a literary phenomenon usually designated as *word play.*[16] Sometimes points will be made in Hebrew and Greek on the basis of words that are similar in pronunciation. Whereas these usages involve repetition, they can be more subtle. Although this phenomenon may be difficult for nonnative readers to see, the discovery of a word play can be a serendipitous event in the art of biblical interpretation. So keep looking! Here is an example to help you get a feel for it.

Isaiah 5 talks about the vineyard of the Lord, contrasting the divine hopes and expectations for the vineyard with the bitter and disappointing reality. The vineyard is producing wild grapes instead of good fruit. In verse 7, the author makes clear the analogy between the vineyard/Israel, the wild grapes/violence and the cry of the oppressed. Isaiah 5:7 (NRSV) reads:

כִּי כֶרֶם יְהוָה צְבָאוֹת בֵּית יִשְׂרָאֵל וְאִישׁ יְהוּדָה נְטַע שַׁעֲשׁוּעָיו

וַיְקַו לְמִשְׁפָּט וְהִנֵּה מִשְׂפָּח
לִצְדָקָה וְהִנֵּה צְעָקָה׃

> he expected justice לְמִשְׁפָּט, but saw bloodshed מִשְׂפָּח;
> righteousness לִצְדָקָה, but heard a cry צְעָקָה.

Look at the last part of the verse. Notice how similar the two pairs of key words look and sound in Hebrew.

You should read through your passage to catch the subtleties of the author's use of language. In Isaiah 5:7 the similarity in the look and sound of the words adds to the poignancy of the divine disappointment. The play on these word pairs underlines the contrast between what God hoped for and what God actually got. Also the failure of justice emphasized by this word play creates empathy for God's point of view.

GRAMMATICAL PATTERNS

Finding and marking semantic repetitions and patterns is an important heuristic beginning point for discovering a text's contours. In the course of searching for these patterns, you also noticed grammatical and syntactic patterns, as we did in several of the examples given above. However, patterning at the level of grammar and syntax deserves attention on its own. First, you need to consider more broadly and systematically the distribution of the grammatical and syntactical features found in a text.

In looking for grammatical and syntactic patterns, *begin with the verb*. Note how tenses, voices, and moods are used or distributed in your passage. If there is a shift in tense, voice, or mood mark these shifts on your worksheet, at least tentatively.

After checking the verbal forms, next observe whether there is a pattern in variations of number and person. Are most of them singular or plural? Is there a shift from singular to plural or plural to singular? Is there a singular where you might expect a plural or a plural where you might expect a singular?[17] Here is an example from Leviticus 1:2-3.

דַּבֵּר אֶל־בְּנֵי יִשְׂרָאֵל וְאָמַרְתָּ אֲלֵהֶם
אָדָם כִּי־יַקְרִיב מִכֶּם קָרְבָּן לַיהוָה מִן־הַבְּהֵמָה
מִן־הַבָּקָר וּמִן־הַצֹּאן תַּקְרִיבוּ אֶת־קָרְבַּנְכֶם׃
אִם־עֹלָה קָרְבָּנוֹ מִן־הַבָּקָר זָכָר תָּמִים יַקְרִיבֶנּוּ
אֶל־פֶּתַח אֹהֶל מוֹעֵד יַקְרִיב אֹתוֹ לִרְצֹנוֹ לִפְנֵי יְהוָה׃

> Speak to the people of Israel and say to them: When any one of YOU bring an offering of livestock to the Lord, YOU shall bring your offering from the herd or from the flock. If the [his] offering is a burnt offering from the herd, he shall offer a male without blemish; he shall bring it to the entrance of the tent of meeting, for acceptance in his behalf before the Lord.

We find here a puzzling alternation of person and number. The passage begins with Israel in the third-person plural ("say to them"). However, in the next line the people are addressed, with a singular subject ("anyone of you"). The second-person "you," now a plural, continues in the next line ("you shall bring"). Then the text switches to the third singular ("if his offering") for the remainder of the text cited above.

What is the expressive force of this variation? Perhaps the reason for these changes lies in the situation. Moses is depicted as addressing these laws to the whole nation face-to-face. Normally laws are formulated in the third person, "if anyone does so and so," but here because they are addressed to an audience, the second person (you) is suitable.[18] This intermixture of second person with the third turns formal legal language into second-person, personal address.

After examining the verbs in your text, consider patterns in the use of participles and infinitives. How frequently do these forms appear? Where do they appear? Do they predominate in a particular segment of the text? Frequently a series of participles or infinitives are used in parallel or similar ways in successive clauses. If their distribution seems significant, mark these features on your layout.

In 1 John 2:9-11, each verse begins with a present, active participle—"the one saying"; "the one loving"; "the one hating." In the following translation, we use "whoever" to translate these participles. Notice the rhythm that is established with this grammatical usage.

> *Whoever claims* to be in the light,
> while hating his brother,
> is still in the darkness.
>
> *Whoever loves* his brother
> dwells in the light,
> and there is no scandal in him.
>
> *But whoever hates* his brother
> is in the darkness,
> and he walks in the darkness,
>
> and he does not know where he is going
> because the darkness blinded his eyes.

This pattern of using present active participles to begin each of these sentences marks the distinction between walking in the light and hating the brother.

SYNTACTIC PATTERNS

In chapter 2 you noted the different types of clauses used in your passage. Now observe how they are distributed in your text. For example, ask, Do nominal and verbal clauses alternate or cluster in a significant way? In chapter 2, you also observed which clauses displayed an unusual word order. At this point, check to see whether there is some pattern emerging in the variation of the word orders.

The story of Anna the prophet in Luke 2:36-38, which contains virtually no repetition of words, marks its main contours by the distribution of clause types. What follows is the contoured Greek text and its explanation.

Καὶ ἦν Ἅννα προφῆτις, θυγάτηρ Φανουήλ, ἐκ φυλῆς Ἀσήρ·
αὕτη προβεβηκυῖα ἐν ἡμέραις πολλαῖς,
ζήσασα μετὰ ἀνδρὸς ἔτη ἑπτὰ ἀπὸ τῆς παρθενίας αὐτῆς,
καὶ αὐτὴ χήρα ἕως ἐτῶν ὀγδοήκοντα τεσσάρων,

ἣ οὐκ ἀφίστατο τοῦ ἱεροῦ νηστείαις
  καὶ δεήσεσιν λατρεύουσα νύκτα καὶ ἡμέραν.
καὶ αὐτῇ τῇ ὥρᾳ ἐπιστᾶσα ἀνθωμολογεῖτο τῷ θεῷ
καὶ ἐλάλει περὶ αὐτοῦ πᾶσιν τοῖς προσδεχομένοις
  λύτρωσιν Ἰερουσαλήμ.

In this text, there are only four finite verbs—three finite plus the copula εἰμι (to be). They are all imperfect. The first two are active, the second is a middle deponent, and the third is also middle, probably deponent. Therefore all the verbs, in addition to being imperfect, are functionally active. They are all indicative in mood. Although there is therefore very little variation in the verbs, they are distributed in an interesting manner. In the first four of the eight clauses, there is only one finite verb and it is the copula. Since the verb of being is not a "real" verb, the three "real" verbs are all contained in the last four clauses of the text.[19] In contrast to the last four clauses, in the first half of the text, besides the copula, there are two nominal clauses and a participial clause. A strong contour line marks the transition from the first half of this passage to the second. This line also raises the question, Why the switch? On the surface, nominal clauses are static, active verbal clauses are dynamic. In this unit, the movement is from the character of Anna to her actions.

CONTOURING THE TEXT

When you have tentatively noted and marked the repetitions and patterns that seem important on the first of the copies of your lined text that you made at the beginning of the chapter, you are ready to prepare your contoured layout of the text. An individual contour is simply a visual representation of an observation of a repetition or pattern. In constructing your contoured text, guard against cluttering your text with so many markings that you distract attention from the major features. You are not interested in marking contours for the sake of marking contours, but because they help you understand the text better. Ask yourself why *this* feature is important enough to justify a contour.

When you are ready to begin contouring your text use the second copy of your lined text. Begin with the contour that you consider to be the most important one for understanding your passage or that seems the clearest and most significant marker. Then proceed to mark the next feature in importance and so on until your markings begin to detract from the most important feature or features of the text, or you have no more features to represent. If you are working with a word processor, it is relatively easy to try out different compositions of contours. Play with the text, good contours develop out of trial and error.

If you were contouring the text of Luke 2:36-38 just presented, you would first make clearly visible the division between the two segments of the unit. You might do this by double spacing between them. If you found other features in the passage, you would then mark them in order of importance. For example, you might next highlight the finite verbs, marking the copula differently. Then you might mark the nominal clauses in a distinctive fashion. Your final product might look like this:

Καὶ ἦν Ἅννα προφῆτις, θυγάτηρ Φανουήλ, ἐκ φυλῆς Ἀσήρ·
αὕτη προβεβηκυῖα ἐν ἡμέραις πολλαῖς,
ζήσασα μετὰ ἀνδρὸς ἔτη ἑπτὰ ἀπὸ τῆς παρθενίας αὐτῆς,
καὶ αὐτὴ χήρα ἕως ἐτῶν ὀγδοήκοντα τεσσάρω,

ἣ οὐκ ἀφίστατο τοῦ ἱεροῦ νηστείαις
 καὶ δεήσεσιν λατρεύουσα νύκτα καὶ ἡμέραν.
καὶ αὐτῇ τῇ ὥρᾳ ἐπιστᾶσα ἀνθωμολογεῖτο τῷ θεῷ
καὶ ἐλάλει περὶ αὐτοῦ πᾶσιν τοῖς προσδεχομένοις
 λύτρωσιν Ἰερουσαλήμ.

In contouring a text use a variety of techniques. Different type faces can be used. But the most striking way to make features visible is with color. On screen or with a color printer you can produce some exciting and insightful contours. On paper or on overhead transparencies you can obtain the same results with markers or highlighters.

Below, we provide two quite different examples of contoured texts. Our first example is from Amos 3:13-15. In this passage there are several repeated words. We have indicated a contour for only the most important ones. First, notice how the word בַּיִת (house) runs through this passage, from the beginning to the end. It clearly seems to be the dominant word in this passage. Because of its dominance, it would seem to deserve a contour. Second, the phrase "Oracle of the LORD" occurs in both the second and last line of the layout, although in slightly different form. This phrase seems to form something of an inclusio. This is usually a significant feature, so we should place this feature on a contour as well.

Third, looking at the verbs, we see that there are two first-person-singular verbs that highlight the action of God. In the following clauses, indicating the results of this action, we find either intransitive or passive verbs. This pattern would seem to place emphasis on these first-person verbs and their subject, God, as the exclusive actor. So this feature can reasonably be assigned a contour. Finally, examining the sound patterns in the passage, we see that the "f" sound (the פ)is prominent. We have marked this lightly so as to not detract from the more important contours already mentioned. Also, it is unclear what the expressive function of this feature might be, and so it may not deserve a contour.

שִׁמְעוּ וְהָעִידוּ בְּבֵית יַעֲקֹב
נְאֻם־אֲדֹנָי יְהוִה אֱלֹהֵי הַצְּבָאוֹת׃
כִּי בְּיוֹם פָּקְדִי פִשְׁעֵי־יִשְׂרָאֵל עָלָיו
וּפָקַדְתִּי עַל־מִזְבְּחוֹת בֵּית־אֵל
וְנִגְדְּעוּ קַרְנוֹת הַמִּזְבֵּחַ
וְנָפְלוּ לָאָרֶץ׃
וְהִכֵּיתִי בֵית־הַחֹרֶף עַל־בֵּית הַקָּיִץ
וְאָבְדוּ בָּתֵּי הַשֵּׁן
וְסָפוּ בָּתִּים רַבִּים
נְאֻם־יְהוָה׃

To summarize, the major contours that we have marked in this passage are: (1) the theme word בַּיִת, which runs throughout the passage; (2) the inclusio "Oracle of the Yahweh"; and (3) the two active first-person verbs that have God as their subject. We have also indicated one minor contour, the sound "f," of whose function we are uncertain.

If you study the passage a bit, you can find other repetitions, such as the ending צ at the end of the first major section of the passage and at the end of the line that begins the second. Is this repetition significant enough to warrant a contour? Would marking it detract from the contours already marked? Note that the first verb, פקד, also occurs at the beginning of the chapter in verse 2. Do these two oracles, 3:1-2 and 3:13-15, form an inclusio for the chapter?

In 1 Peter 2:21-24, we find a rather intricate, although well-formed set of contours. Because of its complexity, marking its contours makes this text visible and our comprehension of it greatly improves. What before was unseen and unnoticed is now seen and becomes the basis for a more insightful and richer understanding of this text. We have presented this contoured layout in English so that you might easily grasp the illustration. In practice, as noted above, layouts are done in the language of the text.

A For to this **you have been called,**

because Christ ***suffered*** also for you, leaving you an example,

B So that you should follow in his steps—

C WHO did not do a *sin,*

and in whom there was found no deceit (in his mouth).

X WHO, being abused, did not reply with a curse,

Suffering did not threaten,

But entrusted himself to the one who judges justly.

C´ WHO himself bore our *sins* (in his body on the tree),

B´ So that free from sins, we might live for justice.

A´ By his wounds **you have been healed.**

The center of the hymn is a chiastic cluster of three relative clauses introduced by the pronoun ὅς (who). The first and third of these clusters say something about sin. The first one is "who did no sin" and the third is "who bore our sins." The cluster of clauses at the center of this arrangement have to do with the nonretaliatory manner in which Christ acted—not replying in kind, but entrusting himself to the just judge.

The next concentric circle of the chiasm is evident in the purpose clauses constructed with the Greek word ἵνα (so that). These clauses have been underlined and they form another ring if we move out from the center of the hymn. Finally, the first line and the last line both contain an aorist passive construction—"you have been called" and "you have been healed." This is a grammatical inclusio (aorist passive verbs) that marks the frame of the chiasm. Clearly, this text is carefully constructed of concentric circles, a pattern of symmetry partly established through the patterning of the function and structure of its clauses.

There are also other, minor, patterns to be noted. "In his mouth" and "in his body" are not only grammatically parallel, but "mouth" and "body" are, in Greek, phonologically similar. In the second line from the top, "suffered" has its echo in the line "suffering did not threaten" in the "who" clause at the center of the chiasm. Similarly, the word "justice" in the second line from the bottom is an echo of the word "justly" used in the central (X) "who" clause.

It is the arrangement of all these features, semantic, grammatical, and syntactical that guides us to the heart of the hymn—the example of the Christ who did not retaliate in kind but trusted himself to the ultimate judge of justice. These features are an important part of what the text communicates—that the call and healing of believers flows out from the nonretaliatory Christ at the center.[20]

CHECKPOINT

At this point you should have an additional page to add to your notebook, a contoured layout of your passage that represents your judgment of the most important contours for understanding the text. Along with your contour, you may wish to write a paragraph or two explaining features that need comment. Before placing your work in your notebook, check it one last time. Ask yourself *why* the repetitions and patterns you have marked might be significant for understanding your text. Your goal is not to mark features for their own sake, but to mark features that may lead you to deeper insights into the message of the passage. It is not just the presence of repeated words or features that is important, but their location and arrangement that determines their significance for communication. This is why it is essential to determine and be able to state, if only tentatively, how a feature might serve the communicative thrust of the text. Although a conclusion about the significance of a contour for understanding cannot always be drawn until you have studied the passage further, remember that you are not simply tilling the ground of understanding for the pleasure of working the soil, but in order to reap insights and inspiration. The following chapter will help you sort out the significance of the features you have found in your text. At this point, at the end of this chapter, it is enough to have a contoured text and brief rationale for the contours you have marked.

CHAPTER 4

PLOTTING THE TEXT

From observing how your passage expresses itself, the present chapter moves to the question of how its content is organized or arranged. A key perspective for the work of this chapter is the notion that texts communicate dynamically through unity and progression. Texts both "hang together" and "go somewhere." In going somewhere they also communicate by detours, by what they leave out, by what is not there as well as what is there. Consequently, the way a text is organized should be viewed as a dynamic arrangement of continuity and discontinuity.

Analyzing the continuities and discontinuities of your text will help you uncover its organization and flow, what we are calling the plot of the text. Your goal is understanding how the individual parts of a text contribute to the development and communicative impact of the whole. In this work, you will first need to uncover the *regions*, the subparts, of your text. This task will call for you to analyze how your text establishes a topic and how it shifts from one topic to another. Also, you will need to pay attention to the structural markers that signal a text's organization and movement. Second, you will be asked to assess the pace of the text and look for gaps in its flow.[1]

With this information, you will be able to see, mark, and assign titles to the regions of your text—those clauses that are more tightly bound to one another than they are to the clauses that border them. The product of this analysis is a **textual topography**—a contoured layout on which you have marked regions and indicated how the parts work to express the message of the whole.

To begin plotting your text, you should have in hand a copy of your contoured text.[2] Using a pencil you can mark and correct your decisions about the structure and flow of your text on it. As the last step in this chapter, you will convert your penciled divisions and tentative assessment of their function into a topography. With a topography of your text in hand you will be ready to venture beyond the confines of the text itself.

REGIONS

Simply put, a **region** is a cluster of clauses more tightly bound to one another than to the clauses that border them. A passage is normally composed of a series of these segments that show internal organization. In deciding where to draw the line between regions of a text, you are working with a continuum—ties of greater cohesion and coherence compared to ties less binding; of greater organization over against weaker organization; borders where several contours coincide, contrasting with lesser-marked boundaries. Since these judgments are qualitative ones, they will call for more conscious and careful reflection on why some clauses form a cluster as over against another set of clustered clauses. Since each textual region, while composed of its own distinctive features, contributes to the unity and progression of the text, you should consider: (1) what characterizes the *coherence* of the individual regions; and (2) what characterizes their *function* within the larger text of which they are a part.

We have chosen the word *region* to describe the subsections of a text because it has a certain ambiguity and fuzziness. In geography, one region may fade gradually into another. Where does the Midwest begin or end? So also the communicative parts of a text may shade together. Likewise, regions may vary greatly in size. The Western United States is certainly a much vaster area than New England. A unit might be formed by an extensive paragraph. Or, each phase or point of an argument might be a region. It may even be a "Rhode Island," a clause that functions in a special way, such as an introductory phrase like "Thus says the LORD."

The regions that you discover should be marked and labeled on your layout. Since you are considering both the literary features as well as the content of the passage, pay attention to the ebb and flow of what is being communicated in the dynamic organization of the text. The role of a textual region in this movement will help you label it.

If you do your work carefully, the repetitions and patterns of contouring and the continuities and discontinuities of plotting should converge in a clear sense of the shape and character of the text. Your topography should make visible the dynamic communicative organization of your text.

Topic and Comment

In reading texts, we expect to find a thread that carries us along and gives coherency to a literary unit. Indeed, without continuity of topic, language becomes disconnected and choppy—the ultimate expression of discontinuity is a dictionary. There is not much plot or sustained argument there!

The concepts of topic and comment are helpful in discovering continuity and discontinuity between clauses. The **topic** is what the clause is about, usually its grammatical or logical subject. Placing an element in the subject slot of a clause has the effect of saying, "look at me, I'm what this sentence is about."

The function of the topic is to present "old" information. It refers to something already mentioned. Since topics represent information "in play," they maintain continuity with what has preceded them. For example:

> "What happened to John?"
> "Well, he dropped out of school last year and got married."

In the second sentence, "he" is the topic, referring to John mentioned in the previous sentence. The fact that "he" refers to old information gives coherency to these two sentences—it binds them together into a question and answer relationship. It would not be fair for the "he" of the second sentence to refer to someone else. If the conversation continued,

> "Wow, that's sudden, I didn't even know John had a girlfriend."
> "He doesn't, I was talking about Luke."

we would feel deceived. This strong feeling of having been deceived is because coherency is a basic expectation—we expect things to follow.

In addition to old information, topics may also represent information known by both writer and audience. Since author and audience normally share a great deal of knowledge, not everything needs to be said—or should be said. Consequently much information is assumed and left unwritten. For example, if the following sentence occurred in a letter,

Joan got married yesterday,

it is assumed that the addressees know who Joan is. If they do not, they will be mystified by this apparently irrelevant piece of information.

Generally, it is a breech of good communicative etiquette to tell an audience what they already know. For instance, take the following sign:

> NO SMOKING—This means you may not ignite any tobacco products in the space in which this sign is posted. If this sign is in a room, it means no ignition of tobacco products in this room. If it is in a hallway, it means no ignition of tobacco products in this hallway.

We don't find such signs in real life because the audience knows what "no smoking" means and the additional information is insulting.[3]

The **comment** of a clause is the new information about its topic and is usually the predicate. As new information, the comment is the contribution of the clause to what is already known. Take the example given above:

Joan got married yesterday.

This sentence is irrelevant if addressed to the woman who was her bridesmaid! The fault would be that the comment says nothing *new*. It is the function of the comment to add movement or dynamism to a passage by advancing what is known. Using the notion of texts both hanging together and going somewhere, the topic represents "hanging together," whereas the comment is "going somewhere."

In Genesis 13:1-5 (NRSV) an analysis of the topic and comment provides an insight into the communicative thrust of the passage. The topics—what is being commented on—are in larger bold letters, their pronouns are in bold.

> So **Abram** went up from Egypt, he and his wife, and all that he had, and Lot with him, into the Negeb.
>
> Now **Abram** was very rich in livestock, in silver, and in gold.
> **He** journeyed on by stages from the Negeb as far as Bethel,
>
> to **the place** where his *tent* had been *at the beginning,* between Bethel and Ai,
> to **the place** where **he** had made an *altar at the first;*[4]
>
> and **there Abram** called on the name of the LORD.
>
> Now **Lot,** who went with Abram, also had flocks and herds and tents.

Abram is the beginning topic and remains on stage until he arrives near Bethel. Then the spotlight switches to "the place," which gets considerable comment. After the author seems satisfied that the reader will know exactly which place is meant—little is presumed—the focus returns to Abram, "and there Abram called . . . ." But attention yet lingers on "the place," which is the antecedent of "there" because, like a topic, it assumes old information. Finally Lot gets the spotlight. We might also note, that although Sarah is mentioned—"his wife"—in the first clause, she herself never becomes a topic of a clause.

It seems significant that so much information is given about "the place." What impact might this bulge have on our understanding of the passage? I suspect that in reading this passage we follow the action and thus skip lightly over the lines about place.

However, in terms of the number of words devoted to a topic, "place" is quite important. As we know from the following narrative, place will be as important as the major actors, Abram and Lot. Indeed we might say the following narrative is all about place! This is foreshadowed by the prominence of the topic "the place" in this unit.

On-line and Off-line

The concepts of on-line and off-line have to do with the progression of the text's action or argument. Some actions or arguments carry the reader along and integrate a passage. They carry the passage forward, they make progress; they are its backbone, so to speak. The clauses or lines that function in this way, giving coherence to the text, we term *on-line* material. Other parts of a passage seem more like detours. They seem neither to advance the narrative in time nor to advance the thrust of an argument. *That is not to say that this material is extraneous or unimportant.*[5] It is just that, in relation to the forward-moving action of the plot, or thrust of the argument, it is circumstantial, explanatory, preparatory, summarizing, or reflective. The material giving information in service of the on-line chain of clauses, we term *off-line.*

In determining what is on-line and what is off-line, the most important question is what actions or arguments are in the foreground and forward moving, temporally or logically, and what are in the background in support of the forward movement. The differences in material are usually marked by formal clues.

Be aware of shifts in tense. For example, in Hebrew narrative, a change from the preterit (*wayyiqtol* form) to the perfective (*qatal* form) can signal a change from foreground to background information. In Greek narrative, frequently the shift from on-line to off-line is signaled by a switch from the aorist to the imperfect tense. The aorist carries the backbone of the narrative action and plot progression while the imperfect fills in off-line information.

Nominal clauses or subordinate clauses are another shape that off-line material may take. Nominal clauses tend to be descriptive and static. They often fill in the plot around the backbone. Likewise, subordinate clauses often describe or modify in some way a member of an on-line clause. As descriptive, they may be off-line and slow down the progression of the action or argument.

In Luke 2, we find an example of how verb tense functions to designate on-line and off-line material in a narrative.[6] Luke 2 is a fast-moving narrative of the birth of Jesus, the annunciation to the shepherds, the shepherds' visit to Bethlehem, and the baby's circumcision and presentation in the temple for Simeon's blessing. Following the blessing, there is the vignette about the prophet Anna, the return to Nazareth, and the story of Jesus in the temple at the age of twelve. The chapter covers a great deal of territory and time. As narrative, the predominant tense in this chapter is the aorist tense. The clauses with the aorist are on-line, providing a strong narrative backbone that keeps the action of the text moving straightforwardly from one episode to another and, within episodes, from action to action.

The use of the imperfect in this chapter signals off-line material.[7] The most interesting of these usages occurs in verses 36-38. This is the story of the prophet Anna.[8] We note, first, that this vignette contains the most concentrated use of the imperfect in the chapter. Anna's presence in the temple, her giving thanks to God, and her speaking to all those looking for Jerusalem's redemption are all expressed with imperfect verbs. The off-line narrative function of this text is also signaled by several other features, such as the preponderance of nominal clauses and participial clauses in the text.

To say that this short episode is off-line is not to say that it is unimportant to the events of Luke 2 or to Luke-Acts. After all, it makes a connection between Jesus and Jewish hopes for redemption, a connection that is critical in both the birth narratives and the larger work.[9] Nevertheless, it functions off-line in this context. Rather than contributing to the forward movement of the narrative action, it represents a moment that is both anticipatory and reflective. Noting this function of the unit is essential for understanding its communicative thrust.

As a second example we will examine the first verses of Genesis 13, which we analyzed above for topic and comment. Genesis 13:1-4 (NRSV):

וַיַּעַל אַבְרָם מִמִּצְרַיִם הוּא וְאִשְׁתּוֹ וְכָל־אֲשֶׁר־לוֹ וְלוֹט עִמּוֹ הַנֶּגְבָּה׃	So Abram went up from Egypt, he and his wife, and all that he had, and Lot with him, into the Negeb.
וְאַבְרָם כָּבֵד מְאֹד בַּמִּקְנֶה בַּכֶּסֶף וּבַזָּהָב׃	**Nominal Clause** Now Abram was very rich in livestock, in silver, and in gold. (v. 2)
וַיֵּלֶךְ לְמַסָּעָיו מִנֶּגֶב וְעַד־בֵּית־אֵל	He journeyed on by stages from the Negeb as far as Bethel, (v. 3*a*)
עַד־הַמָּקוֹם אֲשֶׁר־הָיָה שָׁם אָהֳלֹה בַּתְּחִלָּה בֵּין בֵּית־אֵל וּבֵין הָעָי׃	**Perfect Verb** ***to the place*** *where* his tent had been at the beginning, between Bethel and Ai,
אֶל־מְקוֹם הַמִּזְבֵּחַ אֲשֶׁר־עָשָׂה שָׁם בָּרִאשֹׁנָה	**Perfect Verb** ***to the place*** *where* he had made an altar at the first;
וַיִּקְרָא שָׁם אַבְרָם בְּשֵׁם יְהוָה׃	and there Abram called on the name of the LORD. (v. 4*b*)

The clauses that are not indented represent the foreground, the on-line part of the narrative, since they portray sequential action carrying the narrative forward through time. As is normal in Hebrew narrative, these clauses begin with the preterit *(wayyiqtol)* form and are underlined. The indented clauses represent off-line material. They do not advance the action, but give background information. These background comments can also be distinguished formally from the on-line ones. The first is a nominal clause and relates circumstantial information about Abraham's wealth.

The next two are concerned to identify "the place" precisely. These clauses vary in form from the on-line clauses because they are in apposition, contain relative pronouns (in italics), and are dependent clauses. Further, they seem a bit redundant, since they both begin with the phrase, "to the place," although the phrases use different prepositions. Note also, that the shift to off-line also coincides with a shift in topic, as mentioned above. Even though this segment of the narrative is about the action of Abram, place is equally important from the point of view of the entire narrative. Otherwise, why take the long detour between 3*a* and 4*b*?

Speeches

Speeches that are inserted into narrative are a special case. With regard to a larger narrative, a speech slows or stops the forward pressing plot line. Speeches, as in other kinds of literary units, may have their own on-line and off-line material. That is to say they will contain within themselves material that presses the forward movement of their argument or narrative and material that serves as support for their main argument. Nevertheless, they are off-line in relation to the narrative plot in which they are embedded.

Speeches slow down the pace of the narrative to what is sometimes called "real time." It takes very nearly the same amount of time to read a speech (aloud) as it takes to actually give the speech. Also, speeches may function to gather up themes from the larger work and reflect upon them. In that sense, they may be resting places for the reader—a place to review what has already happened in the narrative and to project or anticipate coming action.

Genesis 24 is an example of an extended narrative that contains several speeches. The long speech in verses 34-49 is by Abraham's servant. In it he summarizes the narrative up to that point in time. In one sense, he catches his own audience up to date. However, his recounting of the past is not exact and seems constructed to promote the success of his mission.[10]

Editorial Comments

Editorial comments are a special type of off-line material. In a narrative, such material is off-line with reference to the time of narration. It does not advance, although it may retard, the narrative. An editorial comment is a comment inserted from a time later than the time of the narrative. It provides comments for the reader of the narrative rather than for the narrative itself. As an example, in Genesis 13, editorial comments break into the story line at several points. At the end of verse 7 we find a note that reminds the reader of the circumstances pertaining to the time of the story (enclosed in parentheses below). This comment is made from the point of view of a later time—when the Canaanites and Perizzites no longer lived in the land.

> And there was strife between the herders of Abram's livestock and the herders of Lot's livestock. (*At that time the Canaanites and the Perizzites lived in the land.*)

In 13:10 we find another comment reminding the reader of how things were at that time.

> Lot looked about him, and saw that the plain of the Jordan was well watered everywhere—*this was before the* L*ORD* *had destroyed Sodom and Gomorrah*—like the garden of the LORD, like the land of Egypt, in the direction of Zoar.

The NRSV translation has been rearranged to follow the Hebrew text more closely. The editorial aside has been placed between dashes—as we would do today to indicate explanatory material—in order to show how intrusive the comment is. This information is yet future with regard to the time line of the present narrative. It foreshadows what will happen in the future. It also functions to explain why Lot would have ever chosen that godforsaken area when he could have had the high country of Canaan.

As a last example from chapter 13, in verse 13 we find a comment that reflects the judgment of the narrator and foreshadows later events in the life of Abraham.

> Now the people of Sodom were wicked, great sinners against the LORD. (NRSV)

This information is unnecessary to the story line. It reflects the judgment of the storyteller who knows this from what will happen later in Genesis. At this point the statement is foreboding and foreshadows the trouble that Lot will find there (see Genesis 19).

In didactic or argumentative texts, it is not uncommon to find editorial comments or asides that sometimes express the writer's judgments about what is being related in the foreground.

In 1 Corinthians 8:1 (NRSV) we seem to have such an aside in Paul's argument about eating food offered to idols.

> Now concerning food sacrificed to idols:
> we know
> that "all of us possess knowledge."
> **Knowledge puffs up, but love builds up.**

The last sentence appears to be more of an aside than part of the main argument—a proverb or instruction that Paul added as a subsidiary thought to the main argument. However, this proverb foreshadows the central theme of Paul's argument in this chapter.

Other Markers

Shifts in topic and comment, on-line and off-line, from narrative to speech, and in temporal perspective from the time of the narrative to the time of the audience, will likely be accompanied by structural markers. These markers are transitional phrases, words, or syntactic structures that mark borders and signal relationships. Words like "therefore" often mark a tight connection between clauses or larger segments of a unit, as do other rhetorical words and phrases such as "finally" or "for this reason." In narrative materials, these markers are often a temporal or spatial indicator such as "on the next day," or "as he was passing through." These linguistic markers are like the highway signs that welcome you or bid you good-bye as you cross from one region into another. Now is the time to make sure you pay attention to these signposts by marking the important ones on your layout.

An example of a transition construction that signals the end of one region and the beginning of another is the one found at the beginning of Judges 3:18. A new clause cluster is initiated by a form of the copula, וַיְהִי, literally "And it was," followed by a relative clause.

וַיְהִי כַּאֲשֶׁר כִּלָּה לְהַקְרִיב אֶת־הַמִּנְחָה
וַיְשַׁלַּח אֶת־הָעָם נֹשְׂאֵי הַמִּנְחָה׃

When [he] had finished presenting the tribute,
he sent the people who carried the tribute on their way. (NRSV)

In this instance the copula (represented in the translation, to some extent, by "When [he]") is followed by a relative clause, which gives the setting for the following action. This construction can be readily seen in a more literal translation: "And it was, when he had finished . . . he sent away . . ." This pattern of וַיְהִי followed by a subordinate clause is a very frequent boundary marker in Hebrew narrative.

There are other common phrases that introduce either complete units or subunits within larger units. In Amos 1 and 2 the phrase "Thus says the LORD" begins a series of oracles. (See the illustration of Amos 1:3-5 given above.) Parables are frequently introduced as parables. For instance, "He told them another parable." Whether or not parables are introduced in just this way, the first words of a New Testament parable are usually some variation of the formula—"The Kingdom of Heaven may be compared to a . . ."

FLOW

The last analytical task of this chapter is to consider *flow*. Where does the text go and how fast? Take note of differing **speeds** in the flow of information within a passage. For instance, in Jonah 1:3, the narrative pace is quite fast. A lot of action takes place in a short stretch of narrative. Jonah decides to flee, he makes his travel arrangements, pays his fare, and heads to Tarshish. Look at the layout below:

וַיָּקָם יוֹנָה לִבְרֹחַ תַּרְשִׁישָׁה מִלִּפְנֵי יְהוָה
וַיֵּרֶד יָפוֹ וַיִּמְצָא אָנִיָּה בָּאָה תַרְשִׁישׁ וַיִּתֵּן שְׂכָרָהּ
וַיֵּרֶד בָּהּ לָבוֹא עִמָּהֶם תַּרְשִׁישָׁה מִלִּפְנֵי יְהוָה׃

In the second line, the almost staccato heaping up of Jonah's actions leads to a sense of desperate flight.[11]

By contrast, in the following verses, 4-16, the narrative covers in considerable detail the events of the storm, beginning with the rising fury of the storm and concluding with the sailors throwing Jonah overboard. How much real time does the passage cover? An hour? Storms, especially life-threatening ones, demand quick decisive action, but here time seems to stand still.

All of which is to say that we are looking at the *narrative pace*. In some places the passage may be quite detailed, whereas in other parts it may move by leaps and bounds, omitting details and leaving gaps. In Jonah 1:1-3 the narrative is fast paced. In 1:4-16, the temporal pace is slow, moving through a harrowing episode in detail and looking at the scene from several angles.

If you find differences in the concentration of material or in temporal speed, try to account for them. Consider what the author feels is necessary to explain or justify for the reader. Presumably many arguments are presented if the author feels the audience needs persuading. Few or none might indicate an assumed agreement.

In narrative, hypothesize about why some events are presented in a rapid-fire, staccato manner, keeping the reader's attention, whereas the pace at other places is slower, inviting the reader to mull over what is being communicated. Try to lay out the passage in a way that reflects these differences in speed.

In texts that explain procedures, the difference in detail may be very striking and puzzling. Note the flow of instructions in Leviticus 1:6-9 (NRSV):

1. The burnt offering shall be flayed
2. and cut up into its parts.

3. The sons of the priest Aaron shall put fire on the altar
4. and arrange wood on the fire.
5. Aaron's sons the priests shall arrange the parts, with the head and the suet, on the wood that is on the fire on the altar;
6. but its entrails and its legs shall be washed with water.
7. Then the priest shall turn the whole into smoke on the altar.

We note first of all, that steps 3 and 4 seem to be out of chronological order, since making a fire on the altar would most likely have been done before the worshiper came with a gift. Thus, in strict chronological order, we would have 3, 4, 1, 2. Obviously step 5 is greatly expanded in comparison to the other steps, which are short simple clauses. Steps 1-4 give a staccato-like effect of rapid actions, one falling after another. But with step 5, the passage comes to a crawl with a much longer sentence and greater amount of detail. Who places the offering on the altar and how it is arranged seems quite important. However, when we come to step 6 we discover that we should have separated out the entrails and legs of the gift and washed them before the offering was placed on the altar. We should have done the washing, step 6, before the arranging, step 5. Here is a **gap** for the first-time reader. Only after reading through the passage would we know to wash certain parts before offering them on the altar. However, for the author, this was apparently assumed information. His audience did not need to read the instructions to carry out the ritual.

Going hand in hand with pace, as in the above example, is the matter of **gaps.**[12] Gaps occur because authors do not state what is obvious and common knowledge between them and their audience. But what was obvious and known then may be neither obvious nor known to the modern reader. We experience a break in communication because we do not have this requisite and assumed background information that is necessary to accurately understand the text.[13] We will return to the subject of gaps in chapter 6 where we will discuss the cultural, historical, and intellectual context of texts.

In order to uncover gaps as fully as possible, read carefully through the text asking, What is skipped over? and What is not said? What seems to assume knowledge or information on the part of the reader? Be alert for the places where it is necessary for the reader to fill in information. A list of gaps that seem significant for understanding your passage can be very valuable in focusing your future work on the passage. The watchword is *significant.*

Find a way to make visible, if you can, significant features about the pace of your text and the location of important gaps. Above we have suggested spacing as one way of marking these features. Marginal markings would be another. You might place a question mark in the margin to indicate a significant gap. Or you might choose to represent the flow of the passage on a separate chart, indicating on a graph how much space is given to what length of time. For example, in Genesis 13 hardly any textual space is given to the quarrel between Abraham's and Lot's herders, yet this fracas must have developed over time. On the other hand, a great deal of textual space is given to the resolution of this dispute. These differences could be represented graphically as follows:

> There are four verses on the resolution of the argument which, let us say, took four hours. This estimate would give a ratio of one verse for every hour. Now the precipitating quarrel, let us say, developed over a week. It gets two verses. If the text were proportionate, we should find 144 verses (a six-day week, leaving time for Shabbat) describing the development of the quarrel and the actions of the opposing sides. One way of presenting this by a graph is to compare the quantity of time with its textual space.

144 hours	________________________________	2 verses
4 hours	____	4 verses

Such a chart shows where compression took place and where the story lingers.

Again, it is important to ask the So what? question—what insights have you gained from your observations that seem to make a difference for understanding your text? As suggested, it is also important to keep a list of gaps for further investigation. Filling in these gaps will put you in closer touch with the writer and allow a more empathetic reading.

A Textual Topography

At this point, you are ready to pull your work together and produce a textual topography—a contoured text that represents the observations you have made in this chapter. It is the final product of your close study of the text and it should communicate your insights clearly, to yourself as well as to others. Because of its importance, take care in its construction.

Formatting and Labeling the Regions

You will want to make sure that the regions of your text are shown clearly by your topography, the focus of this chapter. If you have tracked the topical shifts and the shifts in the text's action or argument; if you have noted editorial comments, the speeches, structural markers; if you have learned the text's flow, then you should have an excellent sense of the regions of your passage. At this point it is a matter of refining your perceptions, making your decisions, and then indicating them in a meaningful way. Along with delineating the regions of a text, label them. These labels should indicate the function of a region. Oftentimes they are rather bland, such as "introduction." Don't worry. You are concerned with clarity and descriptive accuracy in labeling the function of a region within the textual unit.

In marking regions on your textual topography, think of space. The most frequent way in which paragraphs are indicated in a printed book is by indentation of the first line or by leaving more space between the first and last lines of adjacent paragraphs than between lines within a paragraph. Traditional paragraphing is a linear arrangement, but you should not limit yourself to a linear presentation of a text. Think of nonlinear arrangements, such as overlapping spheres or circles, diagrams, flow charts, and outlines. But the most powerful representations are those cast in horizontal form.[14] Because we are used to seeing a page from left to right, material organized this way can be more effective than a vertical page. Below is a horizontal workup of Genesis 13:1-5 (NRSV).

ABRAM	PLACE	ABRAM	LOT
So Abram went up from Egypt, he and his wife, and all that he had, and **Lot** with him into the Negeb. [Now Abram was very rich in live- stock, in silver, and in gold.] He journeyed on by stages from the Negeb as far as Bethel,	to the place where **his** tent had been at the beginning, between Bethel and Ai, to the place where he had made an altar at the first;	and *there* **Abram** called on the name of the LORD.	Now **Lot,** who went with *Abram,* also had flocks and herds and tents. . . .

In this topography, it is clear the Abram is the main thread; his name or a pronoun referring to him occurs in each region. Second, it is obvious that place is the second most important element of this narrative. Finally, Lot is mentioned in the first and last regions. The labels given to these regions is their topic. Two regions are about Abram, one about place, and one about Lot.

You can also see that there are elements, besides Abram, that tie the regions together. First, Bethel is found in the first two regions. The third region refers back to place in the second region. Finally, as noted, Lot occurs in the first and last regions.

Regardless of how you decide to show textual regions, your finished product should include their titles. Note how the horizontal arrangement of the regions makes their titles instantly available and shows at a glance the relative amount of space given to each of them.

Your completed topography should be placed in your notebook, following your contoured text. You may also need to accompany it with explanatory notes that indicate the validity and importance of your topography.

Translation

A polished translation is an important act of closure for this part of the study process. You may have made a rough initial translation when you read through the text in chapter 1. You may have translated the text in your head dozens of times. Now, using your study notes, translate the text once more, taking into account how the text has taken shape and come to life in the course of your work with it. Which words, which nuances, which arrangements of phrases and clauses on the page reflect the most accurate and empathetic reading of the text? Your translation may be quite literal or you may want to move in the direction of a dynamic translation. Or, you may want to do both. In any case, the same principle applies—it is important to be true to the text and also to trust the integrity of the work you have done. You have earned both the right and responsibility to nuance, expand, even paraphrase the text because these understandings and interpretations emerge out of disciplined study of the text.

Semantic Content

If the polished translation is a commitment to the passage as a whole, stating the *gist,* or what the text says, is an act of committing yourself to an understanding of the semantic sense of the text. What, above all, did the author wish to get across? What is the central and most compelling message of the passage?

In preparing a statement of the gist of your passage, reflect on what you believe is the communicative center of your text. It will not be your final statement of what the text means, but now is an optimal time to articulate a tentative conclusion about the interpretation of this text. This is not a complete statement of the text's message or meaning, but it should express its communicative content. It's a little like surveying terrain from a hilltop after exploring each nook and cranny of the scene below you.

So take a deep breath, congratulate yourself on a job well done, and go ahead and make a statement about what it all means. You've done the work, the text belongs to you, and you belong to the text. You have earned the right and the responsibility to make a statement! Just what is the gist of this text? Enter your statement in your study journal alongside your translation.

CHECKPOINT

The preparation of a textual topography is a critical stage in exegesis because it represents the culmination of your close study of the text and it forms the baseline for your understanding of it. As the final stage of careful reading and observation, it should make visible your own hard-won understanding of how the text hangs together, goes somewhere, and what it says when it gets there.

Of course, as with every task of biblical study, the results or payoff of these various tasks have varied. Not every type of investigation or observation that you have made has given you great insight into your passage. On the other hand, some of your observations have resulted in important progress in understanding. Now is the time to sift and simplify.

Let us review what resources for understanding you should have available in your notebook. **First,** you should have a copy of the tabled text with your notes on it. This may be accompanied by one or more notes on grammar, syntax, or an analysis of the usage of key words. If there are textual difficulties these are placed in a note to your tabled text or they get their own separate sheet. **Second,** you should have a copy of your contoured text. The page with your contoured text should be accompanied by a narrative that justifies the contours you have drawn and explains their importance for understanding the text. **Third,** you now have a textual topography to place in your notebook along with an explanation of the topography and its significance for understanding your text. **Fourth,** you have a translation of the passage and a statement of its gist as the last stage of your work.

Now is a good time to review your work. Leave out or minimize the observations that seem less fruitful. It is always painful to prune, but it does promote a better product in the end. Highlight those observations that have contributed most to your present understanding of the passage. Take to heart the admonition about straining out gnats while swallowing camels! Don't become so enchanted with minutia or tantalizing possibilities that you undervalue the most significant features of the text and its construction.

As a final step in your review, spend some time sprucing up your textual topography and sharpening or adding to your rationale and explanation of it. You should have an attractive and meaningful presentation, one that communicates clearly your understanding of the text and is expressed in your translation and gist. Now save this polished textual topography in your study journal along with your study notes and reflections, your final translation, and your statement of the gist.

WRITING A PAPER

Your study of a text may be motivated for various reasons. Up to this point we have only asked you to mark the major stages of your study with a product, like a contoured text, together with the notes and explanations needed to support it and make them clear. Placing these in a notebook is an easy and informal way of saving the results of your study and having them easily available for your use. If you are studying a text for a sermon, a notebook of such material may be quite adequate. If you are preparing a lesson, your notebook may likewise be adequate preparation.

If this describes your situation, at this point you may wish to write a short three- to five-page paper. There are some good reasons to make the extra effort. You are largely finished with your own work on the text. You will want to consult commentaries and other secondary sources to compare your discoveries to those of others. There are other academic, experiential, and practical matters to take into account. Still, you have done a substantial piece of work and "writing it up" is a wonderful way to consolidate your thinking and preserve it for further use.

However, if your study is motivated by the need or desire to write a more academic paper, then you must consider how best to utilize the materials you have already produced. Or perhaps the question is, How do I turn the material I have into a paper? We have observed that there are at least two effective ways to do this.

In one format or plan you would begin with a short introduction to the passage and to the paper. In this introduction you would introduce the passage to the reader—you might say that the passage is about Anna and say who she was, for example. It is also good to state why the passage is important for study and what some of the issues are. In this way the reader has a sense of what is to follow. Then, in the second section, you would present a topography of the passage along with your translation, appending to these a series of notes explaining issues of translation and understanding. Along with these notes, or as a preliminary section to them, you might discuss textual problems. This is a format followed by many commentators who begin their discussions with a translation of the passage.

Now that you have presented the text, you should justify your decision about where the text begins and ends as well as what ties the passage together. This would draw on your work in chapter 1 and 3. Next you could discuss the meaning of important words for your passage. This would catch up any lexical studies from chapter 1. Finally, unless you have placed this material in the notes to your topography and translation, you should point out and discuss the importance of the passage's style and its flow, thus incorporating the work of the last two chapters.

A second way to present your work would proceed along the same lines as those described above for the introduction. However, after your initial introduction, you would present your rationale for the boundaries you have chosen for your pericope and what elements bind the text together. Having defined the unit of study, point out to the reader the overall structure or outline of the passage. In this connection you would present your topography and translation with brief notes limited to text-critical observations, a few comments on important difficulties in understanding and translating the text, and perhaps a comment or two on the meaning of words that are uncertain or controversial. This helps the reader understand why you are construing the passage as you are. Next would come the bulk of your comments. You would work through the passage word by word or phrase by phrase.

This format gives much more attention to the language of the text and calls for you to have devoted additional time, perhaps beyond what you spent in chapter 1, to the meaning of words, idioms, and how the topography of the text influences your understanding of its words and flow, drawing on your work from chapters 3 and 4 and extending it.

In this model, after you have worked through the first four chapters and know your text well, you are then in a position to profitably devote further time to the study of its language, style, and plot. It is this advanced study that can furnish much of the material for your discussion of the text. On the other hand, if you have been zealous and explored more fully the ramifications of your observations for understanding the text, you may not need to do much more work at this point.

As you know, writing a paper is a creative and individual task that also needs to be shaped to the requirements of the topic. The two ways of presentation are just that—two ways. Also, the two formats can be blended. Again, be pragmatic: consider what works best for your passage and your goal in studying it.

Be sure to keep track of your bibliography. As you take notes, make sure you have full bibliographical information for them. It is much easier to do this work as you go along than to try and recover it later in the press of writing and deadlines. The amount of bibliography you have at this time will depend on how extensive your comments on the text are.

Finally, keep in mind the three cardinal rules for explanations—and interpretations. The simplest explanation is preferred. Don't choose complicated and overly hypothetical explanations that adduce facts not in evidence. What is the simplest explanation or interpretation of the data you are explaining? Second, the more powerful explanation is preferred. This means an explanation that works not only in your particular instance, but will solve problems elsewhere as well. For example, Deuteronomy uses Horeb for the mount of revelation although earlier Sinai is used. If in your passage Horeb occurred and you explained its occurrence in a way that worked only for your passage, then an explanation that showed why Horeb, rather than Sinai, occurs generally in Deuteronomy is preferred since one explanation can "solve" all the instances of Horeb in Deuteronomy. The later explanation is more powerful and is preferred.

Finally, the more elegant explanation is preferred. An interpretation that coheres well and flows smoothly is preferred to one that seems to be a hodgepodge of suggestions and observations. Simple and powerful explanations tend to be elegant ones—so seek parsimony in your work. Trim out what detracts, leaving in what is necessary for your interpretation and convincing for your audience. Don't claim more than is needed.

At this point your paper will not be complete because you have yet to consider external factors that also have a crucial bearing on how a text is to be understood. These will be the focus of study in the next part, in which you will look at the literary and historical context of your passage. As we said at the outset, understanding a text is not a straight-line process, although our presentation must of necessity be linear. As you turn to other facets of understanding, you will continue to dialogue with your present understanding. Feel free to come back to your completed work and add to it or modify it.

CHAPTER 5

THE LITERARY CONTEXT

In the first four chapters your focus has been on the text itself. In this chapter you will move beyond the boundaries of your unit in order to see it in its literary context. To do this, you will first need to determine the literary form or genre of your passage. Second, you will need to see the passage's location and function in its book and in its section within the book. Third, if your text has other versions or if it is taken from another source, then a redactional perspective needs to be considered.

For these studies, you will be largely dependent on the work of others in commentaries, introductions, reference works, and monographs. These are the tools of the trade. Of course you will not use every tool for every task of biblical exegesis, but we believe that skillful, competent exegesis depends upon having good tools at hand, knowing how they are used, and becoming practiced in their use.

LITERARY FORM

Although the identification of a passage's genre, or type of writing, cannot magically deliver the meaning of the text, it can help you avoid grievous errors in interpretation. Modern hearers and readers usually understand communication by correctly identifying without much thought the type of language being used. But even so, incorrect identification can lead to misunderstanding. A radio play about a nuclear disaster will not be understood correctly by a driver who tunes in and thinks it is the evening news. The reader of a church magazine may be offended by a satire that he or she does not recognize as satire.

One of the most striking examples of such an error in biblical interpretation is understanding the book of Revelation as a literal prediction of future events rather than an apocalyptic vision. As an apocalyptic vision, it is making theological and ethical points about how its readers should understand faith and live life in uncertain and less-than-nurturing times. But interpreters who do not pay attention to its genre will make misinformed judgments about how to construe this text.

To avoid such errors we must use secondary sources to help determine the literary form or genre of a text. In this literature you will, however, encounter a confusing variety of definitions and terms for genre. Some authors use the term *literary form* either instead of or in addition to *genre*. Some interpreters do not make such a distinction, while others may not use the word *genre* at all, preferring to speak of any type of writing, from a book-length work to a two-line maxim, under the general rubric of "literature" or "literary forms."

Given these caveats, the definition given by James L. Bailey is heuristically valuable. He defines genre as "*the conventional and repeatable patterns of oral and written speech, which facilitate interaction among people in specific social situations.* Decisive to this basic definition are three aspects: *patternedness, social setting,* and *rhetorical impact.*"[1]

Notice that Bailey defines genre as conventional and patterned communication. He assumes that a genre or literary form develops out of a social situation and is generally used in similar social situations. Sermons, for example, developed out of early Christian worship settings and continue to be used, primarily, in worship settings. A sermon has a recognizable pattern, social setting, and rhetorical impact.

Although the identifying marks of contemporary genres may be so ingrained that we use them without conscious thought, it is not so easy to identify accurately the genres of ancient texts. We may not know enough about ancient literature to discover or interpret its literary form or type. Take, for instance, the antitheses in Jesus' teaching in the Sermon on the Mount. Are they examples of Old Testament case law or similar to the interpretive formulas used by the rabbis? Or are they examples of "teaching by focal instance," a type of teaching designed to reorient thinking by posing extreme examples?[2]

Because we lack adequate acquaintance with ancient literary forms, the first step of identifying a passage's genre is to check your stable of commentaries and reference works.[3] Look through several commentaries. A good commentary will indicate the genre of material it is explicating. For example, look at commentaries on the call of Jeremiah in 1:4-10. Most will outline the "call" form and compare the narrative of his call to that of others in the Bible. The introduction to a commentary may also offer a discussion of the genres found in the book and point you to other sources. Introductions to the Old and New Testaments are also a rich source of information. They normally contain sections discussing the major genres found in the Bible along with a bibliography. In addition there are whole monographs on *form* criticism and the various literary genres such as parables or types of prophetic speech.[4]

After you have provisionally identified the type of literature your text represents, develop a profile that describes or defines it. Checking the entry in a Bible dictionary is the best place to find a list of the generic characteristics common to the type of literature that you are studying. Next observe whether and how your text conforms to the genre or goes against the genre in some significant way. Does your text differ in pattern, social setting, or rhetorical function from others of its type? For example, how is Jeremiah's call similar to and different from that of Moses?

In comparing texts note whether the vocabulary, style, and arrangement of material in your unit are similar to those in other examples of the genre. Observe the social context and rhetorical function of your text in comparison with other examples. Since genre is established by common ground, look for similarity with regard to those characteristics that mark your genre.[5] However, do not overlook the dissimilarities!

Take parables for example. A parable will have surface characteristics shared by other parables. They usually begin with a comparison such as "The kingdom of God is like . . ." Frequently, they have a short list of characters, a threefold or fourfold plot, and are fairly repetitive. The topics are mundane—common human experience such as putting yeast in bread dough or harvesting grapes. The characters are common folk figures—masters and servants, landlords and tenants, fathers and sons. Parables often end with a concluding statement or question that connects the world of the parable with the world of the audience. These are markers that are there—or not there. Unlike parables generally, your parable may not begin with a comparison or may have politically prominent figures as its characters.

A parable also shares a certain "attitude" with other parables. There is a similarity of tone. Parables are often a bit sly. They have a twist or a surprise. There is also a similarity of logic. Parables are constructed as syllogisms, although one or more of the terms of the syllogism may not be explicit in the parable. As a syllogism, the gist of a parable can be expressed in the formula A is to B as C is to D with respect to. . . .[6] The purpose of parables is didactic and, in service of this purpose, to humor and entertain.

In making a comparison of several examples of a genre you will see the flexibility and variation possible within a genre. Although all parables belong to the same genre, no parable is exactly like another parable.[7] Whereas you will learn a lot about the social situation and rhetorical impact of a text from its genre, you may learn even more by noting how it is different. For example, unlike other letters of Paul, the beginning of Galatians contains no thanksgiving for the believers in Galatia. How might this absence instruct our understanding of this letter, especially the material that follows? Also, is there a relationship between the exclusion of a thanksgiving and the inclusion of an extensive autobiographical account—also unique to Galatians? Again, these would be fruitful channels to pursue.[8]

Expressive Topography

As you compare the profile of the genre of your passage with the specific features of the passage you are studying, indicate or mark the similarities and differences in some way on your topography. Start with a copy of the textual topography that you produced in chapter 4. On your copy you might enter your observations about how the contours and regions of your topography are common to the genre and how they are different. Note whether the features that give your particular text its unique shape occur in regions of the text in which you have already noticed breaks in its pattern of syntax or the clustering of some grammatical phenomenon. It is likely that the places where the text shows originality, or deviation from the genre, will be places that are also marked by variations in semantics and syntax. It may make sense to mark these areas some way to denote their prominence. Your new creation represents an **expressive topography.** Here is an example from Amos.

Previously we had laid out Amos 1:3-5 as having three regions headed by an introduction. The reason for this division was the parallelism and topic of each region. Now in a study of its literary form, we identify it as a prophetic messenger speech of judgment. This type of speech has the following outline:

1. Messenger formula
2. Reason for the judgment
3. The coming judgment

We can now mark these elements of the genre on our layout, using roman typeface for the messenger formula, *italics* for the reason for judgment, and **bold** for the coming judgment.

Thus says the LORD:

For three transgressions of Damascus,
and for four, I will not revoke the punishment;
because they have threshed Gilead with threshing sledges of iron.

So I will send a fire on the house of Hazael,
and it shall devour the strongholds of Ben-hadad.
[and] I will break the gate bars of Damascus,

and cut off the inhabitants from the Valley of Aven,
and the one who holds the scepter from Beth-eden;
and the people of Aram shall go into exile to Kir,

says the LORD. (Amos 1:3-5)

The change from roman to italics to bold print makes clear the divisions of this speech, but also, it indicates that the emphasis lies on the coming judgment.

Having established the genre of your passage and its expressive topography, the last task is to understand how the text functions as a representative of its genre. Does the text arise out of a similar social situation and have the same rhetorical function and impact as other representatives of the genre? Does it thus reinforce the generic expectations of the reader? Or does it arise out of different circumstances and have a different impact, thus subverting the expectations of the reader?

We mentioned earlier that a successful communication depends on a completed contract between author and reader. The writer chooses a genre in accordance with the rhetorical impact desired. The reader correctly interprets the message partly as a result of bringing the right expectations to the reading. However, writers sometimes achieve their desired impact by "messing" with the genre in some way. A sermon consisting solely of a long story confuses the expectations of the congregation—not necessarily in a negative way! In this case, the preacher extends the opening illustration. The story told to get our attention before getting on with the meatier part of the sermon just gets longer and longer until it fills the whole sermon. Still, because it is church and there is a preacher in the pulpit, we not only adjust our expectations to receive the long story as the sermon, but we may try harder to figure out why this story should be received as a sermon *because* our expectations are disturbed. Or in the above illustration from Galatians, the missing thanksgiving may signal to its readers that something is different about this letter from Paul. The letter communicates by the very disturbance of the readers' expectations.

Or consider the lament in Amos 5:1-3. This lament, set in a context in which both Jerusalem and Israel are thriving, has a far different rhetorical impact from the communal mourning in time of devastation, the normal setting for such a lament. It is like reading an obituary for a person who is alive and very much "kicking." Subverting the generic expectations makes the point.

In the example of the antitheses in the Sermon on the Mount cited earlier, we noted that the antitheses have some of the qualities of casuistic law. This form of law begins with an "if" clause that is followed by a "then" clause.[9] That sounds like legal language. We expect laws, however, to make provisions for the circumstances most likely to occur. Viewed in that light, the injunctions to turn the other cheek, give the coat as well as the cloak, and go the second mile are not rational behaviors that would be fitting in the circumstances. Rather these responses are oddly unfitting. There is something else going on here. The dissonance between the legal form and the "silly" content are thought provoking and reorienting.[10] The point is made partly by subverting rather than reinforcing the genre of case law. If the author is playing with the genre, describe how the text deviates from the norm and explain how deviations from the norm change the rhetorical impact or introduce elements of irony or parody.

After considering the genre of your passage and how it functions, polish and refine your expressive topography by weeding out the indicators that do not lead anywhere and enhancing those that seem to be significant. Finally, find a pleasing way to present what you have learned. As noted above, using different types of fonts can become a concise and elegant way to mark the characteristic elements of a genre. The end result of your work will be an **expressive topography,** since your topography now shows expressive features of the text that belong to its type. Below is an expressive topography of a text we used in chapter 3.

Expressive Topography: 1 Peter 2:21-24
Ethical Instruction

For to this you have been called.
Because Christ suffered also for you
Leaving you an example,
So that you should follow in his steps—

Christian Hymn

WHO **did not do a sin,**
And in whom
there was found no deceit
In his mouth.

WHO, being abused, did not reply with a curse,
Suffering did not threaten,
But entrusted himself to the one who judges justly

WHO **himself** bore **our sins**
In his body on the tree,

Ethical Instruction

So that free from sins,
We might live for justice
By his wounds you have been healed.

The form of this passage results from a blending of ethical instructions and a hymn. The patterns that mark this genre are chiastic structure, and semantic and grammatical repetitions. Note how the author has extended the chiastic structure of the three clauses at the center beginning with "who" into the "seams" as shown by the material in italics. By melding the ethical instructions (you have been called, follow in his steps, live for justice) into the style of the hymn, the author achieves a smooth transition. This blending indicates the melding of the contours of chiasm with the characteristics of the hymn.

In this context we find a traditional hymn taken out of its worship setting to function as the centerpiece for a series of ethical instructions about how to live a nonresistant lifestyle in a hostile environment. The power of hymnic praise of God is tied to the didactic purpose of living rightly.

CONTEXT IN THE BOOK

Having analyzed the genre of your passage and its function in its context, the next step is to see your text in its present context within its book. The most important task at this point, but one that is sometimes given short shrift, is simply to *read the book!* Some books are very long, such as Isaiah or Luke and Acts, and you may not have time to do a thoughtful reading of the whole book—and probably not in Hebrew or Greek! Other texts are self-contained independent units collected in an anthology, such as Psalms and Proverbs. In these cases, reading the whole book may not increase your understanding appreciably. For either of these reasons, you may need to modify the process. But, unless your text is a freestanding unit such as a psalm, there is no other way to really understand how your text functions as part of a larger whole unless you read the book.[11]

The Section

Reading the whole book will give you some sense of the flow of the work and you may, even if only intuitively, have begun to divide the book into its major sections as you were reading. But the quickest, reliable way to grasp the structure of the book is to consult a commentary or two. Usually in the introduction a commentator will indicate the major sections and subsections of a work by providing an outline of the book. How the book should be divided into sections and subsections is sometimes a matter of considerable debate. You may, as you check several commentaries, find that you have stumbled into a hotbed of controversy. If one explanation makes more sense to you than another, go with it. But if you cannot make up your mind, try to understand the issues and figure out how the different solutions affect the interpretation of your passage. You do not need to provide a definitive solution to a long-ranging controversy. What you want at this point is a relatively stable notion of the larger literary section of which your text is a part. Where does its section begin and end?

Since a text is affected by and takes on meaning in relation to its larger literary context, when you have determined the section as well as you can, read it closely. Whether biblical authors composed texts or used texts from other sources, they were faced with the task of fitting their material together. If your passage is a speech embedded in a narrative, as we find in Acts, you need to know the events that led up to the speech and the events that followed or resulted from the speech. If the passage under examination contains a character, it is important to know what has just happened to the character as well as what will happen to the character in the succeeding material. To gain insight from a passage's context, analyze how your passage relates to its surrounding literary environment through its **structure, vocabulary,** and its **literary links.**

Structure

First, look for how material is arranged in your section. This issue is admittedly daunting because seeing and understanding the arrangement of a section can only be done with any certainty from the biblical languages. However, your proficiency in Hebrew or Greek may restrict your ability to read the section. If this is the case, conclusions about structure based on translations are necessarily tentative but can be reinforced by the judicious use of commentaries and by checking crucial points in the Hebrew and Greek text. In this way, accurate insightful work is well within reach. We encourage you to make the best use possible of your language skills at this point within the limits of your time constraints. If you are preaching a number of sermons on a section, such as the Abraham narratives or the Sermon on the Mount, you may indeed wish to take the time to read the section in its own language. Whatever you can do will strengthen your interpretation.

Second, determine the position of your passage in the structure of the section. Whether a specific text is placed at the beginning, in the middle, or at the end of its section matters. If it comes first, it may function to set the tone, introduce the content, establish the setting and characters, or state the major themes of the section. If it comes in the middle of the section, it may serve to communicate the body or "meat" of what the author wants the reader to know. If the passage comes at the end, it may serve to recapitulate what has been said.

In chapters 3 and 4, we listed a number of features that mark the organization of an individual passage. Some of those features are also found in sections. Parallelism, inclusio, and chiasm can occur within a section. In Acts 10 and 11, the story of Peter's vision on the rooftop in Joppa is told twice. In 10:9-23, the vision is told in third-person-narrative form and then in 11:5-17, Peter tells the story in first person to the apostles in Jerusalem.

In the section that includes 1 Peter 2:11–3:12, there is a structural chiasm. The *A* part consists of a *general injunction* to all the believers in 2:11-17. They are to be subject to every human institution. The *B* part that follows is a *particular injunction* to slaves in 2:18-20. They are to be submissive to their masters. The *X* part, the hinge or center of the chiasm, is found in the *christological hymn* in 2:21-25. Christ is the one who did not give back revile for revile but trusted himself to the "one who judges justly." The *B prime* part following the hymn, 3:1-7, is again a *particular injunction* addressed to wives of non-Christian husbands.

They are to be submissive to their husbands. And, finally, the *A prime* part, a *general injunction* to all believers, is found in 3:8-12. All are enjoined not to return evil for evil.

In the interpretation of any text within this section, it is important to note that in this structure the particular injunctions are embedded in general expectations for the whole community. All the injunctions, both particular and general, are in turn rooted and grounded in the example of Christ, the one who hands himself over to the just judge.[12]

Other common patterns are the interchange of narrative and dialogue, or narrative and speeches. Acts 10–11, described above as an example of parallel accounts of narrative and speech, also has narrative and dialogue woven into the section. Sometimes it is helpful to sketch out a section of text, delineating between narrative, dialogue, and speeches to see how the parts interact within the section. Although it occurs more rarely, off-line and on-line material may also figure into the arrangement of a section. In Luke's infancy narratives, the passage about Anna is off-line in relation to the rest of the section, as is evidenced by the consistent use of imperfect verbs in that text.

Perspectival Charts

Charting the context of your text from various perspectives is a tool that you will find useful in relating a text to its literary context. Throughout the rest of the chapter we will suggest various ways you might chart the text. We introduce the concept here as a device to give the structure of the section a visual form.

When you have a sense of the organization of the section in which your text appears, construct a **perspectival chart** demonstrating it. Show how your text fits into the structure of the section and functions in the flow of the section. The following illustration is a perspectival chart of 1 Peter 2:11–3:12. The perspective that is being charted is the structure of the section as a chiasm. Its parallelism as well as its hinge can be readily seen from the chart.

There are other ways to prepare such a chart as well as different aspects of the section to illustrate. Use your imagination and experiment with different kinds of illustration in visualizing the structure of the section. Also, as you study the topic of your passage in the context of its section, notice not only the shifts in topic but also how these shifts are made. Some of the seams or transitions between literary units may be woven together tightly and others will be simply basted together. On your perspectival chart you might leave more or less space to indicate these differences.

Perspectival Chart of 1 Peter 2:11–3:12

1 Peter 2:11-17
General Injunctions
Addressees: All
Submit to every human institution.
Live as free people.

1 Peter 2:18-20
Particular Injunction
Addressees: Slaves, especially slaves of unjust masters (non-Christian)
Be aware of God.
Suffer injustice.

1 Peter 2:21-24
Christological Hymn
Follow in his steps: nonretaliatory behavior.
Live for justice.

1 Peter 3:1-7
Particular Injunction
Addressees: Mainly wives of non-Christian husbands
Submit to husbands.
Do good and do not let yourselves be terrorized.

1 Peter 3:8-12
General Injunction
Addressees: All
Do not return evil for evil.
Do not return revile for revile.

Vocabulary

One of the ways coherence is established in a work is with the recurring use of a thematic vocabulary and motifs. In order to link the vocabulary of your unit with that of its section and even with the rest of the book or books in which it occurs, look at the list of words from your lexical work in chapter 2. You may also wish to add words to which the commentaries have alerted you or that you picked up as you read the book. Make a list of the terms that you want to check. Basic word searches may be accomplished by using the search facility of a computer program such as *Bible Windows*[13] or, more reliably, by using a Hebrew or Greek concordance.

Look for two phenomena. First, how frequent or how important is the word or phrase for your section or work? Look for passages relevant to the interpretation of your text. For instance, in a study of Luke's beatitudes and woes (6:20-26), a word search finds a series of passages that cohere around four themes: rich/poor, full/hungry, laugh/mourn, and being spoken well of/being hated. These passages give perspective to Luke 6:20-26 by illustrating and developing these four dichotomies.

Second, how is the word distributed? Is the word found mainly in your section or in a prominent part of the larger work, a part of the work in which the author heavily invests values and convictions—such as the beginning, ending, or the high point of the composition? A search on the word ἔλεος (mercy) from the parable of the good Samaritan shows that the noun form is used repeatedly in the Magnificat and the Benedictus in chapter 1, but nowhere else in the Gospel of Luke or in Acts.[14] This is a significant observation because the infancy narratives are programmatic for Luke-Acts. The example of the good Samaritan, a man held in low regard by many Jews, a man who took upon himself the burdens of a traveler left to die, serves as the only human example of God's mercy as celebrated in Mary's song and Zechariah's song!

Catchwords can link two units together. In Psalm 1:2 the Hebrew verb הגה occurs and is usually translated "meditate." In Psalm 2:1 the same verb occurs in the first verse of the psalm. Since this word is relatively rare in the Psalms, occurring only ten times in the entire book, the use of the word in both psalms may tie together the first two psalms in the book.

Be aware of word groups as well as the repetition of exact words. If you are working with the noun *justice,* for example, remember to check for the related verb and adjectives. Also, you may find word plays as vital thematic connections. In 1 Peter 2:13 the word usually translated "institution" is really the Greek word for "creation," and it resonates with the faithful "Creator" to which the believers are to entrust themselves in 4:19. The play on words lends a certain irony to the point the author is making about submitting to these human institutions.

Depending on how many connections you find and how significant they are, you may want to enter this information on your perspectival chart. For example, you might want to indicate the connection between the good Samaritan story and its related pericopes in the prologue on a chart. Or you might depict the *distribution of a word* on a chart showing the situations and the sections of the work in which it occurs.

Literary Links

Most works, like individual texts, cohere by using both sequential development and by long-range links. The way a text gets from point A to point B is its sequential development. Events or arguments are presented in an order that contributes to an overall coherence. There is logic to the movement, a cause and effect for each instance, something that leads up to a point and away from it.

Long-range links are phenomena like foreshadowing, flashbacks, and echoes.[15] As you read through a text you will encounter scenes and themes that remind you of what went before or what will come later. These scenes and themes are part of the cohesion of the work—the way it hangs together.

Seeing an individual text in relationship to both the sequential development and its long-range links will round out your understanding of how it fits into its literary context. For this task you will depend on three things: your own reading of the whole work, secondary resources, and the lexical work you just did.

First, determine what role your text plays in how the section starts somewhere and goes somewhere. Where and how your text is situated in the larger whole of this forward momentum is important since its movement provides the basic structure for the coherence of the text. To visualize your findings you may want to add them to your perspectival chart, sketching out the major points of the argument or the major events of the plot. Then look at the text you are studying and determine how it fits into the movement and coherence of the book.

Since this task can become unnecessarily time consuming, limit your sketch to what you can reasonably get onto a page or two aligned horizontally. Again, do not feel like you are cheating if you rely on secondary sources. There is little to be gained by reinventing the wheel. On the other hand, you may have your own ideas about the overall structure of the text. However you work, show the major movements of the work, not every minute detail. When you have completed your chart or outline, you will be able to see at a glance how your text fits into the general, linear movement of the narrative text.

Second, look for any long-range links. There may be references in your text to specific events or ideas that will follow. An obvious example is the narrator's reference to the destruction of Sodom and Gomorrah in Genesis 13:10. The actual event occurs in chapter 19. This foreshadowing helps tie together the Abraham cycle of stories in Genesis. Or a text may, at the same time, echo something that happened earlier and foreshadow something that happens later. Simeon's words to Mary in Luke 2:34, "Behold this child is set for the fall and rising of many in Israel and for a sign that is spoken against," looks both backward and forward. It *echoes* the fall and rising that was a theme of Mary's song in 1:46-55. But it *foreshadows* the opposition that this baby will face as he grows into adulthood and assumes his mission.

Your text may also be linked to similar texts within the section or it may be one of a series of texts with similar genres that occur throughout the book. There are many kinds of series—series of quest stories, oracles, legal instructions, feeding scenes, healing scenes, and so forth. The story of the paralytic in Luke 5:17-26 is a quest story and, as Tannehill suggests, there are seven such stories in the Gospel.[16] From an analysis of the placement of these stories, it would appear that three stories take place in the Galilean ministry, three more occur as Jesus enters Jerusalem, and then there is one final quest story at the end of the Gospel—the second thief on the cross. This cycle of stories participates very little in the development of the text from the birth to the death and resurrection of Jesus since they do not advance the plot in any significant way. Yet they do sound a recurring theme of people approaching Jesus and asking for something vital to human well-being. They also, according to Tannehill, illustrate the rising and falling, about which Mary sang and Simeon prophesied. All of the people who succeed in their quest are lowly in some way—not always in wealth, as is evidenced in the story of Zacchaeus, but in some way. The one person who does not succeed in his quest is the rich ruler.[17]

If you have the opportunity to study an entire book, whether as a student or a teacher, you may wish to invest in more complex and informative kinds of perspectival charts. For instance, the amount of space given to an event or argument is helpful in determining to what the author gives the most value. Sometimes it is valuable to indicate the times at which events happen. For argumentative texts, you may want to establish a flowchart of the topics that are addressed and their logical links. Or you may want to explore the relationship between narrative and speech. The possibilities are many, and sometimes the results are worth their weight in gold.

Redactional Perspective

The aim of this section is for you to gain a sense of the redactor's[18] or author's motivations, inclinations, and point of view. Whereas these factors may be seen in individual texts, they are most clearly evident in the work as a whole. The questions begun here will be more fully explored in the next chapter, but for now see what clues you can glean from your text and its work about the communicative purpose or purposes of your material. There are a number of concrete tasks that can get you quickly into the analysis of a biblical book's point of view.[19] It is usually productive to take a good look at the *beginning* and *ending* of the book, because these are places where authors commonly tip their hand.[20] Another way to make your work stand out and thus glimpse what the author is "up to" is to compare the vocabulary of a work with that of similar works.[21]

We should offer a word of qualification here. The tasks we suggest are *suggestions*. Some of them will be more appropriate for some books and passages than for others. So choose the tasks that seem most fruitful. Also, since literary investigation into a text is not so much a science as an art, there may be additional questions that emerge from your reading of the book that you want to pursue. By all means, do so. You are not limited by the suggestions that we make here.

As suggested, the beginning and ending of a work are especially invested with an author's values. Sometimes the purpose of writing is stated explicitly in the beginning paragraphs, but even without an explicit statement of purpose there often is an implied one. Not only does the author set up the purpose of the work, but also establishes a tone, indicates the genre, and in general prepares the reader for what will follow. A term we often use for beginnings is that they are *programmatic.*

For Luke, the first four chapters of the Gospel establish the agenda for the rest of the work and it is necessary to take them seriously in interpreting passages within the Gospel. The history of interpretation is rife with examples of disastrous understandings that are the result of ignoring Luke 1–4 (the prologue), especially regarding the Jews and Gentiles.

In the prologue, Luke states clearly that the purpose of the incarnation is to be a light for revelation to the Gentiles and for glory to the people Israel (2:32). These particular phrases belong to Simeon's first oracle, but the theme is echoed elsewhere in the prologue as well. Simeon's second oracle summarizes the shadow side of this theme of revelation and glory as he tells Mary that the child is "set for the falling and the rising of many in Israel." These oracles are but an example of the clues in the prologue that set Jesus up as a prophetic figure. As a prophet, his purpose is to proclaim the kingdom of God and to challenge both Israel and the "nations" to choose their allegiance. But, as with the prophets who have gone before him as well as those who will follow him, Jesus' proclamation will be rejected as well as received, by both Jews and Gentiles. From Luke's perspective, it is, of course, more tragic that some in Israel reject the prophetic message, because they are the chosen people, the people who know the most about God.

Another example of this principle is Amos 1:2, the initial speech unit of the book, which serves as a sort of motto or heading. We find Yahweh roaring, and as a result nature is devastated. The same verb is used again in Amos 3:4 and 8. In verse 4 it is a lion that is roaring. However, in verse 8 the focus shifts. Let's look at these two passages in juxtaposition:

> The LORD roars from Zion, and utters his voice from Jerusalem; the pastures of the shepherds wither, and the top of Carmel dries up. (1:2 NRSV)

> The lion has roared; who will not fear? The Lord GOD has spoken; who can but prophesy? (3:8 NRSV)

In 3:8 the roaring of a lion is linked with the necessity of prophesying when Yahweh speaks. This connection, especially since it seems to represent an authentication of Amos's prophecy, indicates the importance of this unit in the work. It also illustrates the nature of Amos's oracles; they are oracles of judgment, doom, and disaster.

Sources

Having worked with the literary context of your passage within its work, now compare it to any other occurrences of the content of your text. Whereas not all texts have such parallels, the Lord's Prayer, for example, occurs in both Matthew and Luke. Although there may be no way of knowing which of these prayers is the earlier, it is fairly clear that both reflect, perhaps in fragmentary fashion, the vestiges of Jewish prayers.[22] It is also assumed that both Matthew and Luke are relying on a common source.[23] The question posed by these parallel versions of the same prayer is: Why does the actual formulation of the prayer differ in the two books? Who changed what and why? Why, for instance, does Matthew use "debt" and "debtors" while Luke uses "trespass" and "those who trespass"?

Sometimes an author uses two or more sources to put a narrative or story together.[24] For example, the flood story in Genesis 6–8 is often thought to be a weaving together of two sources by the redactor. In reading through the first nine verses of chapter 7, it seems that in verses 2 and 3 Noah is to take seven pairs of clean animals. However, in verses 8 and 9 Noah makes no distinction between the clean and unclean animals; they all come in pairs. This latter depiction links to God's first speech to Noah in 6:19 where no distinction is made between clean and unclean animals. Noah is to take a pair of all animals. For these and other reasons, the flood story is believed to be a composite.

The question to ask yourself is: Are there indications of the redactor's point of view in the way the sources are combined? In the present flood story the establishment of a covenant both begins and ends the story—6:18 and 8:21–9:17. Along with this feature there are also the sacrifices that Noah makes upon coming out of the ark. For these Noah needs several pairs of clean animals—some for sacrifice and some for reproduction. Thus covenant and worship seem to be concerns of the redactor of this story.

Making careful observations about the ways authors shaped or combined material from outside sources can help you see their point of view or *tendenz*. A good example is the selective use of Samuel and Kings by the chronicler. Chronicles omits the David and Bathsheba affair and the revolt of Absalom. These omissions enhance the reputation of David. An appropriate question to pursue would be how this "rehabilitation" of David helps us understand the *tendenz* of Chronicles and gain insight into the communicative goal of Chronicles.

In grasping the way an author shaped source material, look for the following three clues. First, what did an author deem important to *include* and what could be *left out?* Second, what material from the source should be *emphasized?* And third, *where* is the material placed in the work and how is it *integrated* into it? These three types of information taken together can suggest an author's communicative aim.

As an example of gathering these three kinds of information, let us look a little more closely at the Lord's Prayer. We might notice first that the two prayers are placed in a different literary setting in Matthew and Luke. In Matthew (6:7-15), the prayer is part of the Sermon on the Mount. It is in the middle of the Sermon on the Mount and, in fact, some would say that it is in the pivotal and most important position in the sermon.[25] In Luke (11:1-4), it is entered into the text right after the story about Mary and Martha, and right before the story about the man who asks his friend for three loaves of bread at midnight.

Another note about the differing *contexts* might be that Matthew provides a careful transition from the passage on almsgiving to the passage on prayer. He closes the prayer with a comment on forgiving each other's sins. In Luke the transitions before and after the prayer are much more abrupt.

With respect to *additions and omissions,* we have noted that Matthew's version is the longer of the two. The direct address of the Father is more elaborate in Matthew. In Luke it is simply "Father, hallowed be your name. Your kingdom come," whereas Matthew adds, "on earth as it is in heaven." In the second part of the prayer, Luke has three petitions, but Matthew has four. In addition to the petitions for bread, forgiveness, and not to be led into temptation, Matthew adds the request to be delivered from evil.

As Ulrich Luz notes, these differences are rooted in the devotional observances and theological concerns of Matthew's Gospel. Whereas the prayer may well have been "simply retold as recited" in Matthew's community, nevertheless, the influence of the Gospel's perspective on the prayer is clear.[26]

To compare texts, you may need to photocopy the texts, put them beside each other, and mark what is the same and what is different. For work with the synoptic Gospels, there is a very helpful book, *Synopsis of the Four Gospels,* which can greatly facilitate this work. It has the Gospels lined up side by side so that you can see what is the same and what is different. The most helpful and expensive edition has both the Greek and the English.[27] You might use a color code to facilitate your work. When you have entered the data on your photocopies, comb through them to see whether there are patterns to the data that might reveal the authors' motives in arranging, adding, or omitting material.

In summary, if your text has another version in the biblical canon or in contemporary literature, do the comparative work.[28] Remember that you are not, at this point, necessarily trying to solve the historical issue of which text is the earliest, but trying to get a handle on the values and investments of the author of your text. Studying the different ways other authors handled the same material gives you a "close up and personal" glimpse of some of the choices your author made. This is a unique opportunity to step into an author's workshop. On your expressive topography, it might make sense to note what your author added, what he or she omitted, and differences in the arrangement of the material.

CHECKPOINT

At the end of chapter 4, the product of your study was a textual topography. In chapter 5 you compared your text to other texts of a similar type. You also considered how your text functions within the horizon of its genre, whether in a reinforcing or subverting manner. You used these findings to construct an expressive topography. Refine your expressive topography if necessary and place it in your study notebook.

Next, review your perspectival chart or charts and prepare a final product that clearly shows how your passage fits into and contributes to the flow and structure of its section and perhaps of the book as a whole. Also, you should draft a short statement that summarizes the most valuable of your discoveries and insights. You might discuss: (1) the genre of your passage; (2) the role of your passage in the structure of its section and the work as a whole, and (3) how its context focuses its communicative point. Place this statement along with your perspectival chart in your notebook.

Writing can be extremely helpful both in clarifying your own understanding and preserving your work for future use. It is a fact that we teach ourselves what we think by writing it. Whatever mode you choose, you are the most important audience for your work—try to find a method that will communicate to you as well as to others who are studying with you. Also keep an eye on the future—you want to be able to come back to your work later and be able to understand it clearly.

CHAPTER 6

THE WORLD OF THE TEXT

We turn now to see the text in its historical and cultural context.[1] This world, although exterior to the text, is presupposed in the text. Members of a culture share many tacit assumptions that shape what is said and, more important, what is not said. Much in communication remains unsaid because it is rude to give more information than the audience requires.[2] For example, the referents of words, such as "emperor" or "Rome" or "super apostles" in 2 Corinthians 11 are not spelled out because the audience knew perfectly well what or who Paul was talking about. It would have been rude for him to have written, "Rome, the city located in Italy, the capitol of the Roman Empire." Even we do not need this much explicit information.

Our problem as readers of ancient texts is that we normally are not privy to enough assumed information. Whereas we know what "Rome" was, we do not know who Paul's opponents were, although their identification was obvious to the recipients of the letter. Indeed, the major hurdle for interpreting some texts, such as the apocalyptic texts of Daniel and Revelation, is determining the referents for their "code" words. The modern reader struggles to uncover the historical figures and events presupposed in the text.

An example of unspoken shared assumptions is found in Daniel 2:31-45. In this passage we have the description of a great statue composed of gold, silver, and so forth. Its golden head is interpreted by Daniel as being King Nebuchadnezzar. But the referents for the following parts of the statue are not given. Uncovering the assumed kings and kingdoms to which the different metals refer is the work of historical research.[3]

Such implicit assumptions may be more general, such as assumptions about the way the physical universe works or knowledge of an intellectual or cultural tradition. For example, in the Ancient Near East, the term *shepherd* was commonly applied to the king as a metaphor for a ruler who cared for his subjects as a shepherd cared for his sheep. If we were to read Psalm 23 as tacitly assuming this royal tradition, we would understand this text quite differently than if we imagined its language to be referring to an actual shepherd.[4]

There is no doubt that uncovering this dimension of a text can be a large task. Consequently, it is good to begin with secondary sources for help. The introductions found in commentaries are normally good sources and the place to begin. You should look at several commentaries though, because there may not be a consensus on the cultural, social, or historical setting of the text. For example, in his Amos commentary, John Hayes places Amos in a different historical context than do most commentators. His different contextual assumption underlies his different understanding of Amos.[5] Context definitely affects the understanding of a text!

Other good secondary sources are the *Dictionary of Biblical Interpretation,* Bible dictionaries such as the *Anchor Bible Dictionary,* and scholarly introductions to the Old and New Testaments. In these works you will find discussions of a book's date of composition and its cultural and social setting. Also, histories of Israel may cover both the Old Testament and New Testament periods. Read selectively, they can provide valuable background for the biblical material.

A major difficulty with placing a biblical text within its tacit context is that most biblical writings are anonymous, undated, and their place of origin uncertain. For a text like Job, only a rough approximation can be given for its context, which may not be very helpful for understanding it.[6] As a general rule, since the New Testament documents were written within a much more limited time span and their immediate world is more fully documented, you can expect more information and precision when working in the New Testament than in the Old Testament. However, even in the New Testament, texts like the book of Hebrews may need to be read without knowing much, if anything, about their specific context.

Consequently, as you will discover, providing a context for understanding a text is a *speculative enterprise.* You must weigh the strength of the evidence presented in favor of one context over against another. Be particularly cautious in adapting the sense of the text to fit a historical reconstruction. An interpretation based on a reconstructed background is only as likely as the reconstruction itself. In addition, the argument can easily become circular—the background is reconstructed on the basis of a proposed understanding and this understanding is then "proved" by the reconstructed background. In the best of all interpretive worlds, an interpretation will rest on what is explicit within the text illuminated by what is implicit and tacitly assumed by it.

Finally, although the study of history for its own sake is an important enterprise, here history is at the service of the text. Be pragmatic and keep in mind that *your goal is understanding a text.*[7] You will find that not all historical information is useful in this regard. For example, the name of the pharaoh who enslaved Israel may be important for the writing of Israelite history, but it would add little to our understanding of the Exodus narrative. To avoid such detours, keep asking, What information would the author and audience likely share that is important for understanding this text? In the case of the pharaoh in Exodus, his name most likely would not have been common knowledge to either author or audience. This example stands in strong contrast to the "false apostles" mentioned by Paul in 1 Corinthians 11 who were certainly known to both author and audience.[8]

The exegetical payoff from a discovery of a text's tacit dimension is not only a better understanding of the text, but it is also a prerequisite for describing a vital aspect of the text's meaning—its illocutionary force. What was this text to do? What was it to accomplish?[9]

Consider the case of a child telling her mother, "Mama, Mama, Johnny is playing in the street!" The child is probably not just providing information, but may want her mother to remove Johnny from possible harm. In this case, she is concerned with Johnny's safety and wants her mother to act to protect him. Or, she may be trying to get her brother into trouble. Such "informative" statements are then called "tattling." Depending on your assumptions about what the girl wants to do, you will understand her statement differently. In the second case Johnny may not be in any danger at all—he is just doing something he is not supposed to do.

A description of the illocutionary force of a text, then, is not a summary of its contents, but *a statement of what the text was to do in context*—in short, the point! An explicit statement of the illocutionary force of John's Gospel is found at John 20:31 (NRSV):

> But these are written so that you may come to believe that Jesus is the Messiah, the Son of God, and that through believing you may have life in his name.

That is, the content was given for a purpose; it was to accomplish a certain goal. Failure to consider the illocutionary force of a passage is a common gap in exegesis and may lead to improper interpretations and applications of the text.

GETTING STARTED

First, draw up a list of gaps—what you wish you knew about the text but don't. Among these gaps will be gaps that are due to your lack of information about people, places, and things mentioned in a text. Other gaps will represent lack of knowledge about an author, ideas in a text, and their relationship to ideas found elsewhere.

Second, classify your list of gaps by the type of information needed to fill them in. For example, a gap in 1 Corinthians 11 is the identity of the super apostles that Paul mentions. You want to know to whom this term refers. Or there may be significant words that you would like to understand more precisely.[10] For example, in Amos 1:1 the word translated "shepherd" (נֹקְדִים) is a very rare word in the Hebrew Bible, occurring again only in 2 Kings 2:4 where it is applied to Mesha, king of Moab! If in making your textual topography you were content with the translation "shepherd," now you might ask how these shepherds were different from ordinary shepherds and what these differences in social and economic status might mean for your understanding of

Amos. All these gaps can be filled by a referent—they refer to an individual or group. Classify them together.

A different type of gap is represented by the common word λόγος (word) in the prologue to the Gospel of John. The referent in this passage is clear. λόγος refers to Jesus. An adequate understanding of the prologue in John 1 depends, however, on discovering the probable reasons for the choice of this word for writing about Jesus. Such an exploration would need to consider how λόγος was used in philosophical and theological writings outside the New Testament.[11] For example, what was the relationship between the use of *logos* in John's prologue and in Philo? Do both authors think that the *logos* was preexistent and present at creation? This type of gap can be filled by a study of the history of ideas and by intellectual history. Classify all such gaps together because such a classification will save you time by indicating the type of information you want and where you should begin looking for it.

Third, prioritize your list of gaps based on your estimate of their potential usefulness. Knowing who the pharaoh of the Exodus was, would be a gap with a very low priority. Recovering the identity of the super apostles would have a high priority. Within the category of high priority, begin with those gaps that would seem easiest to fill. For example, if your commentary has an excursus on the relationship of *logos* in John and in Philo, it would make sense to begin here because of the ready availability of information.

Although generating a list of gaps and prioritizing them is a practical way to focus your efforts, grasping the general historical and intellectual background of a writing remains vitally important and is not to be neglected. Consequently, in our presentation below we will consider what types of information you need for filling gaps and understanding your passage.

Basically, the type of information you will need can be divided into two general categories—*historical information* and *intellectual relationships*. The first section below discusses issues related to the *historical context* of a text. Historical context is taken here to include both social and cultural factors. In the second section we will consider the *intellectual world* of the text. Included in this section are the investigation of specific intellectual traditions and ideas assumed in a text, noting the quotations or allusions, and catching the flavor of an age or culture—the outlook, attitudes, and values prevalent in the intellectual milieu of the time. In the concluding section you will bring your work from this and the previous chapter to bear on the question of the *illocutionary* force of your text—its communicative point.

The Historical Dimension

As just indicated, we are defining the historical situation broadly so as to include not only the political and economic situation, but also the cultural norms and habits of a society. These elements of culture and history are usually uncovered by asking the W questions: *when, where, who, what,* and *why.*[12]

We will use these W questions to order our presentation below, with the exception of *when,* since establishing *when* a text was written often depends upon or is mutually determined by the answers to other W questions, such as *who* wrote it and *why* they did so. As we work with these other questions, we should be able to make informed guesses about the text's date of composition.[13]

Who

Although the authorship and context of a biblical work are usually uncertain, there are instances in which we do know something about the writers and their situation, for example, Jeremiah or Paul. This information obviously should not be neglected. Since many of Jeremiah's speeches and the incidents surrounding them are dated, it is important to have in mind a chronology of events during his ministry and a knowledge of the sequence of his speeches and the events recorded in the book. Here a good commentary should give you a description of his historical situation, and lay out the sequence of events and speeches in the book.[14]

In the case of Paul, who wrote several letters, the place of a letter in the sequence of letters can be significant for our understanding of them. For example, the relationship of an early Pauline writing, Galatians, to a later one, Romans, may be helpful in illuminating both. For Galatians, Romans shows a later and expanded version of Paul's thought. These expansions *may* point to information or understandings that Paul assumed in his earlier work. Or, the later material *may* represent a change on the part of Paul, providing a contrast that can sharpen the focus of a passage in Romans. In either case, for Romans, Galatians provides a baseline for seeing new developments, changes, and clarifications in Paul's thinking.

Since usually little is known about the author of a biblical work, you may at times enter into the realm of scholarly ingenuity, if not fantasy. For example, the authorship of the Gospel of John has been debated at length and written upon extensively, yet without a consensus being reached. Compare, for example, the work of Charlesworth, *The Beloved Disciple,*[15] who argues that the author of John was the apostle Thomas, with that of Brown who believes the Gospel was written in stages by different authors.[16] Given such wide disagreements about the authorship of John, it would be foolish to hang an interpretation only upon a hypothesis about its authorship.

For Whom Is the Text Speaking?

Since most biblical books are anonymous and their authorship uncertain, a profile of the writer may be given in terms of his or her *social location.* Who most likely would have written like this and when? In the case of the Gospel of John, we could ask where and among what group might a *logos* Christology have arisen. These considerations regarding authorship naturally lead to a consideration of other W questions—*where* might such ideas be at home and *for what reason* might a Gospel writer use them in a prologue to a narrative of Jesus' ministry?[17]

Another way to get at the historical and cultural dynamics tacit within a work is to seek clues to the political and economic climate of the times. You might set out to characterize the time of the work in broad strokes indicating whether it was a time of political decline or of expansion, a time of self-government or of tyranny by a foreign government. For example, Amos is placed in the time of Jeroboam II, according to the heading of the book, which was a time of prosperity, expansion, and optimism.[18] Such a location fits his critique of the elite in Israelite society (6:1-7, etc.) and his advocacy for those whom they marginalized and oppressed by their practices (2:6*b*-8). An analysis of Amos's time in conjunction with a study of his message leads to conjectures concerning the social dynamics that were producing both wealthy persons as well as poor ones.

Another approach to tasting the age of a writing is to flesh out the major groups—the players—that were active in the society. An example of such a reconstruction is found in the work of Moshe Weinfeld on Deuteronomy and its "school."[19] He examines a phrase in Jeremiah 2:8 (NRSV), which lists the following influential groups:

> The **priests** did not say, "Where is the LORD?"
> **Those who handle the law** [Torah experts] did not know me;
> the **rulers** transgressed against me;
> the **prophets** prophesied by Baal, and went after things that do not profit.

Priests, torah experts, rulers, and prophets are listed. Prophets, priests, and rulers are familiar groups known to us from Israelite history—but who are the torah experts? To help answer this question Weinfeld posits a connection between the "handlers of the law" in this passage and those mentioned in Jeremiah 8:8 (NRSV) where we find:

> How can you say, "**We are wise,** and the law of the LORD is with us," when, in fact, the false pen of the **scribes** has made it into a lie?

In this text, the wise are linked to the scribes whose activity lies in the writing of the law. From this connection, Weinfeld concludes that part of the duties of the wise in Jeremiah's time was writing down the law and being expert in it. If this reconstruction is accurate, and if these scribes were connected with the Torah found in the temple during Josiah's reign, then we have gained valuable information not only about the authors of Deuteronomy, but also about Jeremiah's negative judgment regarding the results of this reform.

Further, we can note that Jeremiah came from a line of deposed priests who, according to Deuteronomy, were now among those acceptable to serve as priests in the Jerusalem temple. But, as far as we can tell, these "outside priests" were never allowed to act as priests in the temple. Perhaps, then, Jeremiah is speaking as a disenfranchised priest against those who did not allow him and his kindred priests to retake their place in the temple.

Two comments are in order for budding interpreters. First, a competent expositor should become familiar, in a general way, with the period or era in which a work was composed. For example, for the New Testament you should become familiar with the dominant social and political forces of the first century C.E. You should know about the competing parties within the Jewish community, for what and with whom they stood, as well as their economic position and political clout.[20] You should also be aware of the recent past and consider the "great" events that everyone would know and that would shape their perspective. What knowledge of the past—for example, the Maccabean revolt—would be shared by writer and reader, and what might be their attitudes toward it? Such information is the stuff of New Testament introductions and monographs.

Second, because it seems like entirely too much work and terribly inefficient to explore a history and culture in order to understand a single passage, note that what you do for one text will be helpful for the other texts in the book you are studying as well as for your Bible knowledge more generally. Since historical information transcends any single passage, you might develop a special section in your study journal for cultural and historical information, or develop a separate notebook devoted to historical, cultural, and intellectual matters. This will become a growing resource for your work with a book, a set of books, or even a testament. On the other hand, you may find that certain insights are so closely linked to a specific passage, as in the case of Jeremiah 2:8, cited earlier, that you may wish to attach historical information directly as notes to particular words, phrases, or sentences.

To Whom Is the Text Directed?

Although it is necessary to consider the *who, where,* and *when* questions in connection with the origin of a text, it is often more important to pay attention to its possible recipients. A consideration of its audience usually provides insight into the illocutionary force of a text. Unfortunately, just as the biblical writers are almost always anonymous, so are their audiences. For example, to whom were Ruth or Jonah addressed? In order to answer these questions, scholars often, of necessity, have resorted to reconstructing a *state of mind* to which a text might speak.

For example, it has been suggested that the book of Ruth functioned as a polemic against a narrow, nationalistic audience because it is a story of a Moabite who ends up marrying a prominent Judean, thereby becoming an ancestor of David. When might the book of Ruth have addressed a nationalistic mind-set that forbade mixed marriages? A suitable context for xenophobic attitudes is known from the books of Ezra and Nehemiah. In Nehemiah 13 we have a rather vivid statement of Nehemiah's opposition to marriage with foreigners.

> And I contended with them and cursed them and beat some of them and pulled out their hair; and I made them take an oath in the name of God, saying, "You shall not give your daughters to their sons, or take their daughters for your sons or for yourselves." (Nehemiah 13:25 NRSV)

In this context, the reminder that King David himself had a Moabite ancestor, would have spoken against those wanting to prohibit, and even annul, marriages with "outsiders."[21]

However, against this conclusion, several scholars have argued for a different setting. For example, Campbell, on the basis of the language of the book as well as upon more general assumptions, does not think that Ruth is a polemical work nor does he believe that it was addressed to a postexilic audience, in part because the criterion of universalism versus nationalism cannot carry much weight, in his judgment, in determining an audience.[22]

An argument from the history of the Hebrew language can be used to date a book. Some texts seem to be written in an older or more archaic Hebrew, whereas others seem to show a latter phase of the language. Frederic Bush proposes a fairly narrow time range for the composition of Ruth by comparing the language in the book of Ruth with earlier and later stages of the Hebrew language.[23] The linguistic data leads him to date the book earlier than Ezra and Nehemiah's time.

A word of caution is in order. Debates about the audience of a work may or may not shed light on its meaning and function. For example, scholars debated at length the identity of Paul's audience for the book of Galatians. Was he writing to the South or to the North Galatian churches? In hindsight it seems to make little difference in our understanding of Galatians whether he was writing to the northerners or to the southerners. Even in cases when the recipient is named, you may not find this datum very helpful. Luke and Acts are addressed to Theophilus, but we know nothing directly about him from the text. Surmises as to his social location may be helpful, but are not certain enough to found an interpretation.

What Prompted the Text? Why Now?

A very powerful tool to get at the assumptions and illocutionary force of a text is to ask, What triggered the writing of this text? Sometimes an answer can be drawn from the work you have already done, especially from your work investigating the audience of a text. In the case of the book of Ruth, Yair Zakovitch deduced its motivation and illocutionary force from his understanding of its message—it was triggered by a narrow nationalism that forbade foreign marriages.

Only in a small number of cases is there internal evidence that gives a reason for a text's composition. A classic example is found in the opening verses of the Gospel of Luke.

> Since many have undertaken to set down an orderly account of the events that have been fulfilled among us, just as they were handed on to us by those who from the beginning were eyewitnesses and servants of the word, I too decided, after investigating everything carefully from the very first, to write an orderly account for you, most excellent Theophilus, so that you may know the truth concerning the things about which you have been instructed. (Luke 1:1-3 NRSV)

In his prologue the author informs his audience, Theophilus, why he is sending this document to him: the author wants Theophilus to have accurate information based on the research work that he, the author, has done.

Sometimes the comparative work you did in the last chapter points to triggering circumstances. In the case of 1 and 2 Chronicles, scholars have examined how this retelling of history deviates from the story of Israel as told in 1 and 2 Samuel and 1 and 2 Kings. From these deviations, for example Chronicles leaves out the entire David and Bathsheba episode, conclusions are drawn regarding the motivation for writing another history of Israel. The same question could be asked of the Fourth Gospel since it varies so greatly from the other three. What factors triggered such a different telling of the Jesus story?

Mostly, however, the occasion for writing must be pieced together from the text and its setting. This process is illustrated in Elias's commentary on 1 and 2 Thessalonians.[24] He places the writing of these two letters within the framework of Paul's relationship to the church at Thessalonica. From the contents of these letters he deduces that what triggered Paul to write the letters were several conflicts following his and Silas's initial preaching ministry in Thessalonica.

From the foregoing it is obvious that the inferred circumstances leading to the writing of a text are very closely linked to its illocutionary force—what the text was to accomplish. Take the example of Ruth again. If Zakovitch is correct, then Ruth was meant to function as opposition to the reforms of Nehemiah. Contrary to Nehemiah's attempt to keep the blood line "pure," the story of Ruth argues that it might even be honorable to marry a Moabite, and it was certainly acceptable to have descended from one.[25]

Reflecting on Your Work

Because of the slippery nature of judgments about a text's occasion, you will need to weigh both the positive and negative evidence for a position, as well as to decide between the probabilities of competing opinions. Returning to Ruth, what are the merits of the alternative positions? Are the arguments from language, for example, plausible enough to place the writing of the book of Ruth in an earlier context with a different communicative point in mind as Bush does? Or is Zakovitch's argument that Ruth's message was a protest against enforcing pure marriages more persuasive? Is Zakovitch's claim, contra Bush, that language is an uncertain indicator of time because older styles may be imitated by later writers, suasive?[26] Given the complexities and issues that sometimes lie beyond your competence, you will need to exercise the best judgment of which you are now capable, pick a context, and support it as best you can.[27] Often you will be able to judge the soundness of an argument even though, at this point, you are not capable of constructing such an argument. As you study the Bible more and learn more about it, your areas of competence will continue to increase.

Having used the W questions as an agenda for your investigation of the text's historical landscape and having reflected on alternatives and chosen one, take time now to summarize the **interpretive relevance** of your reconstructed historical and cultural frame of reference. In writing your summary make a clear, integrating statement of the relevance of your resreach to understanding the text. For example, if you accept the argument that the occasion for the book of Ruth was the policy of Nehemiah and Ezra to forbid marriage with foreigners and to break up present mixed marriages, you would state their reform as the occasion for its writing, and the relevance of this occasion for understanding the book and your passage within it.

In the end, return to your list of gaps. See how many of the gaps you have closed or can now close. Pay particular attention to how many of the gaps marked with a high priority you have closed. If significant gaps remain open, you have yet the second part of your historical investigation to complete.

The Intellectual Landscape

In communication, the fund of tacitly shared information extends beyond the who, what, and where to the realm of knowledge, ideas, and beliefs that is shared by writer and audience. Since commonplace knowledge, shared beliefs, and values are taken for granted, they form an invisible ocean of assumptions on which a text floats and which interpreters need to take into account.

Fortunately, a complex of shared assumptions may be communicated by a stereotypical phrase or clause. For example, currently in the United States, the phrase "born-again Christian" has become a cliché that identifies a certain stream of Christian tradition within which it functions as a boundary marker. So when someone asks you if you are a "born-again Christian," they are asking about your belief system and identity. Knowing this, you do not need to ask them what they mean by "born again" nor would you reply that all Christians, by definition, are "born again." Your understanding of this phrase is based on your experience of those with whom it is connected, what theological tradition keeps it alive, and consequently, what connotations it carries because of its particular intellectual and social horizon. Thus, such a phrase may be the tip of an intellectual iceberg that you can use as an interpretive key for a text.

The intellectual furniture of an era also contains general ideas and values that are formative for an entire society or culture. Inasmuch as these foundational assumptions belong to a society or a religious tradition as a whole, they are not tied to any particular group or set of historical circumstances. For example, some ideas would be common to all the writers of the New Testament. Such common ideas would include the death and resurrection of Jesus, the authority of the Hebrew Scriptures, and Jesus as the Messiah.

Because our understanding of many beliefs attested in the New Testament may be different from those of first-century writers and their audiences, we need to be alert to the strong possibility that we may replace the theological landscape of the text's context with our own. One way to guard against or at least to limit this inevitable substitution is to watch for anachronisms. That is, be on the look out for interpretations that assume beliefs and knowledge that emerged at a time later than the text. For example, 1 John 5:7-8 has been understood by some Christian interpreters as a reference to the Trinity. However, since the text has suffered a later insertion to make this interpretation secure,[28] and explicit evidence for the notion of a divine Trinity dates from a later time than the writing of this text, it appears anachronistic to posit belief in a triune God as part of the intellectual landscape assumed by this passage.

In the following section we will look for the roots of ideas and beliefs and then trace their peregrinations through history. Questions appropriate to the task of filling intellectual gaps are: Where was an idea or belief at home in the culture? Who transmitted it? and How did it change through time? We will also discuss finding and working with quotations or allusions.

Tradition History

Use this method of inquiry if there is language within your passage that indicates a special vocabulary, peculiar idioms or expressions.[29] These special turns of expression may extend to the whole book or even to a series of books—the Johannine material, for example, has its own cluster of favorite vocabulary consisting of antithetical pairs that include "light/darkness," "truth/falsehood," and "love/hate."

Such a characteristic and distinctive vocabulary usually points toward a *stream of tradition*. Some group has used it over time with the result that it has become formulaic and characteristic of a way of thinking about the world. Whereas these words and concepts may be abstract, they do have an implied social dimension—someone started expressing themselves in this manner and at some point in time. This special language was subsequently transmitted and picked up by others. The gap to fill for understanding John is, Who used this language and why?

Also there are common ideas and emphases in the Johannine literature. These notions would include the preexistence of Jesus, a "higher" Christology stressing the divinity of Jesus, and a preoccupation with knowledge. Since these similarities probably reflect a common point of view rather than a single author, the designation "school" is used to refer to the anonymous individuals who formulated, fostered, and passed on a particular constellation of ideas and ways of expressing them. An obvious question now is: What streams of tradition or school forms the tacit background for understanding the language and ideas of John?

In New Testament studies, consequently, we find the notion of a "Johannine school," whose ideas, special emphases, and language permeate the Gospel of John and the Epistles of John. Although these books vary in genre they have, as indicated, a common body of ideas, vocabulary, and a characteristically simple, repetitive Greek prose style. (There are good reasons beginning Greek students usually read something from the Johannine literature before trying other Greek texts!) The body of literature produced by the Johannine school also reflects a social situation of tension not only with other religious groups, but also within the Jesus movement itself.[30]

Also, since the Bible was not written, nor did its audience hear it, in a vacuum, traditions and schools of thought from the general culture may form part of a text's tacit dimension. Consequently, it is often necessary to go outside of the Bible in order to find the roots of ideas and expressions found in a biblical text. For example, *Haustafeln* or "household codes" are found both in the writings of Greek philosophers such as Plato and Aristotle as well as in the New Testament epistles of Ephesians, Colossians, and 1 and 2 Peter. These "codes" represent collections of conventional wisdom about the ordering of society. It was assumed that society worked best when households were organized in a hierarchical manner. This tacit assumption is also implicit in the household codes found in the Bible.[31]

Writers do not necessarily, however, take over a tradition lock, stock, and barrel. They may use it selectively, or transform it though a different formulation. The adoption of the household codes in the Bible illustrates this point. We misunderstand these texts unless we also take account of how they differ from the extrabiblical tradition. First, in the Bible, they now occur in a different context from those in which they are found in Greek philosophy. Second, in the Bible, these household codes are worded differently. For example, outside the Bible the household codes address the superior member in the hierarchical chain, whereas within the Bible these codes address the weaker party, the subordinate member in the relationship. This change in addressee reflects a significant change in the assumptions that lie behind the household codes in the New Testament.

This example of the household codes illustrates an important principle in uncovering the traditions behind a text: *ask about the meaning and function of material within the context of its use, not just about the assumptions and use of similar material in the more general and extended tradition to which it may belong.* With regard to the household codes, any interpretation of these passages must be judged by how well it explains these changes in the formulation of this traditional material.[32]

Quotations

Most New Testament authors, if not all, assumed their audience would be familiar with the sacred text of their religious tradition—the Hebrew Bible. Consequently, quotations and allusions to the Hebrew Bible are frequent in New Testament texts. As you discover and compare these references with your present Hebrew text, keep several things in mind.

First, whereas authors may assume their audience knew the Hebrew Scriptures, they could not assume that they could read or check it themselves. Written copies of the text were scarce and could be accessed only at certain places, such as a synagogue. Consequently, much instruction and learning would have taken place orally. In addition, for the Greek-speaking Christians, the Septuagint, a Greek translation, in time replaced the Hebrew Bible as their text. Sometimes, then, a writer may be quoting from the Hebrew text and sometimes from this Greek translation of the Hebrew text.

Second, the writers themselves had limited, if any, access to libraries and so they relied on memory. Paul probably did not carry a Bible on his journeys as we might do. As a result, quotations from the Old Testament may not agree with the Hebrew text that we have in hand because of a slip in memory. But third, the text that biblical writers quoted may have been different from ours today. The possibility of alternative texts means that we cannot always be sure that quotations that appear to be paraphrases of existing manuscripts are not actually accurate renditions of lost manuscripts.

Last, and probably most important, biblical writers had their own notions of what constituted good hermeneutical practice.

For example, the New Testament writers sometimes use an Old Testament quotation with little apparent regard for the context of the quotation or its meaning in its own setting. At other times, there seems to be an intent on the part of the New Testament writer to evoke the Old Testament context with considerable richness, sometimes producing allegorical and typological interpretations.[33]

Beyond comparing the New Testament quote with its Hebrew or Septuagintal original, seek to determine how the quoted passage functioned in the religious or theological context of the author. Usually this means determining if the quoted material or its theme occurs in the intertestamental literature and in rabbinic discussion.

For example, Abraham and incidents from his life are quoted as proof texts in Galatians and Romans, although Paul rarely refers to him in other writings. This immediately raises the question of why Paul drew so heavily on Abraham in these two books. It may be because Abraham was regarded as the father of proselytes since he was born a pagan Gentile and not a Jew. The figure of Abraham thus could prove for Paul that Gentiles could be part of God's people apart from adopting the traditional Jewish boundary-marking practices, for example, a kosher diet and circumcision, because Abraham was chosen as a Gentile before these boundary markers were practiced.[34]

The Intellectual Climate

Besides specific traditions connected with a body of literature or a "school," the general theological and intellectual climate of a period or culture also forms part of the background assumed in writing. In the New Testament, questions about knowledge played a very influential role in the spirit of the age. Questions about what one knows and how one knows it were developed in various ways. Thomas Boomershine argues that the two most important streams of development for understanding the New Testament were the apocalyptic and Gnostic traditions. In many ways, the New Testament represents the manner in which Jewish thinkers were struggling with these broader influences. He notes that Paul, in particular, developed his understanding of the cross in dialectic with both Gnosticism and apocalypticism, refusing to accept either dualism in a simplistic way. And he suggests that the power of many of Jesus' parables for his contemporaries depended on a reversal of their common, apocalyptic expectations.[35]

Sometimes an intellectual milieu is referred to as a *worldview*, a term that has come into English as a translation of the German *Weltanschauung*. The type of assumptions labeled "worldview" are the most fundamental, the most widely shared, and the least expressed because they are constitutive of reality for a society. These assumptions are not normally discussed because they are common sense—they are just the way things were or are. Today, we don't spend much time discussing or proving that the earth is round. Everybody knows this and we assume it.[36]

But these basic presuppositions change over time as our knowledge of the world changes. For example, how might physical occurrences be explained—are they regulated by physical, mechanical laws or do they result from unknown and unpredictable causes, of which God is one? The former is part of our worldview in which the universe operates like a giant machine with lawful regularity—things fall because of the law of gravity, which can be defined mathematically. The later view, however, would be closer to the presuppositions of people living in the first century C.E. who thought, for example, that material behaved according to its nature or essence. It was the nature of a rock to fall.

The type of presuppositions we are considering under the rubric *intellectual climate* also extends to the human world in areas such as historiography. What are the shared assumptions about the causes for historical events? Is fate at work and our path cast before us, or do people determine their own destiny? Or, perhaps, God or the gods bring about events. Is history a drama with a plot and goal? Does our history form the battleground for the conflict between good and evil that will result in the triumph of good?

Obviously, these issues are some of the most sensitive in the interpretation of biblical texts because we are often uncomfortable with how different our worldview may be. Texts having to do with creation, miracles, sexuality, gender relationships, slavery, and individuality, for example, are texts whose meaning and usefulness are affected by the differences between their world and ours. At times our modern assumptions about how things "really are" are assumed to be operating behind biblical texts. It is exactly at this point that harm to the meaning and integrity of the text can happen.

An example of trying to read a text in light of present-day assumptions is the attempt to read Genesis 1 as being consistent with the theory of evolution. In one view, what is described in Genesis as happening in discrete "days" is understood by the modern reader to be the result of a much longer process. Since "days" may be taken figuratively, each "day" in Genesis 1 can be an indefinite amount of time. In this manner a seven-day description of how the universe came to be can be harmonized with the findings of geology that indicate a much longer duration for the earth and lengthy eras in the development of life.

The problem with this understanding is that it is anachronistic. Certainly modern theories were not part of the intellectual landscape for Genesis 1. However, depicting creation as taking place in a seven-day week does assume certain knowledge on the part of the reader. This account, which ends with God resting on the seventh day, serves as a warrant for the command that we should likewise rest on the seventh day.[37] Consequently, it seems most probable that the author was thinking in terms of real, twenty-four-hour days.[38]

When placing a text in its intellectual environment, it is important to note not only the fit but the tensions as well. Ask, "When viewed within this context does the text break new ground?" Consider whether the text modifies a tradition or conserves it. For example, to infer the significance of Paul's view of the law we need to compare it to the variety of views found within Judaism and early Christianity. In the Gospel of John we find wisdom themes from the Hebrew Bible and the intertestamental literature. John's text, however, breaks new ground in his fusion of the Gospel tradition and the wisdom tradition, thereby producing something new.[39]

To sum up your findings from this section, prepare a short description of the intellectual roots and relatives of your passage. Now look at your list of gaps. What additional gaps in understanding are now, at least partially, filled? Finally, describe those beliefs and values that seem implicit in your text, but which we might no longer share today.

CHECKPOINT

The goal of your work in contextualizing your passage is to be able to state the *illocutionary* force of your text—What was it *to do?* What was expected *to happen* when its audience read or heard it? What was the expected or hoped for *outcome?* These questions are function questions and can be answered only by reference to a situation and an audience. **First,** take stock of your results. From the previous chapter you should have in your notebook: (1) an expressive topography that shows how your passage fits, or does not fit, its genre; (2) one or more perspectival charts showing its compositional context and function, including its links to its immediate context and the book as a whole.

From this chapter you have prepared a statement of the relevant historical background and how this information helps your understanding of the text. Also, you have described what links there may be between your passage and traditions or schools of thought. Place these statements in your study notebook.

Second, now describe the most salient features of this context for *author and audience.* As an example of how you might use your background studies to describe the communicative point of a passage, let's consider Amos 1:3-5, the oracle against Damascus. From reading 1 and 2 Kings for historical background, we know that Israel and Damascus were enemies from the time of Jehu until the time of Amos, about an eighty-year period. During this time Damascus devastated Israel and reduced it to a vestige consisting of the capital city of Samaria and its outlying areas. This was indeed a harsh and bitter time for the Northern Kingdom.

In its literary context we find this oracle as the first in a sequence of judgment oracles addressed to foreign nations. In it judgment is promised for Damascus because of the atrocities it committed against Israel. Because this oracle describes punishment on a bitter enemy of Israel, it appears to be good news for Israel. Consequently, we might consider its function to be words of assurance or hope for Israel. Its illocutionary force, on this understanding, would have been to bring cheer and the promise of salvation from their number one enemy, Damascus.

However, in its present literary context we also find words of judgment against both Judah and Israel attached to this sequence of foreign nation oracles. In fact Israel receives the greatest censure of all the nations. Given this literary context, we might conclude that for the author the foreign nation oracles functioned as a rhetorical device to set up the audience for the harsh words that will be pronounced against them at the end of the speech. In this case, the illocutionary force is to raise the positive expectations of the people before they are dashed by their own condemnation.

Finally, since Damascus and the other foreign nations are judged for their atrocities in war while Israel is judged for its social injustices, we might conclude that Amos wants his audience to realize that their social injustices are just as worthy of God's judgment as are atrocities committed by enemy soldiers during a war against Israel. In this case, Amos wants to bring about a different perspective on the part of his audience toward social oppression. He wants them to realize that their fate hangs on how they measure up on the social justice scale. The illocutionary force in this total context is to justify the coming judgment of God on Israel because its social oppression is the moral equivalent of wartime atrocities.[40]

The distinction between semantic meaning, or communicative content, and illocutionary force, or communicative point, makes a considerable difference in how we assess the application of a text, a topic that we will consider in the last chapter. In Matthew 5:38-42 Jesus commends to his disciples not resisting the evil person, the turning of the other cheek, giving both coat and cloak, going two miles when asked to go one, and lending to those who ask. This is a simple summary of the content that a translation of the passage would provide. A literalistic understanding might be, "Well we have five actions commanded by Jesus and so we must do these five, no more and no less." This understanding supposes that Jesus is giving a set of commands that we are to practice. However, if we deduce from the literary form of these injunctions in their present context that Jesus is after something more general, because these specific injunctions are "focal instances" and not a list of required actions, then we will suggest a different illocutionary force. Jesus is attempting to bring about a new perspective for how his disciples are to relate to both the powerful and the lowly. The illocutionary force would then be, "Do not retaliate, do more than you are forced to do, and give more than is required of you." If this is what Jesus was seeking to bring about in the life of his disciples, then you can see how the illocutionary force will be crucial when you come to apply your text in chapter 8.

Now *write a clear statement of the illocutionary force of your passage*. This may be only a sentence or two in length. Make sure that your proposed illocutionary force flows from the context you have just described. Note how in the example just given of Matthew 5:39-42, a decisive factor in determining the intended function of the passage was the literary form of the material. In the case of Amos 1:3-5, the levels of function for the passage drew from both the historical context of Amos and the literary context of the passage in the book.

Chapter 7

A Canonical Perspective

Your studies on the literary and historical contexts have shown that your text was neither written nor received in a vacuum. Neither is it received in a vacuum today. First, any biblical text comes to you as part of a larger collection of writings—the Bible. The individual documents that compose Scripture no longer circulate in isolation or as part of a collection, as the letters of Paul may have done at one time. Rather, they come to you bound together in a book in a certain order. This is their immediate context today and the context within which we read them and interpret them.[1]

Since every biblical text we study comes to us as part of a larger whole and we read it as part of this larger whole, the canon and its role in shaping our understanding and interpretation of texts must be taken into account. In other words, our understanding of individual texts is conditioned by what else the Bible might have to say.

Second, the Bible as canon comes to us mediated by our scholarship, or lack thereof, by our theological tradition, and by social context.[2] We study biblical texts from within a stream of interpretation that defines which texts are the most significant for faith and practice, and how these texts are to be understood. The selectivity carried on within an interpretive tradition may result in an informal "canon within the canon." That is, some texts are simply considered more helpful or more basic to a theological tradition or a community's belief and way of life. It seems obvious that some books and passages form the basis for many sermons whereas other books and passages are seldom used. Such selectivity in the use of Scripture may also predispose our understanding of individual texts in a certain direction since frequently used and heard texts form an unconscious "little canon" as a context for our reading of Scripture.

Our concern in this chapter, in keeping with our method generally, is to maintain a textcentric focus and work pragmatically. Our beginning question, consequently, is: Having worked with an individual text, how does the interpreter make the leap to a canonical reading? This starting point commits us to beginning with the individual text and working outward toward a canonical perspective. The common question often asked by laypersons, "But what about this verse that says . . . ?" can be a useful guide to developing a canonical understanding that can be helpful within the community of faith. Our goal, then, is to determine the significance and function of a text within the canon.

Since, as you know, the Bible contains different kinds of material, written over a considerable length of time, and in several different languages, it might seem that the Bible resembles an anthology, a collection of writings that spans many centuries and many lands.[3] The Bible as a canon, however, differs from an anthology. An anthology is made up of writings selected by an editor or committee, because they are representative or the best exemplars of a person, era, or tradition. The Bible, as a canon, however, is made up of writings that were "selected" for their religious value within a community. They were selected in the sense that they survived a historical process leading to their recognition as authoritative writings by the community that kept them alive. As a result of this historical process of selection, the Bible exhibits a *certain* consistency in fundamental, constitutive points of view and on basic ethical principles and practices. However, this consistency exists within parameters that allow for differing points of view, opposing arguments, and even, apparently, contradictory statements.[4]

Another presumption for the coherency of the biblical canon is the importance of the historical sequence of books entering into the body of authoritative writings. The Torah, the first five books of the Bible, is generally considered the earliest material to gain authoritative status and set the direction for what followed. Next came the Prophets, the books of Joshua, Judges, 1 and 2 Kings, Isaiah, Jeremiah, Ezekiel, and the twelve "minor" prophets. The addition of the prophets did not mean the Torah was superseded, but rather that the additional material was in line with it and further extended or enriched it.[5] Finally, when the Writings were added, these books too joined the authoritative stream headed by the Torah.[6]

In the same way, when the collection of New Testament writings were added to this stream, they were not perceived as separate Scripture, even though at the time of the writing of the New Testament the Hebrew canon was yet in flux. Rather these new books were joined to the authoritative stream of writings headed by the Torah. In this way, the New Testament documents did not replace, but continued, the list of inspired writings.[7] It might even be argued that their continuity with the Hebrew Scriptures was necessary in order for the new Greek writings to be perceived as authoritative Scripture.[8]

The Bible, in its diversity, is a book in tension; it exhibits both centripetal and centrifugal forces—forces that bind the material together into a canon and forces that push toward individuality and fragmentation. Your work as an interpreter will be influenced by both of these opposing forces. How you can maintain your hermeneutical equilibrium within this tension is the subject of this chapter.[9]

Many Christians, perhaps most, have tended to read their Bible from a centripetal point of view. They understand the biblical materials as if they were all speaking with the same voice regardless of time and place of origin.[10] This tendency normally has led to the harmonization of differences that are found between texts. Such harmonization has gone out of style in most scholarly circles. Scholars today often spend a great deal of time recovering or recreating a historical situation for each book and thereby discovering its unique voice within its time-bound context. Consequently, the individuality and contextual historical witness of each writing has been stressed over against previous attempts at homogenization.[11] In this process, centrifugal forces dominate, and finding a common core or integrating center for the documents of the canon can become problematic.[12]

So far, your work has tended to feed the centrifugal forces. You have studied your text's language carefully and established its individuality, noted its literary characteristics such as genre, and determined its historical particularity. Now you will be asked to visualize your text as part of a larger canonical whole, to read your text as part of the canon. Such a reading is a synchronic one in the sense that all biblical texts now become possible conversation partners. As an ancient Rabbinic dictum has it, "There is no before and no after in the Torah." All texts can potentially inform the understanding of your text, not just those earlier in time. However, learning to read a text synchronically with other canonical texts is not easy. The goal of the present chapter is to guide you in reading a text in its canonical context with integrity.

PERSPECTIVE

Before you begin searching for a text's most relevant conversation partners, you first need a sense of the terrain, of canonical geography, so to speak. Individual texts, like places on a map, need to be located with regard to the significant features of canonical geography—its "peaks." Without being able to take a bearing from such a major feature you may become lost in detail and unable to make a judgment about the contribution and limits of a text as a participant in the canon. To avoid wandering about in a "flat and trackless" Bible it is important to have in mind a topography of the Bible that shows its major peaks.

For example, in Matthew 19:3-9, Jesus is questioned by the Pharisees concerning the grounds for divorce. The background for this question is that in Deuteronomy 24:1-4 provision is made for a husband to divorce his wife—he may do so for a "cause." The troubling question of course is what constitutes a "cause"? Different answers were given to this question. Some claimed adultery was the only allowable cause. Others thought there were other, lesser, causes that permitted a man to divorce his wife. Some Pharisees now approach Jesus to see how he will answer this difficult and controversial question. Jesus seems to sidestep the question by quoting first from Genesis 1 and 2. He then draws a general principle from the verses he quotes: "What God has joined, humans should not cut apart."

In essence, by beginning with verses from Genesis 1 and 2, Jesus indicates their value as peaks. From these peaks he derives a bearing—what God has joined, humans should not disjoin.

Deuteronomy 24:1-4 must then be seen within the perspective of the dominating peaks of Genesis 1 and 2.

How might you go about gaining such a canonical perspective? You have considered the literary form of your passage and stated its illocutionary force. These two aspects of a passage are important for telling peaks from valleys, the orienting features from the lesser features of canonical geography. In seeking peaks, look for material that has a generalizing and universal scope, like Genesis 1 and 2, and finds affirmation elsewhere in the Bible.

For example, the Sh^{e}ma in Deuteronomy 6:4-5 (NRSV) is an "Everest."

> Hear, O Israel: The LORD is our God, the LORD alone. You shall love the LORD your God with all your heart, and with all your soul, and with all your might.

From the standpoint of literary form, the first verse is cast in confessional form—a nominal clause. The illocutionary force of this confession is to commit Israel to the service of Yahweh, their God, alone.[13] It is unlimited by time or place. It has served, and continues to serve, as the fundamental, daily confession for Jews. It is to be recited before one undertakes to study the Torah, for without receiving the yoke of heaven, how can one understand the Torah? In Christian tradition, Jesus gives this command the status of the foundational or most basic command in the Bible.[14]

As another example, consider the allowance of animal meat for food in Genesis 9:1-7. This passage comes immediately after the flood and God's realization that humans are inclined to do evil. God now adjusts what is allowed for food—humans may now eat meat, but they must not ingest the blood. This passage meets the criteria for a peak passage, since first, it is universal in scope, as is the promise, which immediately follows, to not send another flood. Consequently, this stipulation is incumbent upon all humankind. Second, its position within the canon is pivotal. It is located at the beginning of a new era that is marked by a covenant between God and all humankind and nature. This covenant is the only such universal covenant found in the Bible. Third, it is picked up and solidified by other significant passages in the Bible.

In Leviticus 17 it forms the beginning of the Holiness Code, and refraining from eating blood is commanded for both the Israelite and the Gentile within the Israelite community. In Acts 15 the Jerusalem council reaffirmed this commandment by stipulating this command as one of those incumbent upon all Christians, Jew or Gentile.

As you now begin the process of building a topography of the canon, list what you consider to be the most significant passages in the Bible. This list may reflect your theological or ethical tradition. It may reflect courses you have had on theology and Bible. These passages may be passages that have become important to you personally. Once you have formed a tentative list, reflect on why you consider them peaks. What evidence can you list for their status as peaks? Are they generalizing principles affirmed by several witnesses?

Don't panic! This list and the reasons for your choices are not chiseled in stone. A broader canonical view is not born in a day, but you do need to begin your conscious construction of it now. As you continue to study Scripture you will develop an increasing sense of how it hangs together, its core convictions, and its basic precepts and perspectives. You will find, consequently, that your list will change from time to time. You will undoubtedly add passages as well as remove some from your initial list. This is not so much a sign that your earlier list was a mistake but that you are slowly being molded by your study of Scripture. This outcome is to be celebrated! A lack of change is a lack of growth.

But now, no matter how tentative, you should have in hand a list of peak passages. Also, set up a section of your notebook for your canonical topography and place your list in it. Since your list will change slowly, you might consider placing it as the first page in your notebook where it will remind you of your biblical topography as you study individual texts.

Threads and Tapestry

Having drawn up your list of peak passages and reflected on their importance, you are now ready to see your text in its canonical context. In order to facilitate your understanding and acquisition of this new skill, we would like to change the metaphor from geography to textiles. In what follows, we will use the metaphor of a tapestry formed by threads of different colors and weights that create a design.[15]

The first step is to find the dialogue partners of your text. What texts come to mind as the most relevant to the topic, teaching, or implications of the passage? The simplest way to find related passages is to look for passages that share the same ideas or theme. For example, Genesis 1:26-27 describes humans as being created as the likeness of God. Do we find this idea elsewhere in the Bible? Using a concordance we find the same phrase again in Genesis 9:5-6 (NRSV):

> For your own lifeblood I will surely require a reckoning: from every animal I will require it and from human beings, each one for the blood of another, I will require a reckoning for human life. Whoever sheds the blood of a human, by a human shall that person's blood be shed; **for in his own image God made humankind.**

Here the notion serves as the grounding for a command regarding the taking of human life.

Passages need not be related by wording. Another related passage is Proverbs 17:5, which expresses an inference from this proposition, "Those who mock the poor insult their Maker." If the human is the image of God, then to mock the image is to mock the one for whom it stands. To this passage could also be added those passages referring to God as the maker of humankind or referring to humans as the handiwork of God. All these passages are the immediate dialogue partners of Genesis 1:27. As such they form a thread in the canonical tapestry.[16]

Sometimes you will find counterthreads. In Genesis 1 creation is described as a good, fertile, and life-sustaining environment. The creation of humankind is the final act of this harmonious creation. Psalm 8 gives poetic voice to this notion with its praise to God whose name is magnificent in all the earth and who is praised in the heavens. Furthermore, the magnificent creator God pays attention to humans, has honored them, and made them rulers over God's created creatures. They are only just lacking being divine.

This is certainly not the creation experienced and described by Job. For him creation was capricious and meaningless, as was existence itself. God was not a God who honored humankind, but was vindictive and persecuted them. In expressing these sentiments, Job offers a parody of Psalm 8:

> I loathe my life; I would not live forever. Let me alone, for my days are a breath. **What are human beings, that you make so much of them, that you set your mind on them, visit them every morning, test them every moment?** Will you not look away from me for a while, let me alone until I swallow my spittle? (Job 7:16-19 NRSV)

The third sentence, verse 17, parodies Psalm 8. It stands God's attention to humankind upside down. Rather than being positive and a marvel as in Psalm 8, for Job, God's attention is negative. Rather than being a blessing, it is a curse. Indeed, for Job the blessing would be if God would cease paying attention to him.

The thread of the good and fertile creation in which humankind is honored and rules, has a counterthread that describes creation as a place of baneful existence haunted by God's attention, in which humans are but the flotsam and jetsam of creation and history. In discussing a passage on either of these threads you need also take into account its counterthread. Such related threads can form a wider group of dialogue partners and include more variegation in the canonical context of a passage.

Because two or more threads may be closely related but counter one another, arguments about the teaching of Scripture may arise. One side may take one thread and the other takes its counter. This phenomenon has been apparent, for example, in the discussion of the roles of women in Christian ministry, because opponents in this debate cling to different threads. Using one thread, some argue that women should exercise their capacities as they feel called to use them. Using another thread, others argue that the ministry of women should be limited or prohibited. A canonical perspective would read neither thread out of the Bible, but seek to place them in dialogue and to discover the strengths and limits of each thread as part of the same whole. As in the case of the two threads on creation and the glory of humankind, a decision needs to be made as to which of the two or more threads is the dominant thread within canonical tapestry and which is the counterthread that may supplement or highlight its counterpart.

In the case of Psalm 8 and Job 7, we might say that the psalm represents a confessional thread. This is our confession about the universe and humankind. In Job 7 we have an experiential thread. This is, in fact, how the world and our place in it is at times experienced. Neither thread should be ignored. Rather they need to be held in tension and both affirmed—yes, this is our belief about the world and ourselves, and, yes, our experience may be quite different. The richness of the canonical tapestry would be impoverished if we were to remove either thread from the canon.

In making your judgments about which threads are dominant and which are subdominant, which are heavy threads and which are slight threads, you must revisit your list of peak passages because they will play an important if not decisive role. Since your peak passages provide you with an overall orientation, when you discover that you have more than one thread in a conversation, ask yourself how these threads appear in the perspective of your peak passages.

The example we have been using, Genesis 1, with its notion of humankind created as the image of God, represents for us a peak passage. Using this peak passage to judge between Psalm 8 and Job 7, we would conclude that Psalm 8 expresses the dominant thread and Job 7 the subdominant one. Usually the threads you are working with do not contain any of your peak passages. However, as in the example above, sometimes you will have a thread that contains a peak passage. These threads are obviously dominant threads in the canonical design. Other threads, like subordinate hues in a tapestry, are to be understood canonically in light of these more dominant threads. To return to the counterthreads on women in ministry, they would both need to be judged by the dominant thread that asserts that everyone, as a human being, exists as the image of God and to insult or demean another person is to insult their maker, God. Any discussion of women's roles in ministry must be informed by this perspective.

As suggested, the notion of dominant threads can be understood as threads that compose the tapestry's design. The subdominant threads in turn fill out the patterns and make their contribution to the overall design of the tapestry within the matrix of the dominate threads. These subdominant threads sometimes reinforce dominate ones and sometimes they contrast with them. In either case, they highlight the design formed by the major threads.

Several threads may bundle together complementing and reinforcing one another in the tapestry's design. For example, the thread concerning humans as the image of God is reinforced by the thread of the incomparable value of human life in biblical law. In the New Testament, Jesus' teaching in Matthew 25:31-46 could also form part of this thread bundle. So also those passages that affirm that God is the One who takes care of the marginalized, as in Psalm 146:7-9 (NRSV):

> Who executes justice for the oppressed; who gives food to the hungry. The LORD sets the prisoners free; the LORD opens the eyes of the blind. The LORD lifts up those who are bowed down; the LORD loves the righteous. The LORD watches over the strangers; he upholds the orphan and the widow, but the way of the wicked he brings to ruin.

We also find statements regarding the equality of all humans, and the need to aid them, based on their common manufacture by God, as in Job 31:13-17 (NRSV):

> "If I have rejected the cause of my male or female slaves, when they brought a complaint against me; what then shall I do when God rises up? When he makes inquiry, what shall I answer him? **Did not he who made me in the womb make them? And did not one fashion us in the womb?**
>
> "If I have withheld anything that the poor desired, or have caused the eyes of the widow to fail, or have eaten my morsel alone, and the orphan has not eaten from it—"

Since each individual is created by God, Job is no better than his slaves or the marginalized in his society. Consequently, God will judge him by his justice and generosity toward them. We can add this thread to the bundle at whose core is the notion that each human represents God's image. This growing bundle of threads, by its thickness, emerges as central to the tapestry's design.

As you continue your biblical studies you will gain a clearer picture of the bundles of threads that make up the canonical design. Depending on your knowledge, you may be ready to relate the threads you have developed to larger bundles and to consider this perspective in discussing the canonical significance of your passage. If you cannot assign your threads to a larger bundle at this point, let it go for now.

Besides peak passages, dominate threads, minor threads (both counter and supporting ones), and bundles of threads working together, there are also background threads. Obviously not all passages in the Bible seem as significant as others. Some passages, in fact, seem never to be referred to outside of scholarly literature. The genealogies at the beginning of 1 Chronicles are an example of infrequently used passages. This type of passage, a valley in canonical geography, so to speak, forms background threads for the Bible's tapestry. They are necessary, but they are not that to which our eye is drawn. However, without a background we would find only dangling colorful threads without a context, without a contextual anchor to hold fast their design. By forming background threads, these passages are necessary to the tapestry of the canon, but they do not constitute its design.

So far, in discussing canonical threads and design, we have not differentiated between Old Testament and New Testament material. In fact, it may have surprised you that we have chosen examples mainly from the Hebrew Bible. In reading a passage within a canonical perspective we do not need to distinguish between material from the Old or New Testaments, since the thread to which a passage belongs and how its thread fits into the tapestry's design is the basis for a canonical dialogue. A passage needs to be read with regard to the thread to which it belongs rather than stopping at the border of a Testament.

ASSESSMENT

Seeing texts in a canonical perspective is also important in preventing us from getting lost by focusing on matters of lesser importance. We need the perspective of the "big picture" to discuss the matters of prime importance. We need the sense of proportion that a canonical topography can give us. Using terms like *lesser* and *greater,* and making assessments concerning the *lesser* and the *greater,* implies a value judgment. As we have seen, in the Bible itself not all voices are given equal weight. On the issue of divorce Jesus relied more on Genesis 1 and 2 than on Deuteronomy 24. In making this assessment, Jesus drew a distinction between the ideal that God intended and the remedial that was necessary because of human imperfection. In this hermeneutical perspective the ideal is the orienting peak and its thread has more significance in the tapestry's design than does the remedial passage.

In Matthew 23, Jesus draws attention to the problem of canonical perspective and the need for assessment in his attack on the practice and interpretation of some Pharisees. His speech begins:

> The scribes and the Pharisees sit on Moses' seat; therefore, do whatever they teach you and follow it; but do not do as they do, for they do not practice what they teach. (Matthew 23:2-3 NRSV)

Jesus from the beginning affirms the Pharisees' status and teaching. However, he does not agree with their canonical hermeneutics as illustrated by a later charge:

> Woe to you, scribes and Pharisees, hypocrites! For you tithe mint, dill, and cummin, and have neglected the weightier matters of the law: justice and mercy and faith. It is these you ought to have practiced without neglecting the others. You blind guides! You strain out a gnat but swallow a camel! (Matthew 23:23-24 NRSV)

The nub of the problem, put in our terms, is that these Pharisees have not assessed the threads and design of the Scriptures properly. The major threads have to do with justice, mercy, and faithfulness, and not with tithing mint, dill, and cummin (not that these are to be dropped, but they belong to a lesser thread than the ones about justice, mercy, and faithfulness). As a result, although these Pharisees' teaching and interpretation of individual passages may be correct, their practice is not shaped by the dominant threads and pattern of the Torah. This critique by Jesus underlines an important principle in a canonical reading: the pattern formed by the dominant threads indicate the design of the tapestry. These are the orienting threads for our lives. It is from the peaks and pattern that we take our bearing lest we hang the tapestry upside down![17]

The need for perspective and assessment leads to a further consideration: the design formed by the dominant threads enables judgments regarding what is more congruent and what is less congruent with the canonical design. When assessing the role of your passage within the canon's tapestry, try to be clear about whether it is a dominant thread, a subdominant one, a counterthread, or part of the tapestry's background. Above all, do not extrapolate from a text in a way that fades the vibrancy of the canonical pattern or that mutes or mars it.

The muting of the canonical pattern can result when the Bible is applied in ways that seem to grow more out of unworthy motives, such as anger, rejection, prejudice, or fear than out of faithfulness, mercy, and justice.[18] In the same passage in which Jesus criticizes the Pharisees' interpretation of scripture, he also criticizes their motivation. Below are selections from Matthew 23:25-28 (NRSV):

> "For you clean the outside of the cup and of the plate, but inside they are full of greed and self-indulgence. . . . First clean the inside of the cup, so that the outside also may become clean. . . . For you are like whitewashed tombs, which on the outside look beautiful, but inside they are full of the bones of the dead and of all kinds of filth. So you also on the outside look righteous to others, but inside you are full of hypocrisy and lawlessness."

Finally, and the most difficult task intellectually and emotionally in constructing a canonical perspective, is the need to consider the role and weight of a counterthread. For example, we find the following, quite enigmatic verses, in 1 Timothy 2:13-15 (NRSV):[19]

> For Adam was formed first, then Eve; and Adam was not deceived, but the woman was deceived and became a transgressor. Yet she will be saved through childbearing, provided they continue in faith and love and holiness, with modesty.

To begin with the final verse, taken at face value, for a woman to be saved through childbearing seems heretical—it certainly goes against the dominant threads regarding salvation elsewhere in the Bible. Salvation is an act of God's grace and not the result of human merit or achievement. The statement is also illogical. Are women who cannot bear children doomed? Should nonmarried women seek impregnation so that they might be saved?

The first two verses seem to form a counter to a main thread, which we found in Genesis 1—all persons, regardless of gender, are made as God's image. Further, this passage implies that Adam was less culpable than Eve, a conclusion not borne out by the punishments they bear in Genesis 3. All the actors in that story suffer as a result of their actions. It is only Adam himself who thinks himself less culpable than Eve, blaming his problem on the woman God gave him! God doesn't buy his argument, holding him accountable for his actions. In fact, it is only the woman who does not explicitly receive a curse!

These verses in 1 Timothy, because they seem to fly in the face of a dominant thread embedded in Genesis 1 and 2, would not be given primary weight in a canonical discussion regarding the salvation of women or their role in the Christian community. They do, however, provide a contrast to the positive pattern found in the canon's tapestry. As such, they highlight the dominant pattern by illustrating what that pattern is not.

Understanding and interpreting a passage in a canonical perspective may seem like a daunting and impossible task.[20] Rather than becoming overwhelmed at the prospect of needing to find the main threads and their dominant pattern, realize first of all that your skill and canonical insight will develop and mature over the years. As suggested at the beginning of this chapter, you will build and modify your list of peak texts as you continue to study Scripture. You will continue to develop threads and join passages to them. You will increasingly become aware of how the threads are woven together to form a larger pattern. But since all of this takes time, relax and make the best judgments of which you are capable in the present. As threads are flexible, so remain flexible in your perception of peak passages, threads, and design.

A consolation is that work done on canonical issues need not be done for each passage studied. Rather, conclusions about threads, their significance, and the patterns they form are transferable from one passage to another. In your study journal keep track of what you are learning and how you are conceptualizing canonical geography. Since each passage you study can contribute to your understanding of the Bible as a whole, keep your section on canonical considerations up-to-date. Remember, it takes time to develop as a biblical theologian just as it takes time to develop the other kinds of skills used in the process of interpretation.

As you come to the end of this chapter, you may think that the conclusions we are asking you to draw in this chapter seem subjective. They are. But they are also conclusions that you can test with others. Justifying your peak texts and tapestry design in conversation with peers is very helpful in sorting out which parts of your reasoning are persuasive and which are not. In addition, read works on biblical theology. Although it is doubtful that these authors will use the vocabulary of peaks and threads, their work of identifying important aspects of biblical thought and religion is basic and relevant to a canonical interpretation. Be aware, however, that each author may go his or her own way in developing a biblical theology, and consequently you will find a diversity of themes and concepts stressed.

By using the metaphor of threads and design we have sought to promote flexibility in understanding the contours woven into the tapestry of the canon. By adopting the notion of contrasting threads and background threads we have tried to avoid the need to weave everything into one grand design. Some threads may seem out of step with the dominant threads and their pattern. They may serve, however, as a contrast, and highlight the dominant pattern. Most important though, through the metaphor of a tapestry and the discovery of threads and assessing them, you have a process by which you can highlight the congruencies that you will find, as well as handle the diversity and counter material that you will also find, in a constructive way. In this metaphor, the canon forms a whole—not a bland, textureless whole, but a vivid, vibrant whole.

The metaphor of threads, design, and tapestry also intimates that a canonical reading is an art; the art of weaving a canonical perspective. It is not woven all at once, because the reader may not yet be aware of all the threads. Its pattern may not emerge clearly because the relationship between threads is not yet perceived or perhaps because not enough background has been formed. As the metaphor implies, the ongoing discovery of the tapestry that is the Bible and its interpretation is something that continues to grow and change—our understanding, after all, is like cloth and threads, not stone or concrete.

CHECKPOINT

Having worked through this chapter, what should you have at this point? **First,** you should have a list of peak passages. Try to limit yourself to ten or less, so that you do not proliferate passages making your list useless because it is not discriminating enough. Don't fret, you can modify your list. Right now it is important that you have one. Place this list at the very beginning of your study notebook because you will refer to it often.

Second, you should have a list of passages that you believe form a thread with your present passage. Indicate why these passages form a thread and give the thread a name. If you believe the thread of this passage relates to other threads, list them also.

Finally, take a bearing on your peaks. Make an assessment of how your passage and its thread relates to the major peaks and their threads. What is the importance of your passage to the canon? This statement should be entered as part of your notes for your passage along with a description of the thread and its passages. This notebook entry brings closure to this stage of study, and prepares you for the work of the next chapter.

CHAPTER 8

INTEGRATING TEXT AND LIFE

In the previous chapters, you focused your attention on text and context. In the first four chapters you read the text itself closely and carefully. In the next three chapters you attended to the matters of the text in its context—literary, historical, and canonical. In this chapter, you will work toward integrating text and life. This integration is the final step in what we expressed at the end of chapter 4 as "owning the text and being owned by the text." In this process, the text becomes a partner in your own growth toward wholeness and your ability to act and interact with your world as a person of faith.

Beyond a certain necessary empathy, owning and being owned by the text is not a concept that is dependent upon a particular doctrine of biblical authority.[1] Owning and being owned by the text has to do with allowing the meaning and significance of a text to become part of your life, part of the repertoire of resources that you bring to the events and relationships that make up your life. Owning and being owned by the text has to do with allowing the text to draw you deeper, more critically and more meaningfully into life and, conversely, with allowing life to draw you deeper, more critically and more meaningfully into the text. This integration can become a bridge between the past and the present, between biblical faith and one's own convictions, between a text that has stood the tests of time and the limitations of one's own life that you can use again and again—if you build it with strength and truth. This chapter is about building that bridge.

THE INTERPRETER

One of the first steps in building this bridge is to step back from the text you have examined so closely and take a look inward.

This is the interpreter's personal work. Although you have no doubt been aware all along that you bring your own values and attitudes to the reading of the text, this is the time and place to examine and evaluate them more formally. None of us, either as interpreters or "consumers" of interpretation, come to a text without expectations of what we hope to find in the text or what we wish it to say. These suppositions are both our strength and our vulnerability. Our experience, our wisdom, and our view of life can provide expectations for new understandings of a text. At the same time, experience, wisdom, and view of life can prevent or skew understanding. In this section, we ask you to assess your own reflexes in relation to the text. It is important to be honest with yourself, but it is also important not to dismiss or diminish what you bring to the task of interpretation as unimportant. The goal is not to get rid of expectations as you read, but to acknowledge them and work with them in your interpretive efforts.[2]

Begin by reflecting on your interpretive process thus far. Use a page in your study notebook to jot down your reactions and questions. Look back over your textual topography—likely the aspect of the study process in which your own individuality was most explicitly expressed. Consider how you felt about the text as you worked with it. Did it resonate with you, or was it difficult to hear or take seriously? Identify areas of tension or empathy with the text. What in the text spoke to you? What was difficult to understand?

This is the place to review how your own convictions, your own ideologies, enter into the art of interpretation. Some of these values will be "old business" for you. They are the understandings of what the Bible is and how it is useful for life. They are understandings of how people relate to each other. They are understandings of basic human realities such as power, sexuality, politics and religion, justice and injustice. It may be helpful to sketch in your notebook the basic convictions that are evoked by the text. It may be helpful to identify these core values and attitudes with the sections of the text that aroused your passions—whether of resonance or resistance, assent or dissent, sympathy or offense. The strident militancy of Mary's hymn in Luke 1 may appeal to the fervor of your liberationist views. Or it may jar your notions of her character and appear to be unseemly in light of how she has been portrayed in art and literature. Take note of your comforts and your discomforts and try to identify them with your core values and beliefs.

In addition to such "old business," your examination of the values and attitudes that have been part of you for a long while, certain texts may help you identify new values or attitudes. Few interpreters emerge from a study of the near sacrifice of Isaac, for instance, without having struggled with basic understandings of culture, obedience, and the relationships of humans in families and with God. In that struggle, some of your own values and attitudes may have shifted or been altered. What new values or attitudes might you have identified or gained from the experience of reading a text? It may be helpful to list and to reflect on these as well.

When you have explored these feelings and listed your responses to some of these questions, consider what your findings indicate about you. Set your experience with a particular text in light of your broader experience. Introspection is difficult, because it is hard to recognize in what ways our beliefs and values set limits and outcomes for interpretation. But be as concrete as possible with perspectives or experiences in your life that may be influencing your hearing of this text. Your gender, social commitments, status, and religious convictions are obvious starting points. Try to draw connections between who you are, how you have lived life, and your interpretation of a text.[3] If you are a pacifist, you may have de-emphasized the violence in a text. If you are a feminist, you may have noticed the women characters in the text with special scrutiny. If you are an exceptionally tidy person, you may have been frustrated with elements of the text that do not fit together well. Again, note that the connections you are noticing are in themselves not "bad interpretation" or "eisegesis." Reflexes of this nature can lead to insight as well as skewing. Your values and attitudes may be a gift as well as a hindrance to understanding. The point is not to eradicate them but to notice them and try to validate or invalidate them.

Finally, in light of this reflection, critique the results of your study. Consider how your interpretive motives affected your translation. This is the point where you can ask yourself whether your own values and attitudes work for or against understanding the text. Your reflections may lead you to affirm an insight as true to your best reading of a text. Or you may now perceive that you were overly conditioned in the way you understood some part of the text. In that case, your reflections may lead you to make some adjustment. Take time to take stock—to test the validity of your reading and then either affirm or adjust it.

The Interpreter in the World

Now that you have done your personal work with the text, continue the reflective and evaluative process by seeking global perspectives to set alongside your own. One of the most valuable tools in building self-awareness is to see the text from the perspective of different social locations as well as different religious perspectives. A good way to lighten your captivity to the filter of your own expectations is to read interpretations based on different circumstances and experiences. This process may have begun already in your survey of how the text has been understood by past generations.

Check the resources that you have been using—what sorts of social location or religious perspectives are represented by your bibliography? Do the items predominantly represent a similar social class, religious tradition, or approach to scripture? Have you consulted interpreters who are women as well as interpreters who are men? Take particular care to find interpretive works and articles that bring Third World perspectives to bear on specific passages. These discussions are often illuminative in ways that are especially important for North Americans. Browse the "new book" shelves in libraries and look for journals that originate in Africa, Latin America, and other places. One of the more recent developments in biblical studies is conferences or consultations that draw people from a variety of viewpoints and perspectives together around a theme or text. The papers from these gatherings frequently are published as books of essays that can be very helpful for this kind of work. More material from a variety of global perspectives is available than formerly and it is a wealth of insight and information that should no longer be overlooked.[4]

Also look for materials from religious traditions that differ from your own. An interpreter of the Sermon on the Mount from a Protestant or Free Church tradition might, for instance, profit from looking at a contemporary Orthodox interpretation.[5]

When you have found and looked through these sources, reconsider your text and your interpretation of it. Again, you may want to affirm some aspects of your reading and adjust others as you look at what you have done in light of what others from different places in the world or different traditions have said.

The Transformation of the Interpreter

When you have done the analysis of your own biases and checked them against interpretations emerging from other social locations, consider more fully how this text might challenge you to grow in spirit. As the emphasis on personal reflection indicates, we believe that the text can and should first of all transform the reader. In a very real sense, your ability to use texts in life grows from your own capacity to let the text become part of your own life. One of the outcomes of disciplined exegetical work is that texts become unforgettable. As we have been saying, in some senses you will "own" the text; in other senses it will "own" you. It is essential that the interpreter allow God to speak to her or him personally through the text.

Bible study is a spiritual adventure on the road toward maturity. The ongoing or progressive nature of this phenomenon should be clear, since transformation is the culmination of many tiny steps. Spiritual maturity may seem like a vague and abstract term, but in fact it has very practical implications. It shows in life. Through the spiritual maturity of both individuals and congregations, God's reign enters into and has an impact on everyday life on earth.

But first, as an expositor, you must hear the text affectively. It needs to percolate within you. It needs to become a part of you. Take stock of the resources the text offers you. Seek the vision and values in the text that move you. You have noted aspects of the text that resonate with your own experience and thinking. Analyze how it stimulates and excites you. Consider how you might use this energy as a resource in your own thinking and acting.

You may also have found the text limiting or difficult to hear in places. Are there ways in which these aspects of the text nevertheless help you understand and experience life more wisely and profoundly? Are there ways in which these aspects of the text nevertheless contribute to your growing understanding of the ways of God in human history? Are there ways in which these aspects of the text nevertheless contribute to your spiritual maturity?

Specifically note how the text might affect you and the way you think and live your life. Don't hurry. It takes time and effort to be reflective and insightful. It is much easier to fall prey to surface moralizing or clever witticisms. Cosmetic changes are like the flu: they may be intense and dramatic, but don't last long. Genuine change begins from the center, from deep thought and reflection, and works outward. It may be quite serendipitous.[6]

Study Journal

It is helpful to keep a record of your personal reflections on and about the text. In your study notebook, record new ideas that the text stimulates in you and note personal convictions that are initiated or strengthened by your work with the text. Give yourself freedom in this exercise. Being concrete about the text, about the particular ideas and emotions it evokes, is important—explicit references will help you recall "where you were" with this text in future years. But also allow yourself to record more global reflections sparked by the text. Give yourself scope to direct your mind and heart wherever the text leads you.

Here is a sample journal entry reflecting on Luke 18:1-8, the text about the widow who pesters the judge until she obtains justice. In the entry the interpreter struggles to accept the reality that God's sense of justice may differ from a human perception of justice:

> I find it difficult to let God be God and God's justice be God's justice. I would prefer to define justice, decide when and how justice needs to happen, and learn to pray effectively so that all this "justice" would happen at the right time for the right people. Instead, what is asked is the habit of looking to God for justice, my own and that of others,

with no assurance that God is going to see matters my way or respond on my time table. At the same time that one is required to let God's justice be God's justice, one must also work for justice, because justice is at the heart of God's character. And one can only work for justice according to one's understanding of what justice is. Where, I ask, is the justice in all of this? Working and waiting; practicing and praying; perhaps one acquires this kind of trust only in a lifetime of walking with God in attendance to the matters of justice. At any rate, there doesn't seem to be much choice. If the cry of the widow and the orphan is what God hears, then energetic and empathetic attention to such matters is necessarily not only part of the work of the kingdom, but part of knowing and being close to God. To know and be close to God means hearing with God the cry of the oppressed.

The Context of Biblical Study

Having become as self-aware in your own interaction with the ancient text as you can be at this point, consider next the context of your work with the text. Although we have used that word in many ways throughout the book, we have usually meant the context of the text. Here we are considering your own context, the context in which you as an interpreter of ancient texts are reading and practicing what you read. This context varies with each interpreter and is as rich and diverse as your own interests, involvements, commitments, and relationships. Whereas the immediate temptation is to leap into questions of practical ministry, there is a prior exercise that can greatly enhance your integration of the text with life and, indeed, your ability to minister with the text.

In physics we learn that work involves movement—distance traveled. Just holding steady doesn't count as work (although at times it requires effort)! In working with a text, the goal is to direct the potential communicative power of the text in ways that move you and others. This entails matching the resources of the text with settings that could benefit from these resources.

One of the first tasks of this exercise is naming the settings.

Many of us as readers tend to limit ourselves unnecessarily at this point. Due to the utilitarian pressures that often lead us to read texts in the first place, we limit the settings in which we imagine using the text to next quarter's Sunday school lessons or that sermon looming on the horizon. But in addition to these formal ministry settings, there are also intellectual and relational settings where a text can be an important resource.

For students, one of the most important contexts of biblical study includes other classes and interactions with other students. How does your biblical study inform your thinking on that theology paper? Or what implications does the text have for the issues being discussed in your ethics class? Does your study of the text offer insight into that thorny question raised in a missiology class? The possibilities here are endless. A text's power may raise questions or suggest solutions to a wealth of intellectual enterprises. For pastors and other professional readers of texts, the connections between the text's resources and intellectual pursuits may be less formal but no less important. The text may help you understand a book you are reading or offer a critical perspective on an idea that has been percolating. It may have bearing on an ethical dilemma or help you think theologically about a church practice such as the Eucharist.

In thinking about these settings, it is important to be as specific as possible. Ask, What would be appropriate ways for the power of this text to move me and others toward transformation in the areas of theology, ethics, mission, or practice to which the text speaks? Or, How does the communicative power of the text move me and others toward transformation on this particular question or issue with which we've been struggling?

In addition to intellectual questions and issues, think about the relational settings that are part of your life context for biblical study—again keeping in mind the key concept of "transformation" and again being specific. Does the text offer resources for your relationship with aging parents as they move toward the conclusion of their lives? Does it have insights to offer in your relationship with a spouse, children, or a friend? Does it give you a new way to think about your voluntary service or a community problem? Does it have implications for a conflict with which you are involved?

Finally, consider various ways to minister to others with the text. Wherc in the life of a congregation might the text best be appropriated? Perhaps it could function for the community in worship. Or consider how the text might give hope to the sick, comfort to the bereaved, or encouragement to those who doubt.

When you have thought carefully about the various settings—intellectual, relational, pastoral—in which this text might offer resources, then attend to these settings with a view toward communicating the power of the text. More simply, consider the audience. The makeup of the audience will determine to a large extent how you communicate the power of the text. The text may offer resources both for a Sunday school discussion and an intimate conversation with your spouse, but it is unlikely that you would use the same methods of communicating in both settings—at least, not successfully. The text may offer resources for a community debate on an ethical issue or a worship service, but you will need to tailor content and process for each setting in order to communicate effectively the power of the text.

Whatever the audience, you will need to take into account how the Bible has been used in that setting, positively or negatively, and other factors of culture, class, and gender that might aid or prevent empathy with the text. Since religious texts speak to our deepest commitments and values, how a text relates to ethical commitments, belief systems, and the basic convictions and values of an audience can raise intense feelings. Be aware of the focal personal and social issues of a setting and audience and how these may promote or impair the hearing of the text.

Developing a Work Plan

So far, in this chapter we have been speaking fairly broadly in terms of the variety of settings and audiences in which a text's communicative power might be employed. But most of us, most of the time, engage in Bible study with specific purposes in mind. In this section we want to deal with the practical process of setting a text in motion—activating its power for the common good.

Having done the personal work, having analyzed your own

context, go back now to the text itself. First, you must decide on the **points of attachment.** What in the text will serve as your initial point of departure? What aspects or features of the text will serve as the anchor points for the rope bridge you are building between text and your audience? Look to anchor your bridge on the following types of attachment points.

A word, phrase, or sentence may be the appropriate connection between the text and the people who will hear your sermon or sit in your Sunday school class. If, for instance, you were preaching on Amos 1:3-4, the phrases "Thus says the LORD . . . says the LORD," which form an inclusio, might be the point of attachment that leads you into a sermon on the role of prophets in God's relationship with the people of God. Or, if the text under consideration is Jeremiah 28:2-4, the sentence "I have broken the yoke of the king of Babylon" could serve to bring the text into a discussion on liberation theology, true and false. Or, from 1 Corinthians 8:1, the phrase "love builds up" might be a point of attachment for bringing Paul's discussion of the conflict in Corinth to bear on a contemporary ethical issue.

Sometimes, rather than specific words or phrases, it might be the gist of the text or its illocutionary force that can best influence a context. The point made by Luke's example story of the good Samaritan, about who is the neighbor, might be the heart of a powerful sermon. Or the struggle to understand God's perspective on justice from the story of the widow and the judge in Luke 18:1-8 could become the basis for a paper on justice and human responsibility. Hannah's story in 1 Samuel could become a focal point for a women's discussion of claiming God's grace for themselves. Or perhaps the illocutionary force of a prophetic oracle of doom spoken in the context of national prosperity could become the point of attachment.

Another type of point of attachment might arise out of your observation of a text's contours. One student discovered that Matthew 21:1-17, Matthew's version of the triumphal entry, is organized as a cycle of movements that track Jesus' progress into, about, and then out of Jerusalem. The focal point of the text's topography is the question that is asked at the edge of the city: Who is this? That contour became her point of attachment for a well-received sermon that she preached as a "journey" from various vantage points in the sanctuary.[7]

More abstractly, the ideas embedded in a text may excite you and set off your thinking and reflecting. The idea of Mary as a voice of liberation for her people, a young woman who understood her personal dilemma as an act of God on behalf of her nation, could become a point of attachment for an Advent meditation. Or the idea that the Lord's Prayer in Matthew makes demands upon God, demands that God start being God (aorist imperatives), in the mode of Jewish theodicy, could become a point of discussion in a paper about the character of God.

Finally, even more broadly, a canonical theme or thread may provide new insights. Even with the most open mind and willing heart, the text of 1 Peter, with its painful admonishment to slaves and wives, is difficult to appropriate. But it makes a difference whether one views this text as a part of the canonical thread that deals with right relationships between people or as part of the canonical thread that deals with what it means to live out the principles of nonretaliation. If we see Peter's admonitions in light of the overarching principles of nonretaliation, we may honor his intentions even though we may reject the particular ways he sought to interpret these principles. Such an insight based on a canonical thread could serve as a discussion starter for a Bible study on either 1 Peter or the theme of nonretaliation.

In working with your text you may want to list several possible points of attachment if you have time. You may only need one for a given task of communicating the power of the text, but you will undoubtedly want to come back to a text that you have studied so hard. Taking the time to list a variety of possible points of attachment will be a resource for life situations still to unfold.

When you have identified a solid point of attachment, you are ready to formulate your work plan for the specific occasion of communication you have in mind. In building the bridge between the text and your audience, try to be as clear as possible about what you are attempting to do. It is often helpful to write out a statement of purpose or an objective that you want to attain. These need not be long or complex, in fact it is better if they are brief and to the point. Trying to do too much with a text is one sure way to kill its communicative power rather than giving it the hearing that it deserves. On the other hand, it is also important that your statement of purpose reflect an honest hearing of the text. While in communicating the power of a text you certainly serve your audience, you also act in service of the text. The art of interpretation and the service of the word are, in fact, a twofold responsibility.

When you have your point or points of attachment and statement of purpose in hand, then attend to the building of the bridge one rope at a time. Your work plan, of course, will differ in accordance with the type of communication you are planning. Lesson plans are usually formulated according to activities—information that you want to give about the text, questions you want to pose, small-group discussion topics or other sorts of activities. Do not forget to include appropriate beginning and ending activities.[8] Sermons are usually formulated as "points" or movements. A narrative text may lend itself to a narrative sermon, although often the most effective sermons combine narrative and more expository approaches. Although thematic and special occasion sermons should be part of your repertoire, for many people the most powerful and moving sermons are biblical. Having done your work with the text carefully, it is a special joy to craft what you have gleaned into a clear and cogent message. There is a wealth of good books to help you move effectively into preaching.[9]

Other communicative genres such as meditations for weddings and funerals, devotionals at summer camp, youth ministry, and retreats all have their own sets of expectations and conventions. The scope of this work simply does not allow for exploration of any of these in detail. However, as you follow the generic "rules," prepare a strategy that releases the communicative power of the text for your ministry context. Bridges are built one rope at a time. Look for ways to foster incremental growth. Remember that for the text to be revelatory, it must be revelatory for someone.

CHECKPOINT

Your work up to this point has been communal in many ways, whether you have had study partners or not. If you have not had actual classmates with whom to work, you have nevertheless been supported by the community of scholars and commentators on your passage. But it is important to recognize at this point that you are moving from the private arena into the public arena. Your setting may be a congregation, a community debate, a sickbed in a hospital, or a conversation with a teenager. But wherever and whenever you bring your insights from texts to bear on life situations, you have accepted a significant public responsibility and you are accountable for how you use the gift of the text and your opportunity to study it. Building bridges between your text and your situation is a creative enterprise, but the bridge needs to be well anchored and constructed if it is to carry traffic. If you are making an oral presentation, be clear about how your exposition flows from the text.

Because in this phase you will be enriching others from your study of the text, you may have several entries for your study notebook from this chapter. One passage may spawn multiple occasions and audiences. Below are some considerations for checking your accountability to the text and to your audience.

Since much work in exposition is intuitive, be critical of your style—are you operating persuasively? Are you giving reasons why your audience should believe what you are saying? Attention to persuasion, giving reasons for saying what you are saying, forces you to become less subjective and authoritarian. Your explanation of the communicative power of the text ought to be accepted because it is persuasive, illuminating, and vital, not because of your own authority, eloquence, or charm. Thus, two valuable questions for critiquing any proposed application are:

1. Does your proposed application reflect an empathetic and honest hearing of the text—even when it is difficult to hear?
2. Are the points of attachment clear, and can they bear the traffic that they are being asked to carry?

Consider how your application fits the spirit of the text's communicative point. Will your presentation of the text enable it to operate in your environment as it might have in its original environment? Or by looking at only the communicative content are you in fact going against the intended function of the text?

Review the discussion under the checkpoint in chapter 6 for illustrations of how the application should preserve the illocutionary force. Is it evident that you have presented an accurate hearing of the text or have you used the text as a springboard for your own agenda?

Your application of the text should reflect your canonical assessment of the text. How are the claims of your text amplified or modified by its thread and counterthread? Have you considered the type of thread to which your passage belongs—is it on a major thread in the design or not? Have you evaluated your passage and its thread in light of your list of peak passages? If so, is your use of the passage true to the direction set by your peak passages?

Be passionate about the text and committed to it. The power of a text is both felt and thought. Minister to the heart. Many factors work together to produce a life-giving message that is perceived as revelatory and that promotes growth. These factors include: the expansion of your own spirit as you work with the text; the engagement of your own compassion; the integrity of the text and its continuing capacity to speak to the present and the future; and the active participation of others in hearing the text. Certainly, studying the biblical text is hard work. Just as certainly, grace abounds. The ultimate payoff for biblical study is spiritual maturity and the extension of the reign of God.

Excursus 1

The Structure of Clauses

The clause is the basic unit of syntax. Words in a clause relate to one another in a rule-governed way. In the clause "the students yawned," the phrase "the students" serves as the subject, while the verb "yawned" serves as its predicate. Having both a subject and a predicate, this clause is a well-formed, syntactic structure—it can stand on its own as a complete expression.[1] This minimal structure can be represented symbolically as:

Subject + Verb

This formula, or rule, represents the minimum necessary "slots" needed to form a clause in English. This definition does not specify the size or complexity of the elements filling these slots. A single word, a phrase, or even another clause may occupy the subject slot in a clause.

But these slots must contain elements of the right kind. A clause in English cannot be formed by two verbs, like "wanted yawned" or two nouns, like "boy food." Our definition of clause structure must be further defined by stipulating what type of words may occur in a slot. Our refined formula for an English clause is:

Noun (Phrase) + Verb (Phrase)

Of course not all clauses have just two slots. For example, "Bill perused the newspaper," is a clause with three slots. Take any of the words away, and the clause is no longer complete.

The number of slots required to form a complete expression

depends on the verb. In English, "yawn" requires only one slot to be filled, the subject slot, while "peruse" needs two slots, a subject slot and an object slot. Since the number of slots depends on the verb, we call the words filling these slots *complements*. They are needed to complement or fill out the verb. We can now further refine our defintion of the English clause as:

Verb (Phrase) + required complements

The number of complements required by a verb in English varies from one to three. "Yawn" is an example of a verb that takes one complement, whereas "perused" needs two. "Put" is a verb that takes three complements; for example, "Bill put the groceries on the table." The expressions "Bill put the groceries" or "Bill put on the table" are either incomplete or say something else, in this case something pretty silly—"Bill put on a table to match his tie" or "Bill puts the groceries about ten meters at his best."

The number of complements a verb requires is termed its *valency*. A verb may have more than one valency and more than one meaning. "Walk" is a verb that usually requires one complement—the man walks every morning. However, "walk" can also have a valency of two—the man walks his dog every morning. This helps us understand what happens in Hebrew when verbs change their stem or pattern from *paal* to *piel* or *hiphil*. The verb increases the number of required complements. For example, in the *paal* the verb בּוֹא takes a single complement, as does "come" in English. However, in the hiphil it takes two complements and is then glossed by the English word "bring." Although Greek does not have a system of stems, or patterns, as Hebrew, there are a few verbs that have different forms in the aorist depending on their valency and meaning. The most common of these is the verb ἵστημι ("I stand" or "set"). Much like the English word "put," the first aorist has a valency of three as in "He stood a child in their midst." The second aorist has a valency of one as in "He stood."

Not only may changes in valency signal a change in the meaning of the verb, but the way in which a predicate links to its complements often designates a change in meaning. For example, some verbs use prepositions to mark their object complement—such complements may be termed an *oblique complement*. The

English verb "lives" has two different senses, depending on how it marks its second complement—"He lives a quiet life" versus "He lives (resides) in Elkhart County." In the latter clause, the second complement is an oblique complement.

Which preposition precedes the oblique complement can also be significant for the meaning of a verb. Note the different meanings of the verb ישב in the following two clauses:

וַיֵּשֶׁב יַעֲקֹב בְּאֶרֶץ מְגוּרֵי אָבִיו בְּאֶרֶץ כְּנָעַן׃

And Jacob resided in the land of his ancestor's sojourning, in the land of Canaan. (Genesis 37:1)

וּשְׁלֹמֹה יָשַׁב עַל־כִּסֵּא דָּוִד אָבִיו

And Solomon sat upon the throne of David, his father. (1 Kings 2:12)

ישב requires an oblique object, but which preposition is used to link the complement to the verb has semantic import. If it is בְּ (in) then the verb has the sense to reside, live, dwell. But if it is עַל (on) then the sense is to sit on something.

In Greek, when a verb acquires an attached preposition, a compound verb, it takes an oblique object and its valency may change. The simple verb ἔρχομαι (come) takes one complement, a subject complement, as in "The king is coming." But when the preposition εἰς (into) is attached to form the compound verb εἰσέρχομαι (come into), it requires two complements and the second is marked by a preposition.

οὐ μὴ εἰσέλθῃ εἰς αὐτήν.

He shall never enter into it [the kingdom of God]. (Mark 10:15)

All of our examples so far have been bare predicate frames—a verb with its complements. But many clauses contain words and phrases that are not part of the predicate frame. We term these words *satellites* because they are hung onto, revolve around, the nucleus of the clause. In the clauses

> the students yawned discretely

or

> the students yawned all afternoon

the words "discretely" or "all afternoon" are not part of "yawn's" predicate frame. These words are syntactically optional; they do not fill required slots within the predicate frame. Note that we are describing these words from a syntactic point of view. This description is not an assessment of their communicative contribution. For example, in answer to the question "How long did the students yawn?" the phrase "all afternoon" would be the essential communicative part of the clause, although not required grammatically.

Clauses, then, consist of two kinds of elements—nuclear elements, which fill slots in the predicate frame, and satellites, words and phrases that are not grammatically necessary. These satellites modify the predicate, like "discretely" (a modifier of the predicate "yawned") or "all afternoon" (which modifies the entire predicate frame, telling when the predicate frame took place).

The Types of Clauses

Unlike English, in Hebrew and Greek the predicate can be either a noun or a verb. Because of this distinction in predicate type, it has been customary to group clauses into two large categories: verbal clauses and nominal clauses. If the predicate is a verb, the clause is a verbal clause. If the predicate is a noun, the clause is a nominal clause. The first example is a verbal clause and the second a nominal clause.

ἡ σκοτία ἐτύφλωσεν τοὺς ὀφθαλμοὺς αὐτοῦ.

The darkness blinded his eyes. (1 John 2:11)

καὶ ἡ κοινωνία δὲ ἡ ἡμετέρα μετὰ τοῦ πατρὸς

And our fellowship [is] with the father. (1 John 1:3*d*)

Using the concept of valency, we can give further precision to the distinction between verbal and nominal clauses. A verbal predicate has valency; it controls the number of complements. In a nominal clause, the predicate has no valency; it does not determine the number of complements. There are no two-valent or three-valent nouns, for example. However, in Hebrew and Greek both participles and infinitives may retain their valency and thus form verbal clauses.

In addition to verbal and nominal predicates, a third predicate type is formed by the verb of being. Clauses containing the copula are distinctive syntactically because the copula serves as a "linker"—hooking a nominal subject to a nominal predicate. A nominal clause remains if it is removed from the clause. In a sense it is a "dummy" verb—it fills the predicate slot but does nothing!

Consider the English clauses, "John is the chairman of the board" and "The chairman of the board is John." The semantic sense of both clauses seems the same. Contrast them with clauses containing a regular verb—"John walked the dog" and "The dog walked John." Clearly these clauses have different semantic senses! In fact, clauses with the copula are similar in semantic structure to nominal clauses since the copula links a subject noun phrase to a predicate one. Where they differ from nominal clauses is in the ability of the copula, as a conjugated verb, to indicate tense, aspect, and mood. We find, then, an opposition between nominal clauses, which cannot designate tense or aspect, and clauses with the copula, which can.

In addition to the copula, in Hebrew we also find two existential particles, one positive, יֵשׁ meaning "there is," and another a negative, אַיִן meaning "there is not." These indeclinable and impersonal particles are used to state the existence or nonexistence of something or someone. In English translation we usually supply the impersonal subject "there" as in the following example:

וְאָדָם אַיִן לַעֲבֹד אֶת־הָאֲדָמָה׃

And there was no one to till the ground. (Genesis 2:5 NRSV)

In Greek, forms of the verb "to be" are used both as a copula and as an existential. In 1 John 1:5*b* (NRSV), the first clause uses the copula. The verb "is" links "God" and "light." The second clause employs ἔστιν (it is) as an existential, usually translated "there is."[2]

ὁ θεὸς φῶς ἐστιν

God is light

καὶ σκοτία ἐν αὐτῷ οὐκ ἔστιν οὐδεμία.

and in him there is no darkness at all.

Syndetic and Asyndetic Independent Clauses

There are additional ways clauses can be categorized. Clauses may be linked together with a conjunction or they may begin without any explicit link to what has preceded them. If a clause begins with a conjunction, they are termed *syndetic.* If they are put together by simple juxtaposition, no conjunction, they are termed *asyndetic.* The following clauses from Genesis 13:11-12 illustrate both of these relationships. The first three clauses are syndetic. The fourth is asyndetic. The final clause is syndetic.

וַיִּבְחַר־לוֹ לוֹט אֵת כָּל־כִּכַּר הַיַּרְדֵּן
וַיִּסַּע לוֹט מִקֶּדֶם
וַיִּפָּרְדוּ אִישׁ מֵעַל אָחִיו׃
אַבְרָם יָשַׁב בְּאֶרֶץ־כְּנָעַן
וְלוֹט יָשַׁב בְּעָרֵי הַכִּכָּר

So Lot chose for himself all the plain of the Jordan, and Lot journeyed eastward; thus they separated from each other. Abraham resided in the land of Canaan, but Lot lived in the cities of the plain.

In Hebrew, as in the example above, the most common way to connect independent clauses together is by using the *waw.*

However, as the only common conjunction used to join independent clauses, *waw* has a wide variety of meanings—both conjunctive "and" and disjunctive "but." Within these two logical categories it can take on many finer shades of meaning. In the last line, the sense of the *waw* is to contrast the actions of Abraham and Lot—Abraham did this, but Lot did that. This contrastive use of the conjunctive *waw* is especially prominent when the initial clause in the sentence is asyndetic, as above.

Also in deciding whether Greek clauses are syndetic or asyndetic, keep in mind that several common Greek conjunctions will appear as the second word of a clause instead of the first word.[3] δέ and γάρ, for instance, never appear as the first word of a clause, although we translate them as the first word of the English clause.

DEPENDENT CLAUSES

Clauses can also be classified on the basis of their hierarchical relationship. Clauses may be equal and independent partners in a larger unit, the sentence, or they may just be strung together to form a paragraph. All of the clauses quoted above from Genesis are independent clauses. Most have simply been yoked together by a *waw.* On the other hand, there are clauses that have a relationship of subordination. They are not equal partners in a sentence. These clauses are called *dependent clauses*—they do not make up a complete grammatical expression and so they cannot stand alone but must depend on a clause that can stand by itself.

We may visualize dependent clauses as nesting in another clause—they are clauses that have been inserted into the structure of another clause. For example, in the sentence, "Joan saw the boy who ate the last piece of blueberry pie" the second complement, "boy" contains the embedded clause, "who ate the last piece of blueberry pie." This clause expands the complement phrase, "the boy." Since this clause forms an expansion with another clause's predicate frame, it can be said to be embedded within it.

Another example of an embedded clause is "Whoever ate the blueberry pie will have a purple tongue." The relative clause

"Whoever ate the blueberry pie" functions as the subject complement of the main clause. This dependent clause fills a slot in another verb's frame. Regardless of syntactic role, these embedded clauses are dependent clauses because they serve another clause in some way. The clause into which dependent clauses are inserted is usually the main, independent clause.

A conjunction may be used to embed one clause into another. These conjunctions act as nominalizers, that is they allow a clause to function like a noun and fill a slot that is normally filled by a noun. In English, "that" functions as a nominalizer.

The father saw his daughter.

The father saw that his daughter won the race.

Here the subordinating conjunction "that" enables the clause "his daughter won the race" to act as a noun and fill the direct object slot of "saw."

In Greek, ὅτι (that) functions in a way comparable to English "that."

> οὐ θέλω δὲ ὑμᾶς ἀγνοεῖν, ἀδελφοί,
> ὅτι πολλάκις προεθέμην ἐλθεῖν πρὸς ὑμᾶς
>
> I want you to know, brothers,
> that I have often intended to
> come to you. (Romans 1:13)

Here the nominalizer allows the clause "I have often intended to come to you" to function as the direct object of "know." In Hebrew, כִּי is the most common word used to convert clauses into complements.

וַיִּרְאוּ אֶחָיו כִּי־אֹתוֹ אָהַב אֲבִיהֶם מִכָּל־אֶחָיו

> And his brothers saw that their father loved him more than all his brothers. (Genesis 37:4)

As seen above, dependent clauses also modify nouns. To perform this function a relative pronoun is used. Relative pronouns in

English are terms like *who, which,* and *where.* For example, note how "who" in the following sentence embeds the clause "who wore the red dress," which modifies the subject complement "The girl" and is included in the subject slot of the main verb:

> The girl (who wore the red dress) ate in the Greek restaurant beside the river.

Or the following example:

> καὶ πᾶν πνεῦμα
> ὃ μὴ ὁμολογεῖ τὸν ᾿Ιησοῦν ἐκ τοῦ θεοῦ οὐκ ἔστιν.
>
> And every spirit
> (which does not confess Jesus) is not of God.
> (1 John 4:3 RSV)

In this case, the relative pronoun ὃ is nominative, neuter, singular because its head is πνεῦμα (spirit).

In Hebrew this embedding function is performed by אֲשֶׁר. Unlike Greek, this relative pronoun always has the same form.

וַתַּגֶּד־לָהּ אֵת כָּל־אֲשֶׁר עָשָׂה־לָהּ הָאִישׁ

> (And) she told her everything (which the man did for her).
> (Ruth 3:16*b*)

In this example, the embedded clause is attached to "everything," which fills the direct object slot. It functions as a modifier giving content to "everything."

The participle in Hebrew, particularly if it is definite, can perform this same embedding function. The participle, like the Greek relative, agrees with its head or antecedent. Note the following example:

יִתֵּן יְהוָה אֶת־הָאִשָּׁה הַבָּאָה אֶל־בֵּיתֶךָ כְּרָחֵל וּכְלֵאָה

> May the LORD make the woman (who is entering your house) as Rachel and Leah. (Ruth 4:11)

The participle "the entering (one)" embeds its clause in the direct complement phrase, modifying "the woman." Notice the agreement between the participle (feminine singular and definite) and "the woman."

Dependent clauses also function as satellites outside of the predicate frame. Temporal clauses function this way—"After he studied the Torah, he heard a commotion." The main clause, "he heard a commotion" is modified by the clause "after he studied the Torah." Clauses of circumstance function in this way as well—"While he was jogging in the park, he thought about his future plans." In this sentence, "while he was jogging in the park" gives the circumstances for the action of the main clause. In Hebrew the infinitive is frequently used to form such satellite clauses.

וַיְהִ֣י בְּבוֹא֔וֹ וַיִּתְקַ֥ע בַּשּׁוֹפָ֖ר בְּהַ֣ר אֶפְרָ֑יִם

> And it was when he came, he blew a blast on the trumpet in Mount Ephraim. (Judges 3:27)

In Greek, participles are frequently used to form satellite clauses.

> ἦλθεν ὁ Ἰησοῦς εἰς τὴν Γαλιλαίαν
> κηρύσσων τὸ εὐαγγέλιον τοῦ θεοῦ

> Jesus came into Galilee, preaching the gospel of God. (Mark 1:14 RSV)

Excursus 2

Greek and Hebrew Word Order

As speakers of English, we are used to a very strict word order in our clauses. Subjects of declarative sentences must come before the verb, and their objects after them. In the sentence "June owes Jane money," it is clear who owes whom money because the subject must come before the verb. In English, "normal" word order is quite readily apparent because few variations in word order are allowed. Consequently, we are not used to seeing alternative syntactic patterns as a valuable means of expression—we have little choice in the matter! However, Greek has great flexibility in word order, made possible by its system of inflections. The same, albeit to a lesser extent, is also true of Hebrew. In these languages, since word order is less prescribed, the writer is freer to use the order of words as a means of expression. What becomes gibberish in English, "Boat Bill bought Bob's," makes perfectly good, expressive Greek!

To understand how word order expresses nuances of meaning, we need to know what the normal orders are, since it is deviations from the norm that call for attention. Keep in mind that we are discussing norms and not laws or rules. We are pointing to what you will expect to find in a clause. By knowing the expected, you can note where a text deviates from the norm and does the unexpected. It is what goes against your expectations that is important for you to note and mark on your layout. It is the unusual that requires comment.

Also be aware that the notion of a normal or standard word order can be a bit tricky because it depends in part on the type of text you are reading. To choose an extreme case, Hebrew narrative has a very common clause structure—*waw* plus verb—which is practically nonexistent in poetry. However, given this disclaimer, it is possible to indicate certain norms and to mark deviation from them as significant for the meaning of texts.

GREEK

The expected word order in Greek verbal clauses is the predicate followed by its complements. Thus, customarily, the verb will be the first building block of a clause followed by the subject complement unless the subject is embedded in the verb. The object complement is next followed by the third complement, if there is one. Satellites, if they occur, either appear with the syntactic unit with which they function or, especially in the case of a prepositional phrase, at the end of the clause after the second or third complement, if there is one.

Here, from the Sermon on the Mount (Matthew 7:6), is an example of customary word order for a clause with a verb and a full array of complements. The first complement (a second-person, plural pronoun) is implicit in the imperative verb. The order is verb (after the negative "not") + the second complement (the holy thing) + the third complement (to the dogs).

[Μὴ] δῶτε τὸ ἅγιον τοῖς κυσίν.
verb 1st 2d 3d

When this customary order of words is not followed, the interpreter should take note. This is especially true when second complements are "fronted"—presented in front of the verb. Such variations may signal a change in topic or a special emphasis and are worthy of exegetical attention.[1]

In the following set of examples, the normal word order is demonstrated in the first set of examples. In the second set of examples the complement or satellite that is "out of place" has been underlined in both Greek and the English translation.

Word order of verb + first or subject complement:

Normal: verb + 1st complement

ὡμοιώθη ἡ βασιλεία τῶν οὐρανῶν ἀνθρώπῳ

The kingdom of heaven may be compared to a person. (Matthew 13:24)

ἦλθεν αὐτοῦ ὁ ἐχθρὸς

His enemy came. (Matthew 13:25)

Unusual: 1st Complement + Verb

ἐὰν <u>ὑμεῖς</u> στήκετε ἐν κυρίῳ.

If <u>you</u> stand fast in the Lord. (1 Thessalonians 3:8 RSV)

<u>αὐτὸς</u> γὰρ σώσει τὸν λαὸν αὐτοῦ ἀπὸ τῶν ἁμαρτιῶν αὐτῶν.

For <u>he himself</u> will save his people from their sins. (Matthew 1:21)

Word order of verb + second or object complement:

Normal: Verb + 2d complement

ἤγαγεν αὐτὸν εἰς πανδοχεῖον

He brought him to an inn. (Luke 10:34)

πόθεν οὖν ἔχει ζιζάνια;

From whence does it have weeds? (Matthew 13: 27)

Unusual: 2d complement + verb

ὅπου <u>αὐτὸν</u> ἐσταύρωσαν,

Where <u>him</u> they crucified . . . (John 19:18)

<u>ἀμπελῶνα</u> ἄνθρωπος ἐφύτευσεν

A <u>vineyard,</u> a person planted. (Mark 12:1)

Satellites in verbal clauses with complements:

Normal: Clause + satellite

καὶ ἐπέσπειρεν ζιζάνια ἀνὰ μέσον τοῦ σίτου

And he sowed tares in the middle of the wheat. (Matthew 13:25)

Unusual: Satellite + Clause

<u>ἐκ Ναζαρὲτ</u> δύναταί τι ἀγαθὸν εἶναι;

<u>Out of Nazareth</u> can anything good come out? (John 1:46)

The variation on word order that is probably most difficult, perhaps even counterintuitive for English speakers, is the splitting of a syntactic unit. A good example is 3 John 4, which the RSV renders as "No greater joy can I have than this, to hear that my children follow the truth." In the Greek, there are three Greek words between "greater" and "joy," yielding a nuance that the RSV tries to evoke by putting it first in the English sentence. Notice how the Greek accomplishes something similar by splitting the grammatical sequence:

μειζοτέραν (τούτων οὐκ ἔχω) χαράν

greater (than these I do not have) joy.

Hebrew

The most frequent prose order in Hebrew verbal clauses is the predicate followed by its complements:

Verbal Predicate + Complements

Genesis 12:10 illustrates this principle: (The verbal predicates are in bold type. The last clause is a nominal clause.)

וַיְהִ֥י רָעָ֖ב בָּאָ֑רֶץ
וַיֵּ֨רֶד אַבְרָ֤ם מִצְרַ֨יְמָה֙ לָג֣וּר שָׁ֔ם
כִּֽי־**כָבֵ֥ד** הָרָעָ֖ב בָּאָֽרֶץ׃

Now there was a famine in the land.
So Abram went down to Egypt to reside there as an alien,
for the famine was severe in the land. (Genesis 12:10 NRSV)

The strong expectation in reading Hebrew narrative prose is that the main clauses will begin with a verb in the *wayyiqtol* form. In cases where, for grammatical reasons, the verb cannot begin the clause (e.g., a negative must precede its verb), a *qatal* form is used. It too precedes its complements, as in the following example from Genesis 13. (The negative plus the verb is in bold type.)

וְלֹֽא־נָשָׂ֥א אֹתָ֛ם הָאָ֖רֶץ לָשֶׁ֣בֶת יַחְדָּ֑ו **כִּֽי־הָיָ֤ה** רְכוּשָׁם֙ רָ֔ב
וְלֹ֥א יָֽכְל֖וּ לָשֶׁ֥בֶת יַחְדָּֽו׃

so that the land could not support both of them living together; for their possessions were
so great that they could not live together.
(Genesis 13:6 NRSV)

Deviations from this word order, *verbal predicate + complement,* should attract your attention.

As for the order of complements, the subject complement (SC) has pride of place. The subject complement normally comes immediately after the verb. Since verbal predicates usually stand first, this leads to the expected sequence (A):

(**A**) PREDICATE, SC

In the unexpected case of the verb coming second in its clause, the subject normally stands immediately before the verb (pattern B).

(**B**) SC, PREDICATE

In either case, the reader's expectation is that the subject will come either immediately before or after the verb. In the example from Genesis 12:10, the subjects come immediately after their verbs, pattern A. Below is an example of pattern B, the subject coming immediately before its verb. This, as the less frequent pattern, forms a deviation from the norm and is a marked alternative to the more frequent pattern and should be noted when it occurs.

וְיִשְׂרָאֵ֗ל אָהַ֤ב אֶת־יוֹסֵף֙ מִכָּל־בָּנָ֔יו

Now Israel loved Joseph more than any other of his children . . . (Genesis 37:3 NRSV)

For direct, indirect, and oblique complements, the usual order is that they follow the subject complement. In the standard order, where the verb comes first and the subject follows, these complements follow immediately after the subject. The expected order is:

(**A**) PREDICATE, SC, DC/IC/OC

When the subject comes first, the expected order is:

(**B**) SC, PREDICATE, DC/IC/OC

The pecking order among these complements is that the direct object has pride of place, coming immediately after the subject in the normal pattern. An example of the expected pattern is found in Genesis 37:5:

וַיַּחֲלֹ֤ם יוֹסֵף֙ חֲל֔וֹם

We can render this literally as "Dreamed Joseph a dream." The verb "to dream" stands first in its clause, as expected. The subject follows immediately after the verb, again the expected pattern, with the direct complement, "dream," coming in third place, again as expected.

Genesis 37:3 illustrates the alternate pattern B in which the subject instead of the verb stands at the head of the clause.

וְיִשְׂרָאֵ֗ל אָהַ֤ב אֶת־יוֹסֵף֙ מִכָּל־בָּנָ֔יו

The subject, “Israel,” begins the clause, followed by the verb, with the direct object, “Joseph,” coming immediately after the verb—again in third position. These are the expected positions in which to find the direct object.

Indirect and oblique objects usually follow the direct object, coming in fourth position in the clause, as illustrated by the following clause:

וַיִּטְבְּלוּ אֶת־הַכֻּתֹּנֶת בַּדָּם׃

and dipped the robe in the blood. (Genesis 37:31 NRSV)

The verb stands at the head of the clause. The subject is implicit in the conjugation of the verb. The direct complement comes next, “the robe,” with the oblique complement, “blood,” coming last. (“Dip” is a three-place verb, taking both a direct object—what is dipped—as well as an oblique object, the medium used for dipping.)

However, the direct, oblique, and indirect object normally displace the subject from its position next to the verb, if they are attached as a pronoun to a preposition or אֵת the direct object marker. In the following example, the direct object, “him,” is a pronoun attached to אֵת and comes immediately after the verb, displacing the subject from second position.

וַיֵּבְךְּ אֹתוֹ אָבִיו׃

Thus his father bewailed him. (Genesis 37:35 NRSV)

A literal order would read: “Bewailed him his father.” Indirect and oblique complements also precede the direct complement if they are represented by an attached pronoun. In the following example, the direct complement formed by the body of the request, “where they are pasturing the flock,” comes after the third complement, “me.”

הַגִּידָה־נָּא לִי אֵיפֹה הֵם רֹעִים׃

Please tell me where they are pasturing the flock. (Genesis 37:16)

Unusual Word Order

Altering the normal or expected word order was one way the biblical authors had to control the focus and the emphasis that they wanted a clause to express. It was their way of spotlighting or highlighting what is on center stage in each clause. This spotlight, as in the theater, is not fixed, but can move from one person, object, or argument to another.

One common way to spotlight a component of a clause is to move it into first place—the place that is usually given to the verb in Hebrew and Greek. In Genesis 1:27, the first clause exhibits normal narrative clause order. In the second, the spotlight moves to the "image of God" and then on its parallel, "male and female" in the third.

וַיִּבְרָא אֱלֹהִים אֶת־הָאָדָם בְּצַלְמוֹ
בְּצֶלֶם אֱלֹהִים בָּרָא אֹתוֹ
זָכָר וּנְקֵבָה בָּרָא אֹתָם׃

Normal	**Predicate**	**1 (Subject)**	**2 (Object)**	**Satellite**
	Created	*God*	*the human*	*in his image*
Marked	**Satellite**	**Predicate**	**2**	
	In the image of God	*he created*	*him*	
Marked	**Satellite**	**Predicate**	**2**	
	Male and female	*he created*	*them*	

In the first line, we find normal narrative sequence: the verb with *waw,* subject, object, and satellite. In the second, the satellite "in the image of God" comes first with the object last. The final line follows the order of the second line. These features can be diagrammed as A B C D/ D′ A′ C′ / D″A″ C″. In the last two clauses the D element has been shifted to the head of the clause. This finely crafted arrangement draws attention to the parallelism between "image of God" and "male and female."

In Hebrew narrative the verb usually occupies first position for grammatical reasons: The *wayyiqtol* verb form must stand first in its clause because it is prefixed with a *waw*. Thus, it is relatively easy to spot deviations. Genesis 13:11 offers an example of the normal narrative word order. The verbs in bold type in the translation come at the beginning of each sentence in the Hebrew.

וַיִּבְחַר־ל֨וֹ ל֜וֹט אֵ֚ת כָּל־כִּכַּ֣ר הַיַּרְדֵּ֔ן
וַיִּסַּ֥ע ל֖וֹט מִקֶּ֑דֶם
וַיִּפָּ֣רְד֔וּ אִ֖ישׁ מֵעַ֥ל אָחִֽיו׃

Then Lot **chose** for himself the whole plain of the Jordan
and Lot **traveled** eastward.
And so each **separated** from his fellow.

This verse contains three main clauses, each headed by its verb with a *waw* prefixed to it. In the next verse, which continues the narrative, we find two clauses in which the subjects come first—an alternative order (pattern B)—with the verbs now placed in the perfective (*qatal* forms).

אַבְרָ֖ם יָשַׁ֣ב בְּאֶֽרֶץ־כְּנָ֑עַן
וְל֗וֹט יָשַׁב֙ בְּעָרֵ֣י הַכִּכָּ֔ר

Abram resided in Canaan but Lot resided in the cities of the plain. (Genesis 13:12)

Here shifting the names to the head casts the spotlight on Lot and Abraham and strongly contrasts the destinies of these two men.

Sometimes an author simply wants to dim the spotlight. The use of the passive is a common way in which the attention of the reader can be redirected. In the passive construction, the object of the active verb is promoted to the subject of the verb. "John loves Mary" puts the focus on John, in contrast to "Mary is loved by John" where Mary is promoted and John demoted. In addition to promoting the object of the active verb to the first complement and demoting the subject, the demoted subject can be eliminated! We can say simply, "Mary is loved" without saying by whom. Consequently, the passive can be used when the agent of the action is not known or when the author wishes to omit it.

In Hebrew, passives rarely mention the agent of the action. Consequently, we expect the agent to be anonymous.

טָרֹף טֹרַף יוֹסֵף׃

Joseph has certainly been torn apart! (Genesis 37:33)

וַתֻּקַּח הָאִשָּׁה בֵּית פַּרְעֹה

The woman was taken to Pharaoh's palace. (Genesis 12:15)

In neither example is the agent of the action mentioned—although it is known to the reader from its previous mention in the text. In the first example, we can fill in the implicit agent, "some wild animal," and in the second case, "the servants of Pharaoh." In these two cases the omission of the agent places the focus on the victim of the action.

The Greek of the New Testament, significantly influenced by Hebrew and Aramaic, also makes use of the passive to omit the agent of the action. In the parable of the leaven (Matthew 13:33 and Luke 13:21), we read:

ἕως οὗ ἐζυμώθη ὅλον.

until the whole was leavened.

In this last clause of the parable, the verb is a passive. It casts the agent of the leavening into the background. Although the agent of the leavening might be implicitly filled in by "the yeast," the omission of the agent places the focus on the process or on the subject of the passive verb, "whole."

Mainly we have been discussing techniques an author may use to shine or dim the spotlight of attention on the subject of a clause. But what happens if something is not the subject, yet the author wishes the reader to pay special attention to it? Several devices stand available for this purpose. Two of them are very similar, although given different names. Topicalization and left (or right) dislocation are used to place words on center stage.

In English the normal active sentence pattern is "Jacob did not send Benjamin." However an alternative strategy is to place the object complement, "Benjamin," at the head of the active sentence, "Benjamin, his father did not send." (If the object, "Benjamin," would have a resumptive pronoun, the clause would read, "Benjamin, his father did not send him." This structural wrinkle is termed *left dislocation.*)

Both Greek and Hebrew can accomplish topicalization and dislocation more naturally than can English. In Greek, the case endings are used to designate grammatical function and in Hebrew, definite direct objects are marked with אֶת. Consequently, both Greek and Hebrew can begin a clause with a direct object without fear that it will be confused with the subject.

Topicalization and dislocation may be more frequent in the biblical languages because they place objects in the foreground of the clause without omitting the subject, the agent of the action, as is normally the case with the passive. In a sense these grammatical structures in Hebrew and Greek accomplish what the passive in English does—they promote the object to prominence within the clause while dimming the spotlight on the subject or agent. Note the following example.

וַיִּרְא֣וּ אֶחָ֗יו כִּֽי־אֹת֞וֹ אָהַ֤ב אֲבִיהֶם֙ מִכָּל־אֶחָ֔יו

His brothers saw
that he their father loved more than all his brothers.
(Genesis 37:4)

Observe how the grammatically incorrect "he" fits first position, the normal subject position in English, and helps make it the focus of attention even though it is actually the object. A more grammatically correct translation would be:

> But when his brothers saw that their father loved him more than all his brothers . . . (NRSV)

However, the cost of a translation with normal English word order and grammar is that the pronoun is now shifted from focal position at the head of its clause to its normal position after the verb, and all communicative significance of the placement of the pronoun in Hebrew is lost.

If we were bold and accepted the suggested hypothesis that topicalization and dislocation in Hebrew functions akin to the passive in English, we could translate this clause with an English passive construction.

> His brothers saw that he was loved by their father more than all the brothers.

Now the translation is grammatically correct in English and retains the pronoun as the focus of the clause. Below are two examples from Greek.

> αὐτὸν ἐσταύρωσαν.
>
> They crucified him. (John 19:18)

If we were to keep the Greek word order we would have, "Him they crucified," which is not really acceptable. However, we can maintain something of the communicative force by using a passive construction, "He was crucified." A passive construction is particularly appropriate here since the agent is out of the spotlight in the Greek clause—not being explicitly mentioned.

The following example translates more directly into English, since the direct object can be topicalized smoothly in an English translation and carries over quite well the communicative force of the Greek.

> ἀλλὰ τὴν κρίσιν πᾶσαν δέδωκεν τῷ υἱῷ,
>
> . . . but every judgment he has given to the son. (John 5:22)

Left dislocation (right dislocation in Hebrew!), as mentioned, is very similar to topicalization, but the element placed in initial position is later resumed by a pronoun. This pronoun indicates the syntactic function of the initial element in the sentence. An English example would be, "Jack, his father sent him to town" as a reply to the question, "Where is Jack?" The resumptive pronoun "him" indicates that "Jack" is really the object of the verb, although it comes first in the clause.

כִּ֣י כָל־הָאִ֗ישׁ אֲשֶׁ֤ר הָלַךְ֙ אַחֲרֵ֣י בַֽעַל־פְּע֔וֹר הִשְׁמִיד֛וֹ יְהוָ֥ה אֱלֹהֶ֖יךָ מִקִּרְבֶּֽךָ׃

Every person which went after Baal Peor, Yhwh your God destroyed **him** from among you. (Deuteronomy 4:3)

Sometimes another element of a clause may be spotlighted. In Greek, satellites and oblique objects normally follow the other complements and thus are usually last in the clause. But in 1 John 3:19, all three clauses differ from the norm in the placement of the prepositional phrase:

[Καὶ] ἐν τούτῳ γνωσόμεθα
ὅτι ἐκ τῆς ἀληθείας ἐσμέν,
καὶ ἔμπροσθεν αὐτοῦ πείσομεν τὴν καρδίαν ἡμῶν.

By this we shall know
that out of the truth we are,
and before him reassure our hearts.

Although the RSV retains the prepositional phrase as the topic or focus in the first clause, to do so in the next two clauses renders the translation quite awkward. Some of the impact is, of course, inevitably lost in the more conventional translation.

Abbreviations

ANET	*Ancient Near Eastern Texts Relating to the Old Testament*
BAGD	*A Greek-English Lexicon of the New Testament and Other Early Christian Literature*
BDB	*Hebrew-English Lexicon of the Old Testament*
DBI	*Dictionary of Biblical Interpretation*
DCH	*Dictionary of Classical Hebrew*
EDNT	*Exegetical Dictionary of the New Testament*
HSO	*Hebrew Syntax in Outline*
ICC	*International Critical Commentary*
IDB(s)	*Interpreter's Dictionary of the Bible (Supplement)*
Lidell-Scott	*A Greek-English Lexicon*
NKBE	*The Hebrew and Aramaic Lexicon of the Old Testament*
NRSV	*New Revised Standard Version*
RSV	*Revised Standard Version*
TLOT	*Theological Lexicon of the Old Testament*
TDNT	*Theological Dictionary of the New Testament*
TDOT	*Theological Dictionary of the Old Testament*

NOTES

INTRODUCTION

1. The commentaries in the *ICC* series would be an example of works written from this standpoint. See, for example, Burton's commentary on Galatians and the extensive discussion of the North and South Galatian hypotheses found in the introduction. E. D. Burton, *The Epistle to the Galatians* (Edinburgh: T & T Clark, 1921).

2. It is instructive to compare the articles "Bibical Criticism" and "Biblical Criticism, History of" in *IDB* (1962) with the articles "Biblical Criticism, OT" and "Biblical Criticism, NT" in the supplementary volume (*IDB*[s], 1976). In 1962, classical historical criticism dominated the articles, and solid confidence was expressed in its power to provide continuing progress in biblical interpretation. However, in the supplementary volume (1976), the first section in the article on Old Testament criticism is titled "The Challenge to Previous Biblical Criticism."

3. René Wellek and Austin Warren, *Theory of Literature* (New York: Harcourt, Brace & World, 1956) is the classic formulation of this point of view. "New Criticism" was a movement in general literary scholarship whose roots lie in the first half of the twentieth century in the work of I. A. Richards and others. It was a powerful critical force in American literary thought following the Second World War. From this arena it eventually influenced American biblical scholarship.

4. Wolfgang Richter, *Exegese als Literaturwissenschaft: Entwurf einer Alttestamentlichen Literatur Theorie und Methodologie* (Göttingen: Vandenhoeck & Ruprecht, 1971) is an early manifesto for a new literary, linguistic approach. Another early harbinger was James Muilenburg, "Form Criticism and Beyond" in *JBL* 88 (1969): 1-18.

5. Hans Dieter Betz, *Galatians: A Commentary on Paul's Letter to the Churches in Galatia* (Philadelphia: Fortress Press, 1979).

6. Stanley Fish is a name associated prominently with this point of view. See his *Is There a Text in This Class? The Authority of Interpretive Communities* (Cambridge, Mass.: Harvard University Press, 1980). For a response to new criticism and reader response theory see Gordon J. Thomas, "Telling a Hawk from a Handsaw? An Evangelical Response to the New Literary Criticism," *Evangelical Quarterly* 71 (1999): 37-50.

7. It seems, at times, that modern criticism has reverted to an old but falacious type of argument—the *ad hominem* argument. Argument is directed against the person or his or her class rather than against the substance of the argument. Labeling a reading "feminist" or "patriarchal," for example, does not deal with its adequacy as an interpretation any more than labeling it "fundamentalist" or "modernist" would. Labeling an interpretation is no substitute for a substantive critique.

8. Compare, for example, the commentaries of Speiser (in the Anchor Bible

Series), von Rad (in the Old Testament Library Series), and Westermann, *Genesis 1–11* (Minneapolis: Augsburg Press, 1984; German 1974). Also, Umberto Cassuto, *A Commentary on the Book of Genesis, Part One: From Adam to Noah,* trans. Israel Abrahams (Jerusalem: Magnes Press, 1961; Hebrew 1953).

9. Compare the view of the "patriarchal period" found in Germany as represented in Martin Noth's *History of Israel* (London: A. & C. Black, 1960), and that found in the United States as represented in John Bright's *History of Israel,* 4th ed. (Louisville: Westminster John Knox Press, 2000).

10. A field of linguistics—pragmatics—has grown up around the effect of context and tacit assumptions on communication. Extralinguistic factors make a difference in our understanding of linguistic communication—both spoken and written. Communication is often by "shorthand," with the audience filling in the gaps. See Jacob L. Mey, *Pragmatics: An Introduction* (Oxford: Blackwell Publishers, 1993). An important area of pragmatics and important for interpreters is "relevance theory." See Barbara Gorayska and Roger Lindsay, "The Roots of Relevance," *Journal of Pragmatics* 19 (1993): 301-23 for a discussion and bibliography. For an overview of the modern description and understanding of language, see John Lyons, *Linguistic Semantics: An Introduction* (Cambridge: Cambridge University Press, 1995), chap. 1, "Meta-linguistic Preliminaries." On page 8 he makes the distinction between semantics, in the narrow sense of the term, and pragmatics.

11. We will present the historical and sociocultural dimension in chapter 6.

12. All of us have said about someone's misunderstanding of our language, "But that is not what I meant!" If a critical theory does not take misunderstanding seriously and try to elucidate it, it is denying one of our most common experiences of language. Consequently, one way to test the validity of an interpretive theory is to ask the question, Is it possible to misunderstand a text? If no allowance is made for misunderstanding linguistic communication, then such a theory—unable to differentiate between understanding and misunderstanding—offers little insight into the process of understanding words, sentences, and texts.

13. Because of the crucial and foundational role played by the wording of a text in correctly understanding it, we devote the first four chapters to teaching how to see those features that enable sensible decisions concerning what a text says—its likely semantic sense. It is also for this reason that the interpretive enterprise *must* begin with the actual language of the text.

14. This does not mean that the exegetical method is taught in a beginning language class, but that the sequence of "language" courses must unfold in a way of interpretation that is based on them. Consequently, the interpretation of texts should be the ultimate goal behind the first semester's course in a biblical language. The proximate goal is gaining the language facility necessary to interpret texts.

15. It is jarring to realize that in the secular university setting, text courses automatically mean courses using the original text. In the seminary, on the other hand, text courses normally work in translation unless explicitly labeled otherwise. In some cases, even exegesis courses are taught from an English Bible. When this happens, students are being shortchanged.

16. There should be no opposition between exegesis and the method presented in this book. The traditional exegesis class has been and should remain a mainstay in a good seminary education. The steps for understanding texts found here are the foundation of good exegetical method—this book can stand on its own as a guide to exegesis. Consequently, we will discuss how to save and use the results of study for exegetical work as well as for study directed toward immediate ministry contexts and goals.

17. Many valuable handbooks covering the traditional methods for the study of the Hebrew and Greek Scriptures have been published. A recent one, translated into English after many years of use in German, is Odil Hannes Steck, *Old Testament Exegesis: A Guide to the Methodology,* trans. James D. Nogalski (Atlanta: Scholars Press, 1995), and is an excellent example. It includes outstanding bibliographies for students at the end of each chapter. These works can provide a useful supplement to the stages and techniques of study offered here.

18. *Dictionary of Biblical Interpretation,* John H. Hayes, ed. (Nashville: Abingdon Press, 1999) is a convenient resource for becoming familiar with the methods and terminology of biblical scholarship. Likewise, *The Cambridge Companion to Biblical Literature,* John Barton, ed. (Cambridge: Cambridge University Press, 1998) is a recent collection of essays discussing modern approaches to biblical studies as well as the study of the biblical material itself, and is very useful for acquainting the student with the field of biblical studies.

19. We will, in fact, refer to many of the tools and approaches that are widely used by scholars in order to aid students in the course of their work with a text.

1. Reading Through the Text

1. In Greek, the first twenty-one verses form a single sentence!

2. In the Nestle-Aland Greek text, for instance, the Sermon on the Mount is divided from the surrounding material by double spacing at the beginning of chapter 5 and at the end of chapter 7. Within the Sermon, the Greek text is divided in several ways. The Beatitudes and the Lord's Prayer are lined out clause by clause. The rest of the material is arranged in paragraphs marked by indentation. Most of these paragraphs constitute an appropriate unit for study, although since it is a collection of teachings resembling wisdom sayings, some are very short.

3. Positing Genesis 12:10-20 to be a basic unit does not mean that it contains no further subdivisions. In looking at this passage we find the same form of the copula, which began the narrative, again in verses 11 and 14, dividing this unit into smaller subunits or segments. Notice that verse 10 also features an inclusio in that the first and last line of this verse contain the words "famine in the land," which reinforces the break between verses 10 and 11. On the other hand, verse 10 does not stand on its own. It presents a problem to be solved. Furthermore, in verse 11 we have the same scene, same process—a journey, same actors, and a further problem. It is clearly dependent on verse 10. What you are looking for here is a reasonably good sense of the beginning and ending point of your text. The grace of the interpretive enterprise allows self-correction at any point.

4. Although it is possible to work with a text manually, by far the best way is to use a computer to copy and manipulate your text. Using a computer is easier, quicker, and allows recovery from mistakes.

5. Since we assume that students may be using this guide on their own, we have provided resources that can enable their study. However, the ability to use these tools is no substitute for facility in the languages. We hope that students will continue to improve their reading comprehension so that this initial stage will become easier and easier.

6. We would recommend this grammar for intermediate students. Its perspective is informed by modern linguistics, which makes it suitable as a grammatical companion for the present work.

7. Although there are some notable cases where the punctuation is debatable, it

is normally reliable as a clause marker. John 1:3 illustrates a debatable case. The verb γέγονεν at the end of verse 3 may be understood as part of either the clause ending verse 3 or the one beginning verse 4.

8. See Merwe, Naude, and Kroeze, paragraph 9.5, pages 44ff. for a brief discussion of the major accent markers and a table of them.

2. Tabling the Text

1. Most computer programs have a feature that allows you to turn selected text into a table. Using this feature, you will end up with as many rows as you have lines of text separated by a return. Once you have your text in rows, add the two additional columns to your table. By dragging cell borders you can resize the columns in order to fit the material. It is sometimes advantageous to align your work horizontally on the page (landscape view), so that you have more room to work.

2. Layouts can be presented in English translation on the basis of work with the Hebrew or Greek text. The layouts in these cases are not done from the English text, although they are presented in English. See the commentary by Jake Elias on 1 and 2 Thessalonians. He presents a layout in English for each passage in these two books. Jacob W. Elias, *1 and 2 Thessalonians* (Scottdale, Pa.: Herald Press, 1995).

3. In English even the order in which categories of adjectives are applied is strict. Note the term *grizzly, brown, big bear* as opposed to *big, brown, grizzly bear.*

4. On the topic of lexicography, the student could read with profit, J. P. Louw, ed., *Lexicography and Translation with a Special Reference to Bible Translation* (Cape Town: Bible Society of South Africa, 1985).

5. The concordance, *A New Concordance of the New Testament,* Abraham Even-Shoshan, ed. (Jerusalem: Kiryat Sepher, 1983), is a good concordance for beginners to use. First of all, the Hebrew text is pointed! Second, and for our purposes here more important, the common collocations and expressions in which the word is used are noted. This makes the job of finding usage patterns much easier. A New Testament study tool that combines some features of both a concordance and a lexicon is the three volume *Exegetical Dictionary of the New Testament,* Horst Balz and Gerhard Schneider, eds., English translation published by Eerdmans, 1990–93. It not only surveys the distribution in the New Testament and other literature, but makes comments about the distribution.

6. *Diachronic* refers to "through time" in opposition to *synchronic,* which means "at the same time."

7. This aspect of a word's meaning has been referred to as its "paradigmatic" context—its synonyms, antonyms, and so forth. The study of word meaning from this perspective involves the concept of a word's "sematic field." For a discussion of this topic, see D. A. Cruse, *Lexical Semantics* (Cambridge: Cambridge University Press, 1986) and the relevant sections in John Lyons, *Linguistic Semantics: An Introduction* (Cambridge: Cambridge University Press, 1995). For examples of lexical semantics and semantic fields applied to biblical studies, see John F. A. Sawyer, *Semantics in Biblical Research: New Methods of Defining Hebrew Words for Salvation* (London: SCM Press, 1972) and Moises Silva, *Biblical Words and Their Meaning: An Introduction to Lexical Semantics* (Grand Rapids: Zondervan, 1983).

8. Black's summary of textual criticism is also helpful. David Alan Black, *New Testament Texual Criticism* (Grand Rapids: Baker Books, 1994).

3. Contouring the Text

1. The subject matter of this and the next chapter usually falls under the rubric of "rhetorical analysis," or "stylistics." The following books provide greater detail on this topic: Phyllis Trible, *Rhetorical Criticism: Context, Method and the Book of Jonah* (Minneapolis: Fortress Press, 1994); Robert D. Bergen, ed., *Biblical Hebrew and Discourse Linguistics* (Dallas: Summer Institute of Linguistics, 1994); Roland Meynet, *Rhetorical Analysis: An Introduction to Biblical Rhetoric* (Sheffield: Sheffield Academic Press, 1998); and Ellen van Wolde, *Narrative Syntax and the Hebrew Bible: Papers of the Tilburg Conference 1996* (Leiden: Brill, 1997). Also see George Kennedy, *New Testament Interpretation Through Rhetorical Criticism* (Chapel Hill: University of North Carolina Press, 1984); Stanley Porter and Thomas Olbricht, eds., *The Rhetorical Analysis of Scripture: Essays from the 1995 London Conference* (Sheffield: Sheffield Academic Press, 1997); and Burton Mack, *Rhetoric and the New Testament* (Minneapolis: Fortress Press, 1990).

2. It is best if you can get your entire passage on a single page so that you can see it all at once. You may need to experiment with font size and line spacing to achieve this. For some passages, length precludes such an attempt.

3. In the example from Romans we have placed a translation beside the text for the sake of those who do not yet read Greek. Your contoured text will have just the text on its own page.

4. Normally, for example, you will omit conjunctions, prepositions, and common verbs such as *is, have, said,* and so forth—but not always. Contouring depends on common sense, keen perception, and a growing awareness of your passage.

5. For a much more detailed list of Greek rhetorical figures see Herbert Weir Smyth, *Greek Grammar* (Cambridge, Mass.: Harvard University Press, 1956), pp. 671-83.

6. For a classical description of Hebrew parallelism see George Buchanan Gray, *The Forms of Hebrew Poetry: Considered with Special Reference to the Criticism and Interpretation of the Old Testament* (New York: KTAV Publishing House, 1972) with a prolegomenon by David Noel Freedman. Originally published in 1915. A very helpful discussion of Hebrew poetry is found in Patrick D. Miller Jr., chap. 3, "Poetry and Interpretation," in *Interpreting Psalms* (Philadelphia: Fortress Press, 1986), pp. 29-47.

7. On the levels of parallelism in Hebrew poetry and for a more linguistic approach, the student is advised to consult Adele Berlin, *The Dynamics of Biblical Parallelism* (Bloomington: Indiana University Press, 1985). On Hebrew poetry more generally, see Berlin's essay "Introduction to Hebrew Poetry" in *New Interpreter's Bible,* vol. 4 (Nashville: Abingdon Press, 1996), pp. 301-15. Her discussion of patterning is found on pages 309-11. A brief article on poetry is found in her entry "Poetry, Hebrew Bible" in *DBI.* On issues in the interpretation of Hebrew poetry, see David L. Peterson and Kent Harold Richards, *Interpreting Hebrew Poetry* (Minneapolis: Fortress Press, 1992).

8. Since we are only illustrating the phenomenon of parallelism and not describing it in detail, the student is encouraged to consult dictionary and encyclopedia articles on poetry and parallelism. An overlooked but very helpful article is Abraham Meir Haberman, "Poetry" in *Encyclopedia Judaica* (Jerusalem: Keter, 1971). The student is strongly encouraged to read the section on biblical poetry.

9. We have kept the term *synthetic parallelism* because the student is likely to encounter it in reading about Hebrew poetry. Today many scholars would find parallelism on the grammatical and syntactic level for those couplets once labeled "synthetic." It seems, however, to form a nice miscellaneous category when parallelism

of any kind is minor or nonexistent as in Amos 1:3*b* (NRSV): "because they have threshed Gilead with threshing sledges of iron."

10. Since parallelism is one of the most accessible stylistic features, even in translation, we have not discussed it at length. For an introductory and helpful discussion of parallelism, see Adele Berlin's article "Parallelism" in *The Anchor Bible Dictionary,* with a very helpful and extensive bibliography. Another very helpful discussion is Klaus Seybold, chap. 3, "The Literary Form of the Psalms," in *Introducing the Psalms,* trans. R. Graeme Dunphy (Edinburgh: T & T Clark, 1990; German, 1986), pp. 59-79.

11. Sometimes the parallelism between the two lines is incomplete, as in the first example. In this case the verb from the first clause is assumed in the parallel clause. The arrangement of the elements in the second clause is, however, in reverse order to that of the first, and thus a chiasm is formed.

12. Whether the movement of a chiastic passage is toward a single central clause, a clause couplet, or in and back out to the perimeter, reading in this manner is going against the grain for many Western readers. Although reading toward the center is strange for us, it would have posed no problem for the historical readers of the biblical text. This model is evident in both the early Semite literature as well as Homer and other early Greek writers. In fact, there is evidence that in the Greek educational system, children learned their alphabet games forwards, backwards, and then from the extremities into the middle. That would be the equivalency of "a, z, b, y, c, x," and so forth. Obviously in that culture, people would have a great deal of experience and practice with chiastic arrangements. For further explanation see John Breck, *The Shape of Biblical Language: Chiasmus in the Scriptures and Beyond* (Crestwood, N.Y.: St. Vladmir's Seminary Press, 1994). But also be aware that chiasm is prevalent in our everyday lives as well as in the biblical text. Mardy Grothe takes a lighthearted and sometimes ribald look at chiasm in modern culture in *Never Let a Fool Kiss You and Never Let a Kiss Fool You: Chiasmus and a World of Quotations That Say What They Mean and Mean What They Say* (New York: Viking Press, 1999).

13. Again, we are presenting the text in English for the sake of those unable to read Hebrew well enough. The student will prepare his or her work with the original text. For purposes of illustration, we will use an English translation where little seems lost.

14. How much alike two elements need to be in order to count as parallel partners in a chiasm is a decision that you will need to make. If your contouring fails to convince others, you have probably overread your passage. In part, your decision will be affected by the pattern of the entire unit. The members C/C′ on their own, perhaps, do not appear to be similar enough. However, since A/A′ and B/B′ are so similar, momentum is built up and the similarity that does exists between C/C′ seems adequate.

15. It is commonplace today for the biblical material to be read as literature, that is, with an eye to the types of expressive features we are presenting in this chapter. A *tour de force* in this regard, is Mary Douglas, *Leviticus as Literature* (Oxford: Oxford University Press, 1999). Or see Wilfried Warning, *Literary Artistry in Leviticus* (Leiden: Brill, 1999).

16. For example, puns are paronomasia.

17. Remember, however, that the conventions of subject/verb agreement are different in Greek than in English. In Greek, a neuter plural subject can take a singular verb. Also, whereas in English a compound subject is always plural, in Greek the number of the verb is governed by the subject element closest to the verb, and may

be either singular or plural. Similarly, in Hebrew, agreement in number between subject and verb is less strict than in English.

18. For the sake of smoothness, a pattern of alternation like this one often is not kept in an English translation. The NRSV, for example, places all verbs in the second person.

19. The verb of being, the copula, functions to link subjects with predicate nominatives or adjectives. For further explanation consult the discussion of clause types in Excursus 2.

20. For further examples of contouring see the work of Phyllis Trible with Jonah, *Rhetorical Criticism,* and Jacob W. Elias's commentary on 1 and 2 Thessalonians, *1 and 2 Thessalonians* (Scottdale, Pa.: Herald Press, 1995).

4. Plotting the Text

1. In this chapter we are touching upon the techniques of literary readings of a text. Much has been published in this area. Here are works for further information and development of your reading skills: Meir Weiss, *The Bible from Within: The Method of Total Interpretation* (Jerusalem: Magnes Press, 1984; Hebrew 1967); Robert Alter, *The Art of Biblical Narrative* (New York: Basic Books, 1981); Adele Berlin, *Poetics and Interpretation of Biblical Narrative* (Sheffield: Almond Press, 1983); Shimon Bar-Efrat, *Narrative Art in the Bible* (Sheffield: Almond Press, 1989; Hebrew 1979); Yitzhak Avishur, *Studies in Biblical Narrative: Style, Structure, and the Ancient Near Eastern Literary Background* (Tel Aviv: Archaeological Center, 1999); Meir Sternberg, *The Poetics of Biblical Narrative: Ideological Literature and the Drama of Reading* (Bloomington: Indiana University Press, 1985). In a linguistic vein, see Robert E. Longacre, *The Grammar of Discourse,* 2d ed. (New York: Plenum Press, 1996) and Roger Fowler, *Linguistic Criticism,* 2d ed. (Oxford: Oxford University Press, 1996). For New Testament see E. V. McKnight, *The Bible and the Reader: An Introduction to Literary Criticism* (Philadelphia: Fortress Press, 1985) and R. Scholes and R. Kellogg, *The Nature of Narrative* (London: Oxford University Press, 1966).

2. Since you will need a clean copy on which to place your final indicators of region and pace, you will always want to have at least one clean copy of your contour available for manipulation and marking.

3. In chapter 6, on the background of a passage, you will find a discussion of tacitly assumed "old" information. A bibliography on relevance theory can be found there.

4. The italicized words show parallelism and indicate that these two lines belong together. This reinforces the determination of these lines as a region, a decision that is made here on the basis of their topic.

5. We stress this point because the division between off-line and on-line material is not a division between important and unimportant material. In Genesis 13:1-5, which we have been analyzing, it is exactly the off-line material that is important to the following narrative. The on-line material seems to be connective in function, linking the episode in Egypt at the end of chapter 12 with the following episode, the separation of Abram and Lot.

6. The larger literary unit is Luke 1–2. We are looking at chapter 2 for pragmatic reasons of time and space.

7. In verse 19 and again in 51, the statements about Mary keeping these things in her heart are expressed in the imperfect. Likewise, the summary statements about

how the child Jesus was growing, in verses 40 and 52, use the imperfect. All of these comments are off-line and should be read as editorial asides.

8. See chapter 3 for a layout and contour of this passage.

9. The connection between Jesus and Jewish hopes is a little ambiguous. Whereas most commentators assume that the antecedent of the pronoun "him" in "She gave thanks to God and spoke of *him* to all who were looking" is the baby, it could also be "God" as the closest noun. But the author juxtaposes Anna coming up "at that very hour" with Simeon's pronouncement over the baby. What seems to be implicit in the arrangement of the text is that Anna is connecting God's action in this child with the Jewish hopes for redemption.

10. For an extended discussion of this passage see Sternberg, *The Poetics of Biblical Narrative,* chap. 4, "Viewpoints and Interpretations," pp. 129-52.

11. Notice the inclusion in line three. The first clause and the last end with the same words. This device sets this stream of action apart from what went before and what comes after. All of Jonah's action is concentrated between these "bookends."

12. The term *gap* is used here in the sense of information that is omitted by the author because it is not relevant in context. See Diane Blakemore, *Semantic Constraints on Relevance* (Oxford: Blackwell Publishers, 1987) and John Lyons, "Text and Discourse: Context and Co-text," in *Linguistic Semantics: An Introduction* (Cambridge: Cambridge University Press, 1995), pp. 234-92. We will return to gaps and relevance theory in chapter 6.

13. Gaps can also occur because the author wishes a reader to fill in the missing information, complete the tacit assumption, or derive the unstated inference. In such cases, the author and the reader form a partnership in the extablishment of meaning. For a theoretical discussion of these gaps see W. Iser, *The Act of Reading: A Theory of Aesthetic Response* (Baltimore: Johns Hopkins University Press, 1978). For a discussion of how readers are "set up" by authors, see Jacob L. Mey, *Pragmatics: An Introduction* (Oxford: Blackwell Publishers, 1993), pp. 256-65 on pragmatic acts. For a discussion of reader response theory from the perspective of linguistics, see Roger Fowler, "The Role of the Reader," in *Linguistic Criticism,* 2d ed. (Oxford: Oxford University Press, 1966), pp. 233-55.

14. See Ned Herrmann, *Creative Brain* (Lake Lure, N.C.: Brain Books, 1989) for the arguments for this proposition.

5. The Literary Context

1. James L. Bailey, "Genre Analysis," in *Hearing the New Testament: Strategies for Interpretation,* ed. Joel B. Green (Grand Rapids: Eerdmans, 1995; 2000). The italics in the definition are Bailey's.

2. Perry B. Yoder, *From Word to Life: A Guide to the Art of Bible Study* (Scottdale, Pa.: Herald Press, 1982), pp. 100-101, with bibliography.

3. One of the steps crucial to your ongoing biblical study is gaining access to a number of good commentaries that work from the Hebrew and Greek text. Try to pick reputable scholars and series. Try also to consult commentaries written from different points of view. We encourage students to buy commentaries—new or used—and to establish relationships with libraries that have commentaries. A shelf of good commentaries will be your friend for life. As a rough guide, certain series are worth investigating. Among these would be: *Word Biblical Commentary, Anchor Bible, Hermeneia, International Critical Commentary, Old Testament Library, New International Critical Commentary of the New Testament, JPS Torah Commentary.*

4. A good place to begin finding tools is a reference work like *DBI*. Look under "form criticism" for articles on the Hebrew Bible and the New Testament. There is also a good bibliography at the end of each article. J. H. Hayes, ed., *Old Testament Form Criticism* (San Antonio: Trinity University Press, 1974) and Gene Tucker, *Form Criticism of the Old Testament* (Philadelphia: Fortress Press, 1971) are older but helpful works. For the father of biblical form criticism, read Hermann Gunkel, *The Legends of Genesis* (New York: Schocken Books, 1964; German 1901). Chapter 2, "Introducing the Foreground," in Phyllis Trible, *Rhetorical Criticism: Context, Method and the Book of Jonah* (Minneapolis: Fortress Press, 1994) relates form criticism to rhetorical criticism.

5. What we are calling "characteristics" is akin to what Wellek and Warren have designated as "outer form" and "inner form." See René Wellek and Austin Warren, *Theory of Literature,* 3d ed. (New York: Harcourt, Brace & World, 1956), p. 231.

6. See John W. Sider, *Interpreting the Parables: A Hermeneutical Guide to Their Meaning* (Grand Rapids: Zondervan, 1995).

7. A word of caution is probably in order here. There is sometimes endless debate about which texts belong to a genre, and parable studies are particularly fraught with this kind of fine-tooth combing. This is not to disparage this endeavor, simply keep in mind that the object is to understand the text. You may be able to profit from the debate about whether the "good Samaritan" is a parable or an example story without needing to resolve the issue before going on with your work.

8. Also, it may be fruitful to compare your passage with similar material in the general culture. For the Old Testament, an instructive work is Yitzhak Avishur, *Studies in Biblical Narrative: Style, Structure and the Ancient Near Eastern Literary Background* (Tel Aviv: Archaeological Center Publication, 1999). For the New Testament, a good example would be Hans Dieter Betz, *Galatians: A Commentary on Paul's Letter to the Churches in Galatia* (Philadelphia: Fortress Press, 1979), in which he compares the profile of Galatians with that of an autobiographical defense used in courts of law.

9. See the slave laws in Exodus 21 for this casuistic legal pattern.

10. Yoder, *From Word to Life,* p. 100.

11. Of course, as you advance in your study of texts, your familiarity with the biblical books will increase. Everything you do is cumulative. Be aware, however, that with the Gospels, many of us have in our heads something like a harmonized text of all the Gospels. Therefore, even if you think you know the book well, it is good to reread it.

12. For a fuller exposition of this thesis, see Mary H. Schertz, "Seek Peace and Pursue It," in *The Love of Enemy and Nonretaliation in the New Testament,* ed. Willard M. Swartley (Louisville: Westminster John Knox Press, 1992).

13. A note of caution: there are errors in the textual databases that are utilized by computer programs. Any accurate check must be done by hand with a printed concordance.

14. The verb form occurs in petitions in Luke chapters 16–18.

15. A commentary that works extensively with such long-range links is Robert Tannehill's two volumes on Luke and Acts, *The Narrative Unity of Luke-Acts: A Literary Interpretation,* 2 vols. (Philadelphia: Fortress Press, 1986, 1990).

16. Ibid., vol. 1, *The Gospel According to Luke,* p. 112.

17. Ibid.

18. *Redactor* is used to indicate someone who puts materials together to form a whole. In this process the redactor may have composed new material and modified and arranged the literary sources that were on hand. Luke 1:1-4 shows the author to be a collector and arranger of material to give his audience a better view of Jesus

and the events of his life. For an overview of redaction criticism see the older work by Norman Perrin, *What Is Redaction Criticism?* (Philadelphia: Fortress Press, 1969). For a recent overview with bibliography, see the articles on redaction criticism in *DBI.*

19. In some cases several books need to be included within the scope of your analysis (e.g., 1 and 2 Kings).

20. Note the statement in John 20:30-31 (NRSV), "Now Jesus did many other signs in the presence of his disciples, which are not written in this book. But these are written so that you may come to believe that Jesus is the Messiah, the Son of God, and that through believing you may have life in his name."

21. The difference in vocabulary between the Gospel of John and the Synoptics is striking.

22. Hans Dieter Betz, *Sermon on the Mount* (Minneapolis: Fortress Press, 1995), pp. 370-72. Betz also notes a version of the Lord's Prayer in the *Didache* 8:2. He agrees that Jesus most likely put this prayer together, in some form, but he did so out of Jewish tradition.

23. Scholars use the letter *Q* to designate a source of Jesus' sayings that are used by both Matthew and Luke. For a painstaking attempt to differentiate redactional material from traditional material taken up by the redactor, see Joachim Jeremias, *Die Sprache des Lukasevangeliums: Redaktion und Tradition im Nicht-Markusstoff des dritten Evangeliums* (Göttingen: Vandenhoeck & Ruprecht, 1980).

24. For a survey and discussion of Pentateuchal sources see Joseph Blenkinsopp, *The Pentateuch: An Introduction to the First Five Books of the Bible* (New York: Doubleday, 1992) and Ernest Nicholson, *The Pentateuch in the Twentieth Century: The Legacy of Julius Wellhausen* (Oxford: Clarendon Press, 1998). On the sources in the flood story see Anthony F. Campbell and Mark A. O'Brien, *Sources of the Pentateuch: Texts, Introductions, Annotations* (Minneapolis: Fortress Press, 1993), pp. 211-23. They have used bold and regular print to differentiate the sources in the story. See also the article "Pentateuchal Criticism" in *DBI,* which has an extensive bibliography.

25. Ulrich Luz, *Matthew 1–7: A Commentary* (Minneapolis: Augsburg Press, 1989), p. 40.

26. Ulrich Luz, *The Theology of the Gospel of Matthew,* trans. J. Bredford Robinson (Cambridge: Cambridge University Press, 1995), p. 10.

27. Kurt Aland, ed., *Synopsis of the Four Gospels: Greek-English Edition of the Synopsis Quattuor Evangeliorum,* 3d ed. (Stuttgart: Wuttembergische Bibelanstalt, 1979).

28. For the Old Testament there are a number of good sources for background literature. The most commonly available one is James Pritchard, ed., *Ancient Near Eastern Texts Relating to the Old Testament* (Princeton, N.J.: Princeton University Press, 1978).

6. The World of the Text

1. Since the historical, cultural, social, and intellectual background has been extensively researched in the twentieth century and for many students has come to be practically equivalent with the scholarly study of the Bible, we do not go into great detail in this chapter. Rather, because of our textcentric focus, we indicate how a student might explore this area, for which many helps and a great deal of literature is available, and how such study relates to a better understanding of the text.

2. Pragmatic principles in communication go back to the philosopher Paul Grice.

For a discussion of his principles see: Roger Fowler, "Some Aspects of Dialogue," chap. 8 in *Linguistic Criticism,* 2d ed. (Oxford: Oxford University Press, 1996); Jacob L. Mey, "Pragmatic Principles," chap. 4 in *Pragmatics: An Introduction* (Oxford: Blackwell Publishers, 1993); Deborah Schiffrin, "Pragmatics," chap. 6 in *Approaches to Discourse* (Oxford: Blackwell Publishers, 1994); and John Lyons, "Text and Discourse: Context and Co-text," chap. 9 in *Linguistic Semantics: An Introduction* (Cambridge: Cambridge University Press, 1995). Barbara Gorayska and Roger Lindsay, "The Roots of Relevance," *Journal of Pragmatics* 19 (1993): 301-23 surveys the development of this notion in the analysis of linguistic communication.

3. John J. Collins, *Daniel: A Commentary on the Book of Daniel* (Minneapolis: Augsburg-Fortress Press, 1993) devotes several pages to this riddle, cf. pp. 166-70.

4. See the brief discussion of this tradition in the Ancient Near East and in Israel in Hans-Joachim Kraus, *Psalms 1–59: A Commentary* (Minneapolis: Augsburg Press, 1988; German 1961, 1978), pp. 306f.

5. John H. Hayes, *Amos the Eighth-Century Prophet: His Times and His Preaching* (Nashville: Abingdon Press, 1988).

6. See, however, the instructive work of Yair Hoffman, *A Blemished Perfection: The Book of Job in Context,* Journal for the Study of the Old Testament Supplement series 213 (Sheffield: Sheffield Academic Press, 1996; Hebrew 1995). In this work Hoffman seeks to provide a setting for Job by examining the intellectual and literary traditions that he believes are exhibited within the book itself and which can be compared with more general Ancient Near East phenomenon.

7. A distinction can be made between using a text for historical purposes (e.g., reconstructing a history of Israel) and for exegetical purposes (e.g., using background information to understand a text). Historical criticism was often more interested in history than in texts. Both enterprises are valid, but different. See Edgar Krentz, *The Historical-Critical Method* (Philadelphia: Fortress Press, 1975) and J. Maxwell Miller, *The Old Testament and the Historian* (Philadelphia: Fortress Press, 1976). For historical criticism as a literary method in its time, see John Barton, "Historical-Critical Approaches" in *The Cambridge Companion to Biblical Interpretation,* John Barton, ed. (Cambridge: Cambridge University Press, 1998), pp. 9-20.

8. This is not to say that you can always decide ahead of time which background data will have an important payoff for understanding the text. Sometimes it is only after you have done the work that you come to see that what you have found is not very helpful. As in other stages of the exegesis process, you will become more efficient in your study of a text's tacit context as you gain experience.

9. The notion of illocutionary force is attributed to John L. Austin, *How to Do Things with Words* (London: Oxford Press, 1962). His notions have been developed by J. R. Searle, *Speech Acts* (London: Cambridge University Press, 1969). Their work is discussed in Fowler, *Linguistic Criticism,* chap. 4, and in Schiffrin, *Approaches to Discourse,* chap. 3, "Speech Act Theory." For the positive application of speech act theory to biblical interpretation see Anthony C. Thiselton, "The Hermeneutics of Pastoral Theology: (2) Further Reading—Situations, Pluralism, and 'Believing Reading,'" chap. 16 in *New Horizons in Hermeneutics* (Grand Rapids: Zondervan, 1992).

10. Refer back to "Lexical Analysis," in chapter 2 for some pointers on word study.

11. A dictionary like Liddell and Scott is invaluable for providing references for usages outside the New Testament. Also, theological dictionaries often provide some information along these lines. On a word like λόγος in John, commentaries will have extensive discussions with a bibliography.

12. For an example of how these *W* questions can be answered in a clear and concise manner, see Jacob W. Elias, *1 and 2 Thessalonians* (Scottdale, Pa.: Herald Press, 1995), pp. 25-31.

13. Rather than specifying exact dates for the biblical writings, a period of time or a relative chronology is all that can be accurately determined. For example, in the Hebrew Bible it is debated as to whether the *J* material dates from the period of the monarchy or from the postexilic period. In the New Testament, sometimes a relative chronology is as important, or even more important, than an exact date. For example, is the sequence of the Gospels' composition Mark, Luke, Matthew, and John? If so, then certain conclusions can be drawn about the relationship of Luke and Matthew to Mark.

14. You may have already done this in the previous chapter when you constructed a perspectival chart. You may have outlined material in a section of Jeremiah and dated its components. If so, then you can build on your work in the present chapter.

15. James H. Charlesworth, *The Beloved Disciple: Whose Witness Validates the Gospel of John?* (Valley Forge, Pa.: Trinity Press, 1995).

16. Raymond E. Brown, S.J., "The Gospel According to John (i–xii)" in *The Anchor Bible,* vol. 29 (Garden City, N.Y.: Doubleday, 1966), pp. xxxiv-xxxix.

17. Although we are using a single, but striking, aspect of the Fourth Gospel in this discussion, any argument as to the place, time, and reason for writing would also need to account for other peculiarities of this Gospel—for example, the many trips to Jerusalem to celebrate festivals there, or the fact that John contains no parables or teachings about the kingdom of God!

18. This can be gathered from comments within the book of Amos, see 3:15, as well as by piecing together the political and economic conditions of the country from the biblical record and archaeology. See John Bright's *History of Israel* (Philadelphia: Westminster Press, 1981) or more recently, Paula McNutt, *Reconstructing the Society of Ancient Israel* (Louisville: Westminster John Knox Press, 1999).

19. Moshe Weinfeld, *Deuteronomy and Deuteronomic School* (Oxford: Oxford University Press, 1972), p. 162.

20. For the New Testament, consult or purchase a brief handbook such as Lester L. Grabbe, *An Introduction to First Century Judaism: Jewish Religion and History in the Second Temple Period* (Edinburgh: T & T Clark, 1996), and become familiar with more extensive reference works like E. Schurer, *The History of the Jewish People in the Age of Jesus Christ,* rev. Geza Vermes et al. (Edinburgh: T & T Clark, 1973–1984), 3 vols. in 4. In the last quarter of the twentieth century there was a veritable explosion of research and publication on the Jewish context of Jesus and the New Testament. In the last decade of the century there was also a florescence of writing on the Dead Sea Scrolls. For an easy read, yet authoritative introduction to the scrolls, see Jonathan Campbell, *Dead Sea Scrolls: The Complete Story* (Berkeley, Calif.: Ulysses Press, 1998). For more detail see the work of Campbell's teacher, Geza Vermes, *An Introduction to the Complete Dead Sea Scrolls* (Minneapolis: Augsburg-Fortress Press, 1999).

21. See the recent commentary by Yair Zakovitch, *Ruth: Introduction and Commentary* (Tel Aviv: Am Oved, 1990), in Hebrew, where Zakovitch argues for understanding the book of Ruth as a polemic against the nationalistic policies of the second temple times, as illustrated by the passage from Nehemiah that we have quoted.

22. Edward F. Campbell Jr., "Ruth: A New Translation with Introduction, Notes, and Commentary" in *The Anchor Bible,* vol. 7 (Garden City, N.Y.: Doubleday, 1975), p. 27.

23. Frederic Bush, *Word Biblical Commentary: Ruth, Esther* (Waco: Word Books, 1996), pp. 16-30.

24. Elias, *1 and 2 Thessalonians,* pp. 28-30.

25. Zakovitch, *Ruth.*

26. See the commentaries of Campbell and Bush mentioned above. The recent commentary by Yair Zakovitch, *Ruth,* argues from an examination of the language, that although the book is written in classical Hebrew, there are enough indicators of deviations from it to show that it was written at a later time. He argues that the author adopted a classical style, but the presence of linguistic features from the author's own time crept in (pp. 16-18). Against a straightforward argument from language, Zakovitch raises the possibility of archaizing. Also, the question arises, can a document be dated by the preponderance of its early forms as over against a minority of later forms, or do the presence of later forms automatically, no matter how few, show the book to be a later composition? Since Zakovitch finds the arguments for an early date for Ruth—from its language—wanting, he understands Ruth as a polemic that was written in second temple times (pp. 18-20, 33-34).

27. Here, as usual, changing your mind is not a moral issue! As you continue to learn, you will become a better judge of historical and social reconstructions.

28. See the discussion in Bruce M. Metzger, *A Textual Commentary on the Greek New Testament,* corrected edition (New York: United Bible Societies, 1975), pp. 715-17.

29. Tradition history has been defined as a study of the transmission of literary material or units, regardless of whether they are written or oral. Here we are using tradition history in a broader sense to include the transmission of ideas and the source of the vocabulary in which they are expressed. Of course vocabulary is not transmitted independently of documents. For a tradition point of view see: Walter E. Rast, *Tradition History and the Old Testament* (Philadelphia: Fortress Press, 1972); R. S. Barbour, *Traditio-Historical Criticism of the Gospels* (London: SPCK, 1972); and the article "Tradition History" in *DBI.* For the linguistic aspect of tradition history, the theological dictionaries with which you became acquainted in the first several chapters are also useful here, for example, *TDOT* and *TLOT* for the Old Testament, and *TDNT* and the *EDNT* for the New Testament.

30. A treatment of issues reflected in this group of texts is Raymond Brown's *The Community of the Beloved Disciple* (New York: Paulist Press, 1979). Also, C. K. Barrett, *The Gospel According to St. John: An Introduction with Commentary and Notes on the Greek Text* (London: SPCK, 1958), pp. 3-8.

31. On the household codes consult D. L. Balch, *Let Wives Be Submissive* (Chico, Calif.: Scholars Press, 1981); D. E. Aune, ed., *Greco-Roman Literature and the New Testament: Selected Forms and Genres* (Atlanta: Scholars Press, 1988), pp. 25-30; J. H. Elliot, *A Home for the Homeless: A Sociological Exegesis of 1 Peter, Its Situation and Strategy* (Philadelphia: Fortress Press, 1981); and Elisabeth Schüssler Fiorenza, *In Memory of Her: A Feminist Reconstruction of Christian Origins* (New York: Crossroad, 1983).

32. In your examination of the traditions assumed in your text, the task of the present chapter, you might discuss the implications that can be drawn from your previous literary discoveries with regard to the text's relationship to historical, social, and intellectual factors.

33. The interpretive methods found in the Dead Sea Scrolls have given new impetus and direction to the study of New Testament quotations and hermeneutic. Several articles in the recent collection *The Scrolls and the Scriptures: Qumran Fifty Years After,* Stanley E. Porter and Craig A. Evans, eds. (Sheffield: Sheffield Academic Press, 1997) are informative in this regard. See, for example, Timothy H. Lim, "Midrash Pesher in the Pauline Letters," pp. 280-92.

34. Although this is an emerging area of scholarship, many New Testament commentaries and introductions will have a section dealing with the authors' understanding of the Old Testament and how it was used in their work. There are also some good articles and monographs being published. See, for example, Craig Evans and James A. Sanders, *Luke and Scripture: The Function of Sacred Tradition in Luke-Acts* (Minneapolis: Fortress Press, 1993). For a broad view of how the Hebrew Scriptures influenced the composition and construction of the Gospels see Willard Swartley, *Israel's Scripture Traditions and the Synoptic Gospels: Story Shaping Story* (Peabody, Mass.: Hendrickson Publishers, 1994).

35. Thomas E. Boomershine, "Epistemology at the Turn of the Ages in Paul, Jesus and Mark: Rhetoric and Dialectic in Apocalyptic and the New Testament," in *Apocalyptic and the New Testament: Essays in Honor of J. Louis Martyn,* ed. Joel Marcus and Marion L. Soards (Sheffield: Sheffield Academic Press, 1989), pp. 147-67. See also Klaus Koch, *The Rediscovery of Apocalyptic* (London: SCAM Press, 1972).

36. The specific beliefs, values, and knowledge that distinguish a particular group or subculture within the larger society are discussed under "traditions." In this section we are discussing presuppositions that are shared by all, or virtually all, members of a culture or historical period. These assumptions about the way the world is and works are not necessarily religious. They just are.

37. See Exodus 20:8-11.

38. This is not to say that a person could not hold both to the description of creation in Genesis 1 and the theory of evolution. For example, the different descriptions could be assigned to different genres of writing that have separate communicative points. Genesis 1 might be considered a polemical theological statement, whereas the theory of evolution is a scientific statement attempting to account for modern findings in geology, paleontology, and biology. As a scientific statement it is limited to considering finite material forces as the causes of events on earth. Genesis 1, as a theological statement, does not suffer from these limitations.

39. Consider the parallels that Elizabeth A. Johnson finds between Jesus and Sophia in *She Who Is: The Mystery of God in Feminist Theological Discourse* (New York: Crossroad, 1992), p. 97.

> Like Sophia, Jesus calls out in a loud voice in public places, uttering blessing and threat (7:28, 37). Like her he speaks in long discourses using the first person singular pronoun, proclaiming his elusive but attractive significance in the singular cadences of the "I am" statements (6:51; 10:14; 11:25). Both Jesus and Sophia are identified with Torah, which is light and life for human beings. The symbols of bread, wine and water, and the invitations to eat and drink relate Jesus to Sophia's nourishing activities. The theme of seeking and finding, so constant in Sophia's interactions with people, resonates even in Jesus' first Johannine words, "What do you seek?" and the happy result for the disciples, "We have found the Messiah" (1:38, 41). Whoever seeks and finds him is promised the gift of life which he has come to give (10:10). More ominously Sophia's warnings about seeking and not finding ring out in Jesus' words to unbelieving hearts (7:34). The idea of truth, of right instruction, of revelation of divine mysteries, and guidance in the paths pleasing to God all cast Jesus in Sophia's life-giving didactic role: he is the way, the truth, and the life (14:6). Disciples are encouraged to follow his path and are even called his children, while rejection of him spells death for the rejecters. Woven round with these elements is the theme of God's love and friendship. As with Sophia, whoever loves Jesus is beloved by God (14:23) and enters into a mutuality so profound that they may be called friends (15:15).

40. See John Barton, *Amos' Oracles Against the Nations: A Study of Amos 1:3–2:5* (Cambridge: Cambridge University Press, 1980).

7. A Canonical Perspective

1. The notion of "canonical criticism" and its development is connected with two names in particular, although they pursue this task differently: Brevard Childs and James Sanders. For Childs's approach, representative works would be: *Introduction to the Old Testament as Scripture* (Philadelphia: Fortress Press, 1979) and *Old Testament Theology in a Canonical Context* (Philadelphia: Fortress Press, 1985). For Sanders see: *Torah and Canon* (Philadelphia: Fortress Press, 1972) and *From Sacred Story to Sacred Text* (Philadelphia: Fortress Press, 1987). For an overview of canonical criticism and the work of Sanders and Childs, see *DBI*, "Canonical Criticism."

2. An articulation of how a theological tradition influences interpretation is the chapter "The Case for Calvinistic Hermeneutics," in Walter C. Kaiser Jr. and Moises Silva, *An Introduction to Biblical Hermeneutics: The Search for Meaning* (Grand Rapids: Zondervan, 1994), pp. 251-70.

3. Not all canons share these characteristics. The Koran, for example, has a single author and a single time of writing.

4. James Dunn, *Unity and Diversity in the New Testament: An Inquiry into the Character of Earliest Christianity,* 2d ed. (Philadelphia: Trinity Press, 1990). Harry Y. Gamble, "The Canon of the New Testament," in *The New Testament and Its Modern Interpreters,* ed. Eldon Jay Epp and George W. McRae (Philadelphia: Fortress Press, 1989), pp. 201-43.

5. For arguments regarding the parallel authority of Torah and prophets, see Stephen B. Chapman, *The Law and the Prophets: A Study in Old Testament Canon Formation* (Tübingen: Mohr Siebeck, 2000).

6. The topic of canonization can be pursued in the following resources: *DBI,* "Canon of the Bible" and the bibliography listed there; Magne Saebo, "From 'Unifying Reflections' to the Canon: Aspects of the Traditio-historical Final Stages in the Development of the Old Testament," in *On the Way to Canon: Creative Tradition History in the Old Testament* (Sheffield: Sheffield Academic Press, 1998; German 1988), pp. 285-309, contains a very rich bibliography in the footnotes; George J. Brooke, "'The Canon Within the Canon' at Qumran and in the New Testament," in *The Scrolls and the Scriptures: Qumran Fifty Years After,* Stanley E. Porter and Craig A. Evans, eds. (Sheffield: Sheffield Academic Press, 1997), pp. 242-66; and Rolf Rendtorff, *Canon and Theology,* trans. Margaret Kohl (Minneapolis: Fortress Press, 1993; German 1991).

7. Second Timothy 3:16-17 speaks of the inspiration of Scripture referring to the Hebrew Scriptures.

8. In distinction to the New Testament, the Koran was not added to the existing biblical canon, but replaced it. It now forms the canon for the Muslim. The argument here is simply that given a set or emerging set of books considered authoritative by a community, those adding to this set would consider the question of fit an important one. At least a perceived fit would be important in gaining acceptance for new writings.

9. Some might argue that historical criticism, since it studies the phylogeny of the literary unit, and canonical criticism, since it stresses the phenotype, are mutually exclusive. This is not necessarily true. To continue our biological metaphors, evolutionary biology or genetic biology does not exclude demographics or field biology. The clash between historical criticism and canonical perspective, it seems, in part at least, is due to a mistaken notion of canon and authority on the part of some historical critics. To ask, Why is the present form of Genesis canonical and not the *J* document as reconstructed by scholars? is akin to asking a similar question with

regard to human evolution: Why do we take modern humans and not *Australopithecus* or one of its descendants as the standard human being? Part of the answer, surely, is that although *Australopithecus* may have been the standard in her day, in our day we have another phenotype that serves as the standard by which we measure "normal." So *J* may have been authoritative in its day, but today we don't have *J*. We have a different phenotype. Or, to use a metaphor from a different realm of science, geology does not exclude geography. You would not want to navigate an airplane according to a geography reconstructed from geology. You might fly smack-dab into the Rocky Mountains! (According to geologists, the present Rocky Mountains, in some shape or form, once were part of a sea bottom. Shark's teeth are now found in these mountains!)

10. Sometimes reading the Bible in a vacuum without regard for its circumstance of writing is called "a flat reading" or having a "flat Bible." Historical criticism has given us a variegated Bible in place of a flat one. Another way in which the Bible is read "flat" is in the failure to distinguish the different genres of material found in it. Such a flat reading is bound to cause misunderstanding of material that is not propositional or is not plain-sense descriptive language. Genesis 1 is a classic test case for whether a reader can differentiate genres in the Bible, or if he or she reads it as if it were all composed of a single genre.

11. Among laity there is a tendency to reduce the biblical material to a single voice or point of view. This type of harmonization may be called "canonical reductionism." A similar reductionist tendency is also at work when only the difference between passages are stressed or it is assumed that differing passages are not a part of a coherent whole. Sometimes differences are exaggerated so as to acerbate the problem of seeing how passages could be part of the same whole. For a counter point of view see Moshe Greenberg, "What Are Valid Criteria for Determining Inauthentic Matter in Ezekiel?" in *Ezekiel and His Book,* Bibliotheca Epheridum Theologicarum Lovaniensium, no. 74, ed. J. Lust (Leuven: University Press, 1986), pp. 123-35.

12. Check the discussion in Gerhard Hasel, *Old Testament Theology: Basic Issues in the Current Debate,* rev. ed. (Grand Rapids: Eerdmans, 1975). For constructive work see, for example, John H. Sailhamer, *Introduction to Old Testament Theology: A Canonical Approach* (Grand Rapids: Zondervan, 1995).

13. Note the proper translation of this passage, as given in the NRSV: "Hear, O Israel: The LORD is our God, the LORD alone." It was a commitment of quality, which is why *love* is the appropriate emotion and attitude that characterizes this commitment. See the repetition of the command to love in Deuteronomy 11:1, 13:3, 30:6; Joshua 22:5 and 11.

14. See Mark 12:30, Matthew 22:37, and Luke 10:27.

15. For an Old Testament theology that uses the metaphor of design, see Elmer A. Martens, *God's Design: A Focus on Old Testament Theology* (Grand Rapids: Baker Books, 1981).

16. A thread is a fuzzy concept that should not be thought of too rigidly as expressing a theme, motif, or concept. Passages expressing a motif or concept may form a thread, but room must be left for other criteria to be used in defining a thread. Also the limits of a thread are soft. Perhaps passages that refer to God as "maker" belong to a separate thread. For example, the metaphor of God as a potter forming humankind is found more than once in the Bible (cf. Isaiah 29:16, Jeremiah 18, and Romans 9:21). Perhaps this forms a separate thread. The judgment as to how fine you make your threads is a heuristic process—what seems best to facilitate a productive dialogue among passages and provide a canonical perspective. You will also find that threads cluster together. For example, in the judg-

ment scene in Matthew 25 we find that we minster to Jesus himself as we minister to the least of these. This notion of Jesus being present in these people probably forms a related, but different, thread.

17. Remember, it is the fruit that counts! See Matthew 7:13-23.

18. The following chapter will develop more fully the motives and reasons behind the utilization of a particular passage. There you will be called upon to assess what is in your cup! None of us is free from a polemical use of Scripture.

19. Many interpretations, often quite ingenious, have been given to these verses, especially the last one, verse 15, in an attempt to "save it." To date, none seems particularly suasive and there is no consensus on how to construe it. For the sake of illustration, we have adopted a plain-sense reading of the verse. For a treatment of 1 Timothy 2:15 that sets it in the context of the conflicts of the third generation of the Christian church, see Susan Heine, *Women and Early Christianity: A Reappraisal* (Minneapolis: Augsburg Press, 1988), pp. 124-46.

20. Depending on your familiarity with the Bible and your theological tradition and education, you will be more or less secure in this enterprise at the beginning. We suggest reading or at least scanning several books on biblical theology. A good place to begin in order to get your bearings would be Robert Morgan, "The Bible and Christian Theology," in *The Cambridge Companion to Biblical Interpretation,* ed. John Barton (Cambridge: Cambridge University Press, 1998), pp. 114-28, and three articles in *DBI,* "Theology, Biblical," "Theology, New Testament," and "Theology, Old Testament." These articles also have a considerable bibliography.

8. Integrating Text and Life

1. A good place to begin with the issues of biblical authority is *Inspiration and Authority: Nature and Function of Christian Scripture,* ed. Paul J. Achtemeier, Patrick H. Alexander, and David Winter (Peabody, Mass.: Hendrickson Publishers, 1999). Other sources are: John P. Burgess, *Why Scripture Matters: Reading the Bible in an Age of Church Conflict* (Louisville: Westminster John Knox, 1998) and William J. Abraham, *Canon and Criterion in Christian Theology* (Oxford: Clarendon Press, 1998).

2. The relationship between one's own horizons and the horizons of a text have been explored most extensively (and densely) by Hans-Georg Gadamer in *Truth and Method,* trans. Barrett Barden and John Cumming (New York: Seabury Press, 1975). For a more accessible introduction see Georgia Warnke, *Gadamer: Hermeneutics, Tradition and Reason* (Stanford: Stanford University Press, 1987), esp. pp. 75-82.

3. Two helpful collections of essays on social location and interpretation are *Reading from This Place,* vol. 1, *Social Location and Biblical Interpretation in the United States,* ed. Fernando Segovia and Mary Ann Tolbert (Minneapolis: Fortress Press, 1995) and *Reading from This Place,* vol. 2, *Social Location and Biblical Interpretation in Global Perspective,* also edited by Segovia and Tolbert (Minneapolis: Fortress Press, 1995).

4. Some examples are: Susan Brooks Thistlethwaite and Mary Potter Engel, eds., *Lift Every Voice: Constructing Christian Theologies from the Underside* (San Francisco: Harper & Row, 1990); R. S. Sugirtharajah, ed., *Voices from the Margin: Interpreting the Bible in the Third World* (Maryknoll, N.Y.: Orbis, 1991); and Virginia Fabella and Sun Ai Lee Park, eds., *We Dare to Dream: Doing Theology as Asian Women* (Hong Kong: Asian Women's Resource Center for Culture and Theology, 1989).

5. Bishop Dmitre, *The Kingdom of God: The Sermon on the Mount* (Crestwood: N.Y.: St. Vladimir's Seminary Press, 1992).

6. Ronald Wallace, in his *On the Interpretation and Use of the Bible: With Reflections on Experience* (Grand Rapids: Eerdmans, 1999), touches on some of these concerns in the latter half of the book.

7. Rachel Miller Jacobs, "Who Is This?" 28 March 1999, College Mennonite Church, Goshen, Indiana.

8. There are many excellent resources for teaching the Bible in the congregation. Here are only a few to get you started. For a proactive book on teaching, see Charles F. Melchart, *Wise Teaching: Biblical Wisdom and Educational Ministry* (Harrisburg, Pa.: Trinity Press, 1998). For a book that takes liberation issues seriously, see Fernando Segovia and Mary Ann Tolbert, eds., *Teaching the Bible: The Discourses and Politics of Biblical Pedagogy* (Maryknoll, N.Y.: Orbis, 1998). A more traditional and practical approach is James Wilhoit and Leland Ryken, *Effective Bible Teaching* (Grand Rapids: Baker Books, 1988).

9. See most recently, Paul Scott Wilson, *The Four Pages of the Sermon: A Guide to Biblical Preaching* (Nashville: Abingdon Press, 1999) and Ronald J. Allen, *The Teaching Sermon* (Nashville: Abingdon Press, 1995). Classic works include: Leander E. Keck, *The Bible in the Pulpit: The Renewal of Biblical Preaching* (Nashville: Abingdon Press, 1978); Eugene L. Lowry, *The Homiletical Plot: The Sermon as Narrative Art Form* (Atlanta: John Knox Press, 1980); John MacArthur Jr., *Discovering Expository Preaching: Balancing the Science and Art of Biblical Exposition* (Waco: Word Publishing, 1992).

Excursus 1

1. A phrase, on the other hand, is an element that is part of a larger whole. It is not an independent grammatical unit. The words "the women," in the example, illustrate a phrase. It is dependent and incomplete. Of course, in usage, phrases or even single words sometimes function as complete expressions. But they do so only because the remainder of their clause is understood from context. In response to the question, "Who read the Torah all last night, Bill or Bob?" a single word is sufficient—Bob. But it is sufficient because the rest of the clause is understood.

2. The copula is also used in this manner in Hebrew. See 1 Samuel 1:1, "There was a man . . ."

3. Occasionally δέ will appear as the third word of a Greek clause. In Luke 10:31, the idiom "by chance" (two Greek words) is followed by the conjunction καί or δέ. In this case the idiom is not interrupted by the conjunction.

κατὰ συγκυρίαν δὲ ἱερεύς τισ κατέβαινεν ἐν τῇ ὁδῷ ἐκείνῃ

By chance, a certain priest was going down in that way.

Excursus 2

1. See David Alan Black, *Learn to Read New Testament Greek* (Nashville: Broadman & Holman, 1994), pp. 182-85, for more on Greek word order and additional examples.

BIBLIOGRAPHY

Abraham, William J. *Canon and Criterion in Christian Theology.* Oxford: Clarendon Press, 1998.

Achtemeier, Paul J., Patrick H. Alexander, and David Winter, eds. *Inspiration and Authority: Nature and Function of Christian Scripture.* Peabody, Mass.: Hendrickson Publishers, 1999.

Aland, Kurt, ed. *Synopsis of the Four Gospels: Greek-English Edition of the Synopsis Quattuor Evangeliorum.* 3d ed. Stuttgart: Wuttembergische Bibelanstalt, 1979.

Allen, Ronald J. *The Teaching Sermon.* Nashville: Abingdon Press, 1995.

Alter, Robert. *The Art of Biblical Narrative.* New York: Basic Books, 1981.

Armstrong, Terry, Douglas Busby, and Cyril F. Carr. *A Reader's Hebrew-English Lexicon of the Old Testament.* Grand Rapids: Zondervan, 1981.

Aune, David E., ed. *Greco-Roman Literature and the New Testament: Selected Forms and Genres.* Atlanta: Scholars Press, 1988.

Austin, L. *How to Do Things with Words.* London: Oxford Press, 1962.

Avishur, Yitzhak. *Studies in Biblical Narrative: Style, Structure and the Ancient Near Eastern Literary Background.* Tel Aviv: Archaeological Center Publication, 1999.

Bailey, James L. "Genre Analysis." In *Hearing the New Testament: Strategies for Interpretation,* ed. Joel B. Green, 197-221. Grand Rapids: Eerdmans, 1995.

Balch, David L. *Let Wives Be Submissive: The Domestic Code in 1 Peter.* Chico, Calif.: Scholars Press, 1981.

Balz, Horst, and Gerhard Schneider, eds. *Exegetical Dictionary of the New Testament.* English translation, Grand Rapids: Eerdmans, 1990–93.

Barbour, Robert S. *Traditio-Historical Criticism of the Gospels.* London: SPCK, 1972.

Bar-Efrat, Shimon. *Narrative Art in the Bible.* Sheffield: Almond Press, 1989 [Hebrew 1979].

Barrett, C. K. *The Gospel According to St John: An Introduction with Commentary and Notes on the Greek Text.* London: SPCK, 1958.

Barton, John. *Amos' Oracles Against the Nations: A Study of Amos 1:3–2:5.* Cambridge: Cambridge University Press, 1980.

______. "Historical-Critical Approaches." In *The Cambridge Companion to Biblical Interpretation,* ed. John Barton, 9-20. Cambridge: Cambridge University Press, 1998.

Barton, John, ed. *The Cambridge Companion to Biblical Literature.* Cambridge: Cambridge University Press, 1998.

Bauer, Walter, William Arndt, Wilbur Gingrich, and Frederick Danker. *A Greek-English Lexicon of the New Testament and Other Early Christian Literature.* A translation of Bauer by Arndt and Gingrich revised by Gingrich and Danker. Chicago: University of Chicago Press, 1957.

Bergen, Robert D., ed. *Biblical Hebrew and Discourse Linguistics.* Dallas: Summer Institute of Linguistics, 1994.

Berlin, Adele. *The Dynamics of Biblical Parallelism.* Bloomington: Indiana University Press, 1985.

______. "Introduction to Hebrew Poetry." In *New Interpreter's Bible,* Vol. 4, 301-15. Nashville: Abingdon Press, 1996.

______. "Paralellism." In *Anchor Bible Dictionary.* Vol. 5, ed. David Noel Freedman, 155-62. New York: Doubleday, 1992.

______. *Poetics and Interpretation of Biblical Narrative.* Sheffield: Almond Press, 1983.

______. "Poetry, Hebrew Bible." In *Dictionary of Biblical Interpretation,* ed. John H. Hayes. Nashville: Abingdon Press, 1999.

Betz, Hans Dieter. *Galatians: A Commentary on Paul's Letter to the Churches in Galatia.* Philadelphia: Fortress Press, 1979.

______. *The Sermon on the Mount: A Commentary on the Sermon on the Mount, Including the Sermon on the Plain (Matthew 5:3–7:27 and Luke 6:20-49).* Ed. Adela Y. Collins. Minneapolis: Fortress Press, 1995.

BibleWindows. Silver Mountain Software, 1993, 1999.

BibleWorks, LCC. Hermeneutika Computer Bible Research Software, 1998–2000.

Biblia Hebraica Stuttgartensia. Stuttgart: Deutsche Biblestiftung, 1967/77.

Black, David Alan. *New Testament Textual Criticism.* Grand Rapids: Baker Books, 1994.

Blakemore, Diane. *Semantic Constraints on Relevance.* Oxford: Blackwell Publishers, 1987.

Blass, Friedrich, and A. Debrunner. *A Greek Grammar of the New Testament and Other Early Christian Literature.* Chicago: University of Chicago Press, 1961.

Blenkinsopp, Joseph. *The Pentateuch: An Introduction to the First Five Books of the Bible.* New York: Doubleday, 1992.

Boomershine, Thomas E. "Epistemology at the Turn of the Ages in Paul, Jesus and Mark: Rhetoric and Dialectic in Apocalyptic and the New Testament." In *Apocalyptic and the New Testament: Essays in Honor of J. Louis Martyn,* ed. Joel Marcus and Marion L. Soards, 147-67. Sheffield: Sheffield Academic Press, 1989.

Breck, John. *The Shape of Biblical Language: Chiasmus in the Scriptures and Beyond.* Afterword by Charles Lock. Crestwood, N. Y.: St. Vladimir's Seminary Press, 1994.

Bright, John. *A History of Israel.* Philadelphia: Westminster Press, 1981.

Brooke, George J. "'The Canon Within the Canon' at Qumran and in the New Testament." In *The Scrolls and the Scriptures: Qumran Fifty Years After,* eds. Stanley E. Porter and Craig A. Evans, 242-66. Sheffield: Sheffield Academic Press, 1997.

Brooks, James A., and Carlton Winbery. *Syntax of New Testament Greek.* Washington D.C.: University Press of America, 1979.

Brown, Francis, S. R. Driver, and Charles Briggs. *A Hebrew and English Lexicon of the Old Testament.* Oxford: Clarendon Press, 1907.

Brown, Raymond E. *The Community of the Beloved Disciple.* New York: Paulist Press, 1979.

______. *The Gospel According to John (i-xii).* In *Anchor Bible.* Vol. 29. Garden City: Doubleday, 1966.

Burgess, John P. *Why Scripture Matters: Reading the Bible in an Age of Church Conflict.* Louisville: Westminster John Knox, 1998.

Burton, Ernst De Witt. *A Critical and Exegetical Commentary on the Epistle to the Galatians.* Edinburgh: T & T Clark, 1921.

Bush, Frederic W. *Ruth, Esther.* Word Biblical Commentary Series. Vol. 9. Waco, Tex.: Word Publishing, 1996.

Buttrick, George, ed. *The Interpreter's Dictionary of the Bible.* 4 vols. Nashville: Abingdon Press, 1962.

Campbell, Anthony F., and Mark A. O'Brien. *Sources of the Pentateuch: Texts, Introductions, Annotations.* Minneapolis: Fortress Press, 1993.

Campbell, Jr., Edward F. "Ruth: A New Translation with Introduction, Notes, and Commentary." In *Anchor Bible.* Vol. 7. Garden City, N.Y.: Doubleday, 1975.

Campbell, Jonathan. *Dead Sea Scrolls: The Complete Story.* Berkeley, Calif.: Ulysses Press, 1998.

Cassuto, Umberto. *A Commentary on the Book of Genesis, Part One: From Adam to Noah*. Trans. Israel Abrahams. Jerusalem: Magnes Press, 1961 [Hebrew 1953].

Charlesworth, James H. *The Beloved Disciple: Whose Witness Validates the Gospel of John?* Valley Forge, Pa.: Trinity Press International, 1995.

Childs, Brevard. *Introduction to the Old Testament as Scripture*. Philadelphia: Fortress Press, 1979.

______. *Old Testament Theology in a Canonical Context*. Philadelphia: Fortress Press, 1985.

Clines, David., ed. *The Dictionary of Classical Hebrew*. 3 vols. Sheffield: Sheffield Academic Press, 1993–.

Collins, John J. *Daniel: A Commentary on the Book of Daniel*. Minneapolis: Augsburg Fortress Press, 1993.

Cross, Frank M., OT ed., and Raymond E. Brown, NT ed. *The Anchor Bible*. Garden City, N.Y.: Doubleday, 1981–.

Cross, Frank Moore, OT ed., and Helmut Koester, NT ed. *Hermeneia: A Critical and Historical Commentary on the Bible*. Minneapolis: Augsburg Fortress, 1971–.

Cruse, D. A. *Lexical Semantics*. Cambridge: Cambridge University Press, 1986.

Dmitre, Bishop. *The Kingdom of God: The Sermon on the Mount*. Crestwood, N.Y.: St. Vladimir's Seminary Press, 1992.

Douglas, Mary. *Leviticus as Literature*. Oxford: Oxford University Press, 1999.

Driver, S. R., A. Plummer, and C. A. Briggs, eds. *The International Critical Commentary*. Edinburgh: T & T Clark, 1895–.

Dunn, James. *Unity and Diversity in the New Testament: An Inquiry into the Character of Earliest Christianity*. 2d ed. Philadelphia: Trinity Press, 1990.

Einspahr, Bruce. *Index to Brown, Driver & Briggs Hebrew Lexicon*. Chicago: Moody Press, 1976.

Elias, Jacob W. *1 and 2 Thessalonians*. Scottdale, Pa.: Herald Press, 1995.

Elliot, John H. *A Home for the Homeless: A Sociological Exegesis of 1 Peter, Its Situation and Strategy*. Philadelphia: Fortress Press, 1981.

Emerton, J. A., C. E. B. Cranfield, and G. N. Stanton, eds. *New International Critical Commentary of the New Testament*. Edinburgh: T & T Clark, 1998–.

Evans, Craig, and James A. Sanders. *Luke and Scripture: The Function of Sacred Tradition in Luke-Acts*. Minneapolis: Fortress Press, 1993.

Even-Shoshan, Abraham, ed. *A New Concordance of the Old Testament*. Jerusalem: Kiryat Sepher, 1983.

Fabella, Virginia, and Sun Ai Lee Park, eds. *We Dare to Dream: Doing Theology as Asian Women.* Hong Kong: Asian Women's Resource Center for Culture and Theology, 1989.

Fish, Stanley. *Is There a Text in This Class? The Authority of Interpretive Communities.* Cambridge, Mass.: Harvard University Press, 1980.

Fowler, Roger. *Linguistic Criticism.* 2d ed. Oxford: Oxford University Press, 1996.

Freedman, David Noel, ed. *Anchor Bible Dictionary,* 6 vols. New York: Doubleday, 1992.

Gadamer, Hans-Georg. *Truth and Method.* Trans. Barrett Barden and John Cumming. New York: Seabury Press, 1975.

Gamble, Harry Y. "The Canon of the New Testament." In *The New Testament and Its Modern Interpreters,* eds. Eldon Jay Epp and George W. McRae, 201-43. Philadelphia: Fortress Press, 1989.

Gesenuis, Wilhelm, and E. Kautzsch. *Gesenius' Hebrew Grammar.* Trans. from German by A. E. Cowley. Oxford: Clarendon Press, 1910.

Good News Bible: The Bible in Today's English. New York: American Bible Society, 1976.

Gorayska, Barbara, and Roger Lindsay. "The Roots of Relevance." *Journal of Pragmatics* 19 (1993): 301-23.

Grabbe, Lester L. *An Introduction to First Century Judaism: Jewish Religion and History in the Second Temple Period.* Edinburgh: T & T Clark, 1996.

Gray, George Buchanan. *The Forms of Hebrew Poetry: Considered with Special Reference to the Criticism and Interpretation of the Old Testament.* London; New York: Hodder & Stoughton, 1915. Reprint, New York: KTAV Publishing House, 1972.

Greenberg, Moshe. "What Are Valid Criteria for Determining Inauthentic Matter in Ezekiel?" In *Ezekiel and His Book,* ed. J. Lust, 123-35. Bibliotheca Epheridum Theologicarum Lovaniensium 74. Leuven: University Press, 1986.

Grothe, Mardy. *Never Let a Fool Kiss You and Never Let a Kiss Fool You: Chiasmus and a World of Quotations That Say What They Mean and Mean What They Say.* New York: Viking Press, 1999.

Gunkel, Hermann. *The Legends of Genesis.* New York: Schocken Books, 1964 [German 1901].

Haberman, Abraham Meir. "Poetry." In *Encyclopedia Judaica.* Jerusalem: Keter, 1971.

Han, Nathan E. *A Parsing Guide to the Greek New Testament.* Waterloo, Ontario: Herald Press, 1991.

Hasel, Gerhard. *Old Testament Theology: Basic Issues in the Current Debate.* Rev. ed. Grand Rapids: Eerdmans, 1975.

Hayes, John H. *Amos the Eighth-Century Prophet: His Times and His Preaching*. Nashville: Abingdon Press, 1988.

Hayes, John H., ed. *Dictionary of Biblical Interpretation.* Nashville: Abingdon Press, 1999.

______. *Old Testament Form Criticism.* San Antonio: Trinity University Press, 1974.

Heine, Susan. *Women and Early Christianity: A Reappraisal.* Minneapolis: Augsburg Press, 1988.

Herrmann, Ned. *The Creative Brain.* Lake Lure, N.C.: Brain Books, 1989.

Hoffman, Yair. *A Blemished Perfection: The Book of Job in Context.* JSOT, 213. Sheffield: Sheffield Academic Press, 1996 [Hebrew 1995].

Iser, Wolfgang. *The Act of Reading: A Theory of Aesthetic Response.* Baltimore: Johns Hopkins University Press, 1978.

Jenni, Ernst, and Claus Westermann. *Theological Lexicon of the Old Testament.* 2 vols in 3. Trans. Mark E. Biddle. Peabody, Mass.: Hendrickson Publishers, 1997.

Jeremias, Joachim. *Die Sprache des Lukasevangeliums: Redaktion und Tradition im Nicht-Markusstoff des dritten Evangeliums.* Göttingen: Vandenhoeck & Ruprecht, 1980.

Johnson, Elizabeth A. *She Who Is: The Mystery of God in Feminist Theological Discourse.* New York: Crossroad, 1992.

Jouon, Paul. *A Grammar of Biblical Hebrew.* 2 vols. Trans. and rev. by T. Muraoka. Rome: Editrice Pontificio Instituto Biblico, 1991.

Keck, Leander E. *The Bible in the Pulpit: The Renewal of Biblical Preaching*. Nashville: Abingdon Press, 1978.

Keck, Leander E., ed. *The New Interpreter's Bible.* 12 vols. Nashville: Abingdon Press, 1994.

Kelly, Page H., Daniel S. Mynatt, and Timothy G. Crawford. *The Masorah of Biblia Hebraica Stuttgartensia: Introduction and Annotated Glossary.* Grand Rapids: Eerdmans, 1998.

Kennedy, George. *New Testament Interpretation Through Rhetorical Criticism.* Chapel Hill: University of North Carolina Press, 1984.

Koch, Klaus. *The Rediscovery of Apocalyptic.* London: SCAM Press, 1972.

Koehler, Ludwig, and Walter Baumgartner. *The Hebrew and Aramaic Lexicon of the Old Testament.* Rev. W. Baumgartner and Johann Jakob Stam. New York: E. J. Brill, 1994.

Kraus, Hans-Joachim. *Psalms 1–59: A Commentary.* Minneapolis: Augsburg Press, 1988 [German 1961/1978].

Krentz, Edgar. *The Historical-Critical Method.* Philadelphia: Fortress Press, 1975.

Liddell, Henry George, and Robert Scott. *Greek-English Lexicon*. 9th ed. Oxford: Clarendon Press, 1940.

Lim, Timothy H. "Midrash Pesher in the Pauline Letters." In *The Scrolls and the Scriptures: Qumran Fifty Years After*, eds. Stanley E. Porter and Craig A. Evans, 280-92. Sheffield: Sheffield Academic Press, 1997.

Logos Library System. Logos Research Systems, Inc., 1995–99.

Louw, J. P., ed. *Lexicography and Translation with a Special Reference to Bible Translation*. Cape Town: Bible Society of South Africa, 1985.

Lowry, Eugene L. *The Homiletical Plot: The Sermon as Narrative Art Form*. Atlanta: John Knox Press, 1980.

Luz, Ulrich. *Matthew 1–7: A Commentary*. Trans. Wilhelm C. Linss. Minneapolis: Augsburg Press, 1989.

______. *The Theology of the Gospel of Matthew*. Trans. J. Bredford Robinson. Cambridge: Cambridge University Press, 1995.

Lyons, John. *Linguistic Semantics: An Introduction*. Cambridge: Cambridge University Press, 1995.

MacArthur, Jr., John. *Rediscovering Expository Preaching: Balancing the Science and Art of Biblical Exposition*. Waco: Word Publishing, 1992.

Mack, Burton. *Rhetoric and the New Testament*. Minneapolis: Fortress Press, 1990.

McKnight, Edgar V. *The Bible and the Reader: An Introduction to Literary Criticism*. Philadelphia: Fortress Press, 1985.

McNutt, Paula. *Reconstructing the Society of Ancient Israel*. Louisville: John Knox Press, 1999.

Martens, Elmer A. *God's Design: A Focus on Old Testament Theology*. Grand Rapids: Baker, 1981.

Melchert, Charles F. *Wise Teaching: Biblical Wisdom and Educational Ministry*. Harrisburg, Pa.: Trinity Press International, 1998.

Metzger, Bruce. *A Textual Commentary on the Greek New Testament*. 2d ed. Stuttgart: Deutsche Biblegesellschaft, 1994.

Mey, Jacob L. *Pragmatics: An Introduction*. Oxford: Blackwell Publishers, 1993.

Meynet, Roland. *Rhetorical Analysis: An Introduction to Biblical Rhetoric*. Sheffield: Sheffield Academic Press, 1998.

Miller, J. Maxwell. *The Old Testament and the Historian*. Philadelphia: Fortress Press, 1976.

Miller, Jr., Patrick D. *Interpreting the Psalms*. Philadelphia: Fortress Press, 1986.

Morgan, Robert. "The Bible and Christian Theology." In *The Cambridge Companion to Biblical Interpretation*, ed. John Barton, 114-28. Cambridge: Cambridge University Press, 1998.

Moule, C. F. D. *An Idiom-Book of New Testament Greek*. Cambridge: Cambridge University Press, 1953.

Muilenburg, James. "Form Criticism and Beyond." *Journal of Biblical Literature* 88 (1969): 1-18.

Nestle-Aland Greek-English New Testament. Stuttgart: Deutsche Bibelgesellschaft, 1994.

Nicholson, Ernest. *The Pentateuch in the Twentieth Century: The Legacy of Julius Wellhausen*. Oxford: Clarendon Press, 1998.

Noth, Martin. *The History of Israel*. London: A & C Black, 1960.

Perrin, Norman. *What Is Redaction Criticism?* Philadelphia: Fortress Press, 1969.

Perschbacher, Wesley. *The New Analytical Greek Lexicon*. Peabody, Mass.: Hendrickson Publishers, 1990.

Petersen, David L., and Kent Harold Richards. *Interpreting Hebrew Poetry*. Minneapolis: Fortress Press, 1992.

Porter, Stanley E., and Craig A. Evans, eds. *The Scrolls and the Scriptures: Qumran Fifty Years After*. Sheffield: Sheffield Academic Press, 1997.

Porter, Stanley E., and Thomas Olbricht, eds. *The Rhetorical Analysis of Scripture: Essays from the 1995 London Conference*. London Conference on the Rhetorical Analysis of Scripture 1995. Sheffield: Sheffield Academic Press, 1997.

Pritchard, James, ed. *Ancient Near Eastern Texts Relating to the Old Testament*. Princeton, N.J.: Princeton University Press, 1978, 1992.

Rast, Walter E. *Tradition History and the Old Testament*. Philadelphia: Fortress Press, 1972.

Rendtorff, Rolf. *Canon and Theology*. Trans. Margaret Kohl. Minneapolis: Fortress Press, 1993 [German 1991].

Richter, Wolfgang. *Exegese als Literaturwissenschaft: Entwurf einer Alttestamentlichen Literatur Theorie und Methodologie*. Göttingen: Vandenhoeck & Ruprecht, 1971.

Rienecker, Fritz. *A Linguistic Key to the Greek New Testament*. Trans. Cleon L. Rogers Jr. Grand Rapids: Zondervan, 1980.

Robertson, A. T. *A Grammar of the Greek New Testament in Light of Historical Research*. 5th ed. New York: Hodder & Stoughton, 1931.

Saebø, Magne. *On the Way to Canon: Creative Tradition History in the Old Testament*. Sheffield: Sheffield Academic Press, 1998.

Sailhamer, John H. *Introduction to Old Testament Theology: A Canonical Approach*. Grand Rapids: Zondervan, 1995.

Sanders, James. *Torah and Canon*. Philadelphia: Fortress Press, 1972.

______. *From Sacred Story to Sacred Text.* Philadelphia: Fortress Press, 1987.

Sarna, Nahum M., gen. ed. *The JPS Torah Commentary.* Philadelphia; New York: The Jewish Publication Society, 1989–.

Sawyer, John F. A. *Semantics in Biblical Research: New Methods of Defining Hebrew Words for Salvation.* London: SCM Press, 1972.

Schertz, Mary H. "Nonretaliation and the Haustafeln in 1 Peter." In *The Love of Enemy and Nonretaliation in the New Testament,* ed. Willard M. Swartley, 258-86. Louisville: Westminster John Knox Press, 1992.

Schiffrin, Deborah. *Approaches to Discourse.* Blackwell Textbooks in Linguistics, 8. Oxford: Blackwell Publishers, 1994.

Scholes, Robert, and Robert Kellogg. *The Nature of Narrative.* New York: Oxford University Press, 1966.

Schürer, Emil. *The History of the Jewish People in the Age of Jesus Christ (175 B.C.–A.D. 135).* 3 vols. in 4. Rev. Geza Vermes, et al. Edinburgh: T & T Clark, 1973–84.

Schüssler Fiorenza, Elisabeth. *In Memory of Her: A Feminist Theological Reconstruction of Christian Origins.* New York: Crossroad, 1983.

Searle, John R. *Speech Acts: An Essay in the Philosophy of Language.* London: Cambridge University Press, 1969.

Segovia, Ferando, and Mary Ann Tolbert, eds. *Teaching the Bible: The Discourses and Politics of Biblical Pedagogy.* Maryknoll, N.Y.: Orbis Books, 1998.

______. *Reading from This Place.* 2 vols. Minneapolis: Fortress Press, 1995.

Seybold, Klaus. "The Literary Form of the Psalms." In *Introducing the Psalms.* Trans. R. Graeme Dunphy, 59-79. Edinburgh: T & T Clark, 1990 [German 1986].

Sider, John W. *Interpreting the Parables: A Hermeneutical Guide to Their Meaning.* Grand Rapids: Zondervan, 1995.

Silva, Moises. "The Case for Calvinistic Hermeneutics." In Kaiser, Jr., Walter C., and Moises Silva, *An Introduction to Biblical Hermeneutics: The Search for Meaning,* 251-70. Grand Rapids: Zondervan, 1994.

______. *Biblical Words and Their Meaning: An Introduction to Lexical Semantics.* Grand Rapids: Zondervan, 1983.

Smyth, Herbert Weir. *Greek Grammar.* Rev. ed. by Gordon Messing. Cambridge, Mass: Harvard University Press, 1956.

Speiser, E. A. *Genesis. The Anchor Bible.* Vol. 1. Garden City, N.Y.: Doubleday, 1964.

Steck, Odil Hannes. *Old Testament Exegesis: A Guide to the Methodology.* Trans. James D. Nogalski. Atlanta: Scholars Press, 1995.

Sternberg, Meir. *The Poetics of Biblical Narrative: Ideological Literature and the Drama of Reading.* Bloomington: Indiana University Press, 1985.

Sugirtharajah, R. S., ed. *Voices from the Margin: Interpreting the Bible in the Third World.* Maryknoll, N.Y.: Orbis/SPCK, 1991.

Swartley, Willard. *Israel's Scripture Traditions and the Synoptic Gospels: Story Shaping Story.* Peabody, Mass.: Hendrickson Publishers, 1994.

Tannehill, Robert. *The Narrative Unity of Luke-Acts: A Literary Interpretation.* 2 vols. Philadelphia: Fortress Press, 1986, 1990.

Thiselton, Anthony C. *New Horizons in Hermeneutics.* Grand Rapids: Zondervan, 1992.

Thistlethwaite, Susan Brooks, and Mary Potter Engel, eds. *Lift Every Voice: Constructing Christian Theologies from the Underside.* San Franscisco: Harper & Row, 1990.

Thomas, Gordon J. "Telling a Hawk from a Handsaw? An Evangelical Response to the New Literary Criticism." *Evangelical Quarterly* 71 (1999): 37-50.

Tov, Emanuel. *Textual Criticism of the Hebrew Bible.* Minneapolis: Augsburg Fortress, 1992.

Trible, Phyllis. *Rhetorical Criticism: Context, Method and the Book of Jonah.* Minneapolis: Fortress Press, 1994.

Tucker, Gene. *Form Criticism of the Old Testament.* Philadelphia: Fortress Press, 1971.

Van der Merwe, Christo H. J., Jackie A. Naudé, and Jan H. Kroeze. *A Biblical Hebrew Reference Grammar.* Sheffield: Sheffield Academic Press, 1999.

Vermes, Geza. *An Introduction to the Complete Dead Sea Scrolls.* Minneapolis: Augsburg Fortress, 1999.

Von Rad, Gerhard. *Genesis: A Commentary.* Old Testament Library Series. Philadelphia: Westminster Press, 1972.

______. *Deuteronomy: A Commentary.* Old Testament Library Series. Philadelphia: Westminster Press, 1966.

Wallace, Daniel B. *Greek Grammar Beyond the Basics: An Exegetical Syntax of the New Testament.* Grand Rapids: Zondervan, 1996.

Wallace, Ronald. *On the Interpretation and Use of the Bible: With Reflections on Experience.* Grand Rapids: Eerdmans, 1999.

Waltko, Bruce, and M. O'Conner. *An Introduction to Biblical Hebrew Syntax.* Winona Lake, Ind.: Eisenbrauns, 1990.

Warnke, Georgia. *Gadamer: Hermeneutics, Tradition and Reason.* Stanford, Calif.: Stanford University Press, 1987.

Weinfeld, Moshe. *Deuteronomy and the Deuteronomic School.* Oxford: Oxford University Press, 1972.

Weingreen, Jacob. *Introduction to the Critical Study of the Hebrew Bible.* Oxford: Clarendon Press, 1982.

Weiss, Meir. *The Bible from Within: The Method of Total Interpretation.* Jerusalem: Magnes Press, 1984 [Hebrew 1967].

Wellek, René, and Austin Warren. *Theory of Literature.* New York: Harcourt, Brace & World, 1956.

Westermann, Claus. *Genesis 1–11: A Commentary.* Trans. John J. Scullion. Minneapolis: Augsburg Press, 1984 [German 1974].

Wilhoit, Jim, and Leland Ryken. *Effective Bible Teaching.* Grand Rapids: Baker, 1988.

Williams, Ron. *Hebrew Syntax in Outline for Hebrew.* Toronto: University of Toronto Press, 1976.

Wilson, Paul Scott. *The Four Pages of the Sermon: A Guide to Biblical Preaching.* Nashville: Abingdon Press, 1999.

Wolde, Ellen van. *Narrative Syntax and the Hebrew Bible: Papers of the Tilburg Conference 1996.* Leiden; New York: Brill, 1997.

Yoder, Perry B. *From Word to Life: A Guide to the Art of Bible Study.* Scottdale, Pa.: Herald Press, 1982.

Young, Richard A. *Intermediate New Testament Greek: A Linguistic and Exegetical Approach.* Nashville: Broadman & Holman Publishers, 1994.

Zakovitch, Yair. *Ruth: Introduction and Commentary.* Tel Aviv: Am Oved, 1990 [Hebrew].

Zerwick, Max, and Marg Grosuenor. *A Grammatical Analysis of the Greek New Testament.* Rome: Biblical Institute Press, 1981.

Scripture Index

Subject Index